60 Quick Knitted Toys

FUN, FABULOUS KNITS IN THE 220 SUPERWASH® COLLECTION FROM CASCADE YARNS®

THE EDITORS OF SIXTH&SPRING BOOKS

sixth&springbooks NEW YORK

3 9082 13141 4974

sixth&springbooks

161 Avenue of the Americas, New York, NY 10013

sixthandspring.com

Editor
CAROL J. SULCOSKI

Editorial Assistant
JACOB SEIFERT

Yarn Editor
MATTHEW SCHRANK

Supervising
Patterns Editor
CARLA SCOTT

Patterns Editors
MARI LYNN PATRICK
RENEE LORION
ROSEMARY DRYSDALE
LORI STEINBERG

ART DIRECTOR
JOE VIOR

Photography
JACK DEUTSCH

Stylist
JOSEFINA GARCIA

Hair and Makeup
ELENA LYAKIR

Vice President/
Editorial Director
TRISHA MALCOLM

Publisher
CAROLINE KILMER

Production Manager
DAVID JOINNIDES

President
ART JOINNIDES

Chairman
JAY STEIN

Copyright © 2017 by Sixth&Spring Books/Cascade Yarns

Library of Congress Cataloging-in-Publication Data

Names: Sixth & Spring Books.
Title: 60 quick knitted toys : fun, fabulous knits in the 220 Superwash collection from Cascade / by The Editors of Sixth&Spring Books.
Other titles: Sixty quick knitted toys
Description: First Edition. | New York : Sixth&Spring Books, 2017. | Includes index.
Identifiers: LCCN 2016034099 | ISBN 9781942021445 (pbk.)
Subjects: LCSH: Knitting—Patterns. | Soft toy making--Patterns.
Classification: LCC TT829 .A15 2017 | DDC 745.592—dc23
LC record available at https://lccn.loc.gov/2016034099

Manufactured in China

1 3 5 7 9 10 8 6 4 2
First Edition

CASCADE YARNS
DISTRIBUTOR OF FINE YARN

cascadeyarns.com

contents

Creating the PERFECT TOY

The bestselling 60 Quick Knits series is back
—and this time we've compiled a fabulous collection of knitted toys,
sure to charm little and big kids alike.

A talented cadre of designers has created this diverse collection
of knitted playthings, including dolls, animals, puppets,
games, pillows, and blocks. There is no better line of yarn to turn to
than the versatile 220 Superwash® family of yarns from Cascade Yarns®:
100 percent superwash wool in worsted weight, 100 percent superwash
merino wool in sport and Aran weights, and a
multitude of colors and effects, all of them soft and durable.
Whether in need of snuggly teddy bears, knitted tools,
a life-size doll, or a dragon puppet, you'll enjoy every
minute spent creating the perfect toy that will become
an instant family heirloom.

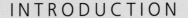

To locate retailers that carry Cascade Yarns®
220 Superwash® collection visit cascadeyarns.com.

Friendly Fox

This charming fox is friendly, not fierce,
and eager to become your child's new and cherished lovey.

DESIGNED BY AUDREY DRYSDALE

Knitted Measurements
Approx 12"/31cm high, when sitting

Materials
■ 2 3½oz/100g balls (each approx 220yd/200m) of Cascade Yarns *220 Superwash* (superwash wool) in #823 Burnt Orange (A) ⟨3⟩
■ 1 ball each in #873 Extra Creme Cafe (B) and #815 Black (C)
■ One size 6 (4mm) circular needle, 16"/40cm long, *or size to obtain gauge*
■ One set (4) size 6 (4mm) double-pointed needles (dpn)
■ Stitch markers
■ Polyester stuffing

Notes
1) Wind small balls of yarn for each block of color.
2) When changing colors, twist yarns on WS to prevent holes in work.
3) Change to circular needle when sts no longer fit comfortably on dpn.

Head
Beg at center back of head, with A and dpn, cast on 4 sts. Do *not* join.
Set-up row (RS) [Kfb] 4 times—8 sts. Divide sts over 3 dpn (2 sts, 3 sts, 3 sts). Join, taking care not to twist sts, and pm for beg of rnd. Cont to work in rnds as foll:

Rnd 1 *Kfb; rep from * around—16 sts.
Rnd 2 and all even-numbered rnds Knit
Rnd 3 *K2, M1; rep from * around—24 sts.
Rnd 5 *K3, M1; rep from * around—32 sts
Rnd 7 *K4, M1; rep from * around—40 sts.
Cont in this way to inc 8 sts every other rnd, working 1 more st between incs every inc rnd, until there are 104 sts. Knit 7 rnds even. Piece measures approx 4"/10cm from beg. Cut A.

SHAPE SNOUT
Cont to work back and forth in rows as foll:
Row 1 (RS) Join B and k25; join A and k54; join 2nd ball of B and k25. Turn.
Row 2 (WS) With B, p25; with A, p54; p25 B.
Dec row 3 With B, k23, ssk, pm; with A, k2tog, k50, ssk, pm; with B, k2tog, k23—4 sts dec'd.
Row 4 and all WS rows Purl, matching colors.
Dec row 5 With B, k to 2 sts before marker, ssk, sm; with A, k2tog, k to 2 sts before marker, ssk, sm; with B, k2tog, k to end—4 sts dec'd.
Next 11 RS rows Rep dec row 5. There are 52 sts at end of last row—12 sts B, 28 sts A, 12 sts B.

Gauge
22 sts and 30 rnds to 4"/10cm over St st using size 6 (4mm) needles.
Take time to check gauge.

Friendly Fox

Row 28 (WS) Purl, matching colors.
Dec row 29 With B, k1, k2tog, k to 2 sts before marker, ssk, sm; with A, k2tog, k to 2 sts before marker, ssk, sm; with B, k2tog, k to last 3 sts, ssk, k1—6 sts dec'd.
Next 3 RS rows Rep dec row 29. There are 28 sts at end of last row—4 sts B, 20 sts A, 4 sts B.
Row 36 (WS) Purl, matching colors.
Dec row 37 With B, k4, sm; with A, k2tog, k to 2 sts before marker, ssk, sm; with B, k4—2 sts dec'd.
Next 4 RS rows Rep dec row 37. There are 18 sts at end of last row—4 sts B, 10 sts A, 4 sts B.
Row 46 (WS) Purl, matching colors.
Dec row 47 With B, [k2tog] twice, sm; with A, [k2tog] 5 times, sm; with B, [k2tog] twice—9 sts.
Row 48 (WS) Purl, matching colors.
Dec row 49 With B, k2tog, sm; with A, [k2tog] twice, k1, sm; with B, k2tog—5 sts.
Cut yarns and draw A tightly through rem sts.
Beg at point of nose, sew seam leaving opening to insert stuffing. Stuff head. Sew opening closed.

EARS (Make 2)
With A, cast on 18 sts, pm; with B, cast on 18 sts—36 sts in total.
Row 1 (RS) With B, k18, sm; with A, k18.
Row 2 and all WS rows Purl, matching colors.
Dec row 3 With B, k1, k2tog, k to 2 sts before marker, ssk, sm; with A, k2tog, k to last 3 sts, ssk, k1—4 sts dec'd.
Next 6 RS rows Rep dec row 3—8 sts rem after last row, 4 sts B and 4 sts A.
Row 23 (RS) With B, k1, k3tog, sm; with A, k3tog, k1—4 sts.
Row 24 (WS) With A, p2tog, sm; with B, p2tog.
Cut yarns and draw A tightly through rem 2 sts.

Fold ears and sew sides tog. Sew ears to head (see photo).

Body
Note Body is worked back and forth in rows.
With A, cast on 8 sts.
Row 1 (RS) *Kfb; rep from * to last st, k1—15 sts.
Row 2 and all WS rows Purl.
Row 3 *Kfb; rep from * to last st, k1—29 sts.
Row 5 *Kfb, k1; rep from * to last st, k1— 43 sts.
Row 7 *K3, M1; rep from * to last st, k1—57 sts.
Row 9 With A, k16, pm; join B and k25, pm; join a 2nd ball of A and k16.
Row 10 and all WS rows Purl, matching colors.
Row 11 With A, k1, [M1, k3] 4 times, M1, k3, sm; with B, k5, [M1, k7] twice, M1, k6, sm; with A, k3, [M1, k3] 4 times, M1, k1—70 sts.
Row 13 With A, k1, [M1, k4] 5 times, sm; with B, k5, [M1, k8] twice, M1, k7, sm; with A, k3, [M1, k4] 4 times, M1, k2—83 sts.
Row 15 With A, k1, [M1, k5] 5 times, sm; with B, k5, [M1, k9] twice, M1, k8, sm; with A, k3, [M1, k5] 4 times, M1, k3—96 sts.
Row 17 With A, k1, [M1, k6] 5 times, sm; with B, k5, [M1, k10] twice, M1, k9, sm; with A, k3, [M1, k6] 4 times, M1, k4—109 sts.
Row 19 With A, k1, [M1, k7] 5 times, sm; with B, k5, [M1, k11] twice, M1, k10, sm; with A, k3, [M1, k7] 4 times, M1, k5—122 sts.
Row 20 With A, p41; with B, p40; with A p41.
Work even in St st (k on RS, p on WS), matching colors, until piece measures

4½"/12cm from beg, end with a WS row.
Dec row (RS) With A, [k4, k2tog] 6 times, k5, sm; with B, [k4, k2tog] 6 times, k4, sm; with A, k5, [k2tog, k4] 6 times—104 sts.
Work even in St st, matching colors, until piece measures 6½"/17cm from beg, end with a WS row.
Dec row (RS) With A, [k3, k2tog] 6 times, k5, sm; with B, [k3, k2tog] 6 times, k4, sm; with A, k5, [k2tog, k3] 6 times—86 sts.
Work even in St st, matching colors, until piece measures 8½"/22cm from beg, end with a WS row.
Dec row (RS) With A, [k2, k2tog] 6 times, k5, sm; with B, [k2, k2tog] 6 times, k4, sm; with A, k5, [k2tog, k2] 6 times—68 sts.
Purl 1 row, matching colors.
Dec row (RS) With A, [k1, k2tog] 7 times, k2, sm; with B, [k1, k2tog] 7 times, k1, sm; with A, k2, [k2tog, k1] 7 times—47 sts.
Purl 1 row, matching colors.
Dec row (RS) With A, [k2tog] 8 times, sm; with B, [k2tog] 7 times, k1, sm; with A, [k2tog] 8 times—24 sts.
Purl 1 row, then bind off, matching colors
Beg at base, sew center back seam, leaving an opening for stuffing.
Stuff the body, then sew rem seam.
Leave top edge open (it will be covered by the head).

Legs (Make 4)
With C, cast on 4 sts.
Row 1 (RS) [Kfb] 4 times—8 sts.
Divide sts over 3 dpn (2 sts, 3 sts, 3 sts). Join, taking care not to twist sts, and pm for beg of rnd. Cont to work in rnds as foll
Rnd 1 *Kfb; rep from * around—16 sts.
Rnd 2 and all even-numbered rnds Knit.
Rnd 3 *K2, M1; rep from * around—24 sts

Rnd 5 *K3, M1; rep from * around—32 sts.
Rnds 6–14 Knit.
Rnd 15 *K3, k2tog; rep from * to last 2 ts, k2—26 sts.
Knit 14 rnds. Cut C. Join A and knit 18 rnds.
Next rnd *K3, k2tog; rep from * to last t, k1—21 sts.
Knit 1 rnd. Stuff leg.
Next rnd *K1, k2tog; rep from * around—14 sts.
Knit 1 rnd.
Next rnd *K2tog; rep from * around—7 sts.
Cut A and draw tightly through rem sts.

Tail

With B, cast on 4 sts.
Row 1 (RS) [Kfb] 4 times—8 sts.
Divide sts over 3 dpn (2 sts, 3 sts, 3 sts). Join, taking care not to twist sts, and pm or beg of rnd. Cont to work in rnds as foll:
Rnd 1 *Kfb, k1; rep from * around—12 sts.
Rnds 2 and 3 Knit.
Rnd 4 *K3, M1; rep from * around—16 sts.
Rnds 5 and 6 Knit.
Rnd 7 *K4, M1; rep from * around—20 sts.
Rnds 8 and 9 Knit.
Cont in this way to inc 4 sts every 3rd rnd, working 1 more st between incs every inc rnd, until there are 40 sts.
Work even in St st until tail measures 4½"/11.5cm from beg.
Next rnd *K6, k2tog; rep from * around—35 sts.
Knit 4 rnds. Cut B. Join A and knit 6 rnds.
Next rnd *K5, k2tog; rep from * around—30 sts.
Knit 6 rnds.
Next rnd *K4, k2tog; rep from * around—25 sts.
Knit 6 rnds. Stuff tail.
Next rnd *K3, k2tog; rep from * around—20 sts.
Knit 1 rnd.
Cont in this way to dec 5 sts every other

rnd, working 1 less st between decs every dec rnd, until there are 5 sts.
Cut A and draw tightly through rem sts.

Finishing
Sew head, legs and tail to body (see photo). Secure head with extra sts at the front neck.

NOSE
With B, cast on 3 sts.
Row 1 (RS) [Kfb] 3 times—6 sts.

Row 2 Knit.
Row 3 [Kfb] 5 times, k1—11 sts.
Row 4 Knit.
Row 5 [Kfb, k1] 5 times, k1—16 sts.
Bind off. Sew side edges tog to form a circle. Sew nose around point on face.

EYES (Make 2)
Work same as nose. Sew to face. With B, embroider straight sts (see photo). ∎

Castle Set

Fortify the ramparts—the knitted ramparts, of course!
Want a bigger castle? Keep knitting until you've created your ideal palace.

DESIGNED BY MEGAN KREINER

■■■▭

Knitted Measurements
Arch 3"/7.5cm tall and 8"/20.5cm wide
Block 2½"/6.5cm tall and 3"/7.5cm wide
Round 2½"/6.5cm tall and 4½"/11.5cm diameter

Materials
▧ 2 3½/100g balls (each approx 220yd/200m) of Cascade Yarns *220 Superwash* (superwash wool) each in #877 Golden (A) and #821 Daffodil (B) 🔟
▧ 1 ball in #815 Black (C)
▧ One set (5) size 4 (3.5mm) double-pointed needles (dpn), *or size to obtain gauge*
▧ Stitch markers
▧ Scrap yarn
▧ Polyester stuffing
▧ Polyester cushion foam 1"/2.5cm thick

Stitch Glossary
M1L Insert LH needle from front to back under the strand between last st worked and next st on LH needle. Knit into the back loop to twist the st.
M1R Insert LH needle from back to front under the strand between last st worked and next st on LH needle.
Knit into the front loop to twist the st.

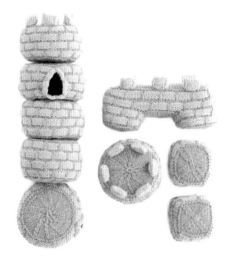

Slip Stitch Pattern
(over a multiple of 5 sts)
Rnd 1 With A, knit.
Rnd 2 With B, *k3, sl 1 wyib, k2; rep from * around.
Rnds 3–6 With B, *p3, sl 1 wyib, p2; rep from *around.
Rnds 7 and 8 With A, knit.
Rnd 9 With B, *sl 1 wyib, k5; rep from *around.
Rnds 10–13 With B, *sl 1 wyib, p5; rep from *around.

Rnd 14 With A, knit.
Rep rnds 1–14 for slip st pat.

Notes
1) Castle set pictured consists of 1 arch, 2 castle blocks, and 6 castle rounds, plus 18 merlons and 2 windows.
2) Knit as many pieces, adding as many merlons and windows, as desired for your ideal castle.

Merlons (Make 18)
With B, cast on 14 sts and divide over 3 dpn (4 sts, 5 sts, 5 sts). Join, taking care not to twist sts, and pm for beg of rnd.
Rnds 1–6 K1, p5, k2, p5, k1.
Divide sts evenly over 2 dpn and join sts tog using 3-needle bind-off (see page 182).
Stuff merlon, lay aside for attaching during finishing.

Windows (Make 2)
With C, cast on 7 sts. Work back and forth in rows as foll:
[Knit 1 row, purl 1 row] 4 times.
Row 9 Ssk, k3, k2tog—5 sts.
Row 10 Purl.
Row 11 Ssk, k1, k2tog—3 sts.
Cut yarn, draw tail through sts twice, and pull tightly to finish.

Gauge
24 sts and 34 rnds to 4"/10cm over St st using size 4 (3.5mm) needles.
Take time to check gauge.

Castle Set

I-CORD TRIM
With dpn and B, cast on 5 sts.
*Row 1 (RS) K5, slide sts back to beg of needle to work next row from RS. Bring yarn around from back. Rep from *for I-cord for approx 5¼"/13cm or to fit around entire outer edge of the window. Pin around the window and sew in place before binding off, adjusting length if necessary.
Lay aside for attaching during finishing.

Castle Blocks (Make 2)
With A, cast on 8 sts and divide evenly over 4 dpn. Join, taking care not to twist sts, and pm for beg of rnd.
Rnd 1 Kfb in each st—16 sts.
Rnds 2, 4, 6, and 8 Knit.
Rnd 3 [M1L, k4, M1R] 4 times—24 sts.
Rnd 5 [M1L, k6, M1R] 4 times—32 sts.
Rnd 7 [M1L, k8, M1R] 4 times—40 sts.
Rnd 9 [M1L, k10, M1R] 4 times—48 sts.
Rnd 10 Purl.
Rnds 11–38 Rep rnds 1–14 of slip st pat twice. Cont with A only.
Rnd 39 Purl.
Rnd 40 [Ssk, k8, k2tog] 4 times—40 sts.
Rnds 41, 43, 45, and 47 Knit.
Rnd 42 [Ssk, k6, k2tog] 4 times—32 sts.
Rnd 44 [Ssk, k4, k2tog] 4 times—24 sts.
Cut three 2½"/6.5cm square pieces of the cushion foam and stack inside castle block.
Rnd 46 [Ssk, k2, k2tog] 4 times—16 sts.
Rnd 48 [Ssk, k2tog] 4 times—8 sts.
Cut yarn, draw through sts twice, and pull up tightly to finish.

Castle Rounds (Make 6)
With A, cast on 5 sts and divide over 3 dpn (2 sts, 2 sts, 1 st). Join, taking care not to twist sts, and pm for beg of rnd.
Rnd 1 Kfb in each st—10 sts.
Rnds 2, 4, 6, 8, 10, and 12 Knit.
Rnd 3 [K1, M1] 10 times—20 sts.
Rnd 5 [K1, M1, k1] 10 times—30 sts.
Rnd 7 [K1, M1, k2] 10 times—40 sts.
Rnd 9 [K1, M1, k3] 10 times—50 sts.
Rnd 11 [K1, M1, k4] 10 times—60 sts.
Rnd 13 [K2, M1, k3] 12 times—72 sts.
Rnd 14 Purl.
Rnds 15–42 Rep rnds 1–14 of slip st pat twice. Cont with A only.
Rnd 43 Purl.
Rnd 44 [K2, ssk k2] 12 times—60 sts.
Rnds 45, 47, 49, 51, and 53 Knit.
Rnd 46 [K1, ssk, k3] 10 times—50 sts.
Rnd 48 [K1, ssk, k2] 10 times—40 sts.
Rnd 50 [K1, ssk, k1] 10 times—30 sts.
Rnd 52 [K1, ssk] 10 times—20 sts.
Cut three 4"/10cm diameter circles of the cushion foam and stack inside castle round.
Rnd 54 [Ssk] 10 times—10 sts.
Rnd 55 Knit.
Cut yarn, draw through sts twice, and pull up tightly to finish.

Arch
PILLARS (Make 2)
With A, cast on 8 sts and divide over 3 dpn (3 sts, 3sts, 2 sts). Join, taking care not to twist sts, and pm for beg of rnd.
Work rnds 1–23 same as castle block. Change to A.
Rnd 24 With A, k36, bind off 12 sts and fasten off last st. Cut yarn and transfer sts to scrap yarn.
CENTER
With A, cast on 8 sts and divide evenly over 4 dpn. Join, taking care not to twist sts, and pm for beg of rnd.
Work rnds 1–9 same as castle block.
Rnd 10 P12, bind off 12 sts, p12, bind off 12 sts—24 sts.
Joining rnd 11 K12, match up the center bind-off edge with the first pillar bind-off edge, k36 from pillar, k12 from arch center, match up the bind-off edge with 2nd pillar bind-off edge, k36 from 2nd pillar—96 sts. Change to B.
Rnds 12–23 Work rnds 2–13 of slip st pat. Cont with A only.
Rnd 24 Knit.
Rnd 25 Purl.
Rnd 26 [K22, k2tog, ssk, k8, k2tog, ssk, k10] twice—88 sts.
Rnds 27, 29, 31, and 33 Knit.
Rnd 28 [K21, k2tog, ssk, k6, k2tog, ssk, k9] twice—80 sts.
Rnd 30 [K20, k2tog, ssk, k4, k2tog, ssk, k8] twice—72 sts.
Rnd 32 [K19, k2tog, ssk, k2, k2tog, ssk, k7] twice—64 sts.
Rnd 34 [K18, k2tog, ssk, k2tog, ssk, k6] twice—56 sts. Bind off all sts.
Cut five 2½"/6.5cm squares and one 2½ x 7½"/6.5 x 19cm rectangle of cushion foam. Stack 2 squares inside each pillar, 1 square in center, and then rectangle over center and pillars.
Sew seam.

Finishing
Sew 6 merlons to arch top and 6 merlons to top of each castle round (see photo). With B, sew windows to castle rounds and then I-cord to windows with 2 sets of long sts at 6 points (see photo). ∎

Green Dragon

More cute than ferocious, this dragon toy provides drama and laughs for every royal.

DESIGNED BY MEGAN KREINER

Knitted Measurements

Approx 6"/15cm tall and 7"/18cm long, including tail

Materials

- 1 3½oz/100g ball (each approx 220yd/200m) of Cascade Yarns *220 Superwash* (superwash wool) each in #906 Chartreuse (A), #864 Christmas Green (B), and #824 Yellow (C) (4)
- Small amount of black yarn for face
- One set (4) size 4 (3.5mm) double-pointed needles (dpn), *or size to obtain gauge*
- One pair size 4 (3.5mm) needles
- Stitch marker
- Tapestry needle
- Polyester stuffing
- Polyester cushion foam, 1"/2.5cm thick

Body and Head

With A, cast on 5 sts and divide over 3 dpn (2sts, 2 sts, 1 st). Join, taking care not to twist sts, and pm for beg of rnd.
Rnd 1 [Kfb] 5 times—10 sts.
Rnds 2, 4, 6, 8, 10, and 12 Knit.
Rnd 3 [K1, M1] 10 times—20 sts.
Rnd 5 [K1, M1, k1] 10 times—30 sts.
Rnd 7 [K1, M1, k2] 10 times—40 sts.
Rnd 9 [K1, M1, k3] 10 times—50 sts.
Rnd 11 [K1, M1, k4] 10 times—60 sts.

Rnd 13 Purl.
Rnds 14–30 Knit.
Rnd 31 [K1, ssk, k3] 10 times—50 sts.
Rnds 32, 34, 36, 38, and 40 Knit.
Rnd 33 [K1, ssk, k2] 10 times—40 sts.
Rnd 35 [K1, ssk, k1] 10 times—30 sts.
Cut a 3½"/9cm diameter circle of cushion foam and insert into the base.
Rnd 37 [K3, ssk, k1] 5 times—25 sts.
Rnd 39 [K3, ssk] 5 times—20 sts.
Stuff the body.
Rnd 41 [K1, ssk, k1] 5 times—15 sts.
Rnds 42–48 Knit.
Rnd 49 [K1, M1, k2] 5 times—20 sts.
Rnd 50 Knit.

Rnd 51 [K1, M1, k1] 10 times—30 sts.
Rnds 52–58 Knit.
Rnd 59 [K1, ssk] 10 times—20 sts.
Rnds 60–62 Knit.
Stuff the head.
Rnd 63 [Ssk] 10 times—10 sts.
Cut yarn, draw end through rem sts twice, and pull tightly to finish.

Muzzle

With A, cast on 20 sts and divide over 3 dpn (7 sts, 7 sts, 6 sts). Join, taking care not to twist sts, and pm for beg of rnd.
Rnds 1–4 Knit.
Rnd 5 [K1, M1, k1] 10 times—30 sts.
Rnds 6–8 Knit.
Rnd 9 [K1, M1, k4] 6 times—36 sts.
Rnds 10–12 Knit.
Rnd 13 [K1, ssk, k3] 6 times—30 sts.
Rnds 14 and 15 Knit.
Rnd 16 [K1, ssk] 10 times—20 sts.
Bind off. Using mattress st, close bound-off edge for mouth. Sew cast-on edge to head, stuffing muzzle before closing seam.

NOSTRILS (Make 2)
With A, cast on 10 sts and divide over 3 dpn (3 sts, 3 sts, 4 sts). Join, taking care not to twist sts, and pm for beg of rnd.
Rnd 1 Purl.

Gauge

24 sts and 34 rnds to 4"/10cm over St st using size 4 (3.5mm) needles.
Take time to check gauge.

Green Dragon

Rnds 2 and 3 Knit.
Cut yarn, draw end through sts twice, and pull tightly to finish. Sew to muzzle with the cast-on edge as outer edges (see photo).

Ears (Make 2)
With A, cast on 20 sts and divide over 3 dpn (7 sts, 7 sts, 6 sts). Join, taking care not to twist sts, and pm for beg of rnd.
Rnd 1 Purl.
Rnds 2 and 3 Knit.
Rnd 4 [Ssk] 10 times—10 sts.
Cut yarn, draw end through rem sts twice, and pull tightly to finish. Pinch one end of ear and secure the sts held tog with a few sewn sts to form the dimensional ear shape (see photo). Attach pinched end of each ear to side of head.

Tail
With A, cast on 30 sts and divide evenly over 3 dpn. Join, taking care not to twist sts, and pm for beg of rnd.
Rnds 1–5 Knit.
Rnd 6 [K1, ssk, k3] 5 times—25 sts.
Rnds 7–10 Knit.
Rnd 11 [K1, ssk, k2] 5 times—20 sts.
Rnds 12–17 Knit.
Rnd 18 [K1, ssk, k1] 5 times—15 sts.
Rnds 19–24 Knit.
Rnd 25 [K1, ssk] 5 times—10 sts.
Rnds 26–28 Knit.
Cut yarn, draw end through rem sts twice, and pull tightly to finish.
Sew cast-on edge to body, stuffing tail before closing seam.

Wings (Make 2)
With B, cast on 8 sts and divide over 3 dpn (3 sts, 3 sts, 2 sts). Join, taking care not to twist sts, and pm for beg of rnd.
Rnd 1 Knit.
Rnd 2 [K1, M1, k2, M1, k1] twice—12 sts.
Rnd 3 Knit.
Rnd 4 [K1, M1, k4, M1, k1] twice—16 sts.
Rnd 5 Knit.
Rnd 6 [K1, M1, k6, M1, k1] twice—20 sts.
Rnds 7–12 Knit.
Divide sts evenly over 2 dpn and hold parallel, matching shaping, ready for next row.
Next row *With 3rd dpn, k1 st from back needle tog with 1 st from front needle; rep from * across—10 sts.
Next row k1, sl st from RH to LH needle, cast on 3 sts, bind off 7 sts; sl st from RH to LH needle, cast on 4 sts, bind off 8 sts; sl st from RH to LH needle, cast on 3 sts, bind off 4 sts.
Pinch beg row of wings tog and secure with a few sewn sts.
Sew wings to body (see photo).

Tummy Panel
With C, cast on 5 sts and divide over 3 dpn (2 sts, 2 sts, 1 st). Join, taking care not to twist sts, and pm for beg of rnd.
Rnd 1 Kfb in each st—10 sts.
Rnds 2, 4, 6, and 8 Knit.
Rnd 3 [K1, M1] 10 times—20 sts.
Rnd 5 [K1, M1, k1] 10 times—30 sts.
Rnd 7 [K1, M1, k2] 10 times—40 sts.
Rnd 9 [K1, M1, k3] 10 times—50 sts.
Rnd 10 Knit. Bind off.

Finishing
Sew tummy panel to dragon front.
With B, embroider 4 pairs of long sts across tummy panel. With black yarn, embroider eyes and eyebrows using long sts.

BACK SCALES
With straight needles and B, cast on 50 sts.
Row 1 *Cast on 3 sts, bind off 6 sts, sl st from RH to LH needle; rep from * until 2 sts rem.
Bind off rem sts. Pin cast-on edge of back scales in place along center back, beg at top of head and end at tip of tip, then sew in place. ■

4,5

Royal Couple

A roly-poly king and queen, with crowns and ermine-trimmed robes,
are ready to rule their knitted castle—and vanquish a dragon, if necessary.

DESIGNED BY MEGAN KREINER

Knitted Measurements
Approx 4"/10cm tall and 3"/7.5cm wide

Materials
▥ 1 3½oz/100g ball (each approx 220yd/200m) of Cascade Yarns *220 Superwash* (superwash wool) each in #804 Amethyst (A), #228 Frosted Almond (B), #871 White (C), #821 Daffodil (D), #1920 Pumpkin Spice (E), and #815 Black (F)
▥ One set (4) size 4 (3.5mm) double-pointed needles (dpn),
or size to obtain gauge
▥ Stitch markers
▥ Tapestry needle
▥ Polyester stuffing
▥ Polyester cushion foam, 1"/2.5cm thick

Body
With A, cast on 5 sts and divide over 3 dpn (2 sts, 2 sts, 1 st). Join, taking care not to twist sts, and pm for beg of rnd.
Rnd 1 Kfb in each st—10 sts.
Rnds 2, 4, 6, and 8 Knit.
Rnd 3 [K1, M1] 10 times—20 sts.
Rnd 5 [K1, M1, k1] 10 times—30 sts.
Rnd 7 [K1, M1, k2] 10 times—40 sts.
Rnd 9 Purl.
Rnds 10–23 Knit.

Head
Change to B.
Rnds 24 and 25 Knit.
Rnd 26 [K3, ssk, k3] 5 times—35 sts.
Rnds 27, 29, 31, and 33 Knit.
Rnd 28 [K3, ssk, k2] 5 times—30 sts.
Rnd 30 [K3, ssk, k1] 5 times—25 sts.
Rnd 32 [K3, ssk] 5 times—20 sts.
Rnd 34 [K1, ssk, k1] 5 times—15 sts.
Rnd 35 Knit.
Cut one 2¾"/7cm diameter circle of cushion foam. Insert into base of body. Stuff body. Cut yarn, draw through sts twice, and pull up tightly to finish.

Robe Trim
With C, cast on 6 sts.
*Row 1 (RS) K6, slide sts to beg of needle to work next row from the RS and bring yarn around from back. Rep from * for I-cord for approx 18"/45.5cm. Do *not* bind off. With F, embroider long sts randomly around trim for ermine effect. Beg at center back, pin trim in place around to center front along joining of the A and B sections, curved to go down front, and then curved to go to back along bottom edge to meet in back (see photos). Adjust length of I-cord, if necessary, and bind off.

Nose
With B, cast on 6 sts and divide evenly over 3 dpn. Join, taking care not to twist sts, and pm for beg of rnd.
Rnd 1 Kfb in each st—12 sts.
Rnds 2, 4, and 6 Knit.
Rnd 3 [K1, M1, k1] 6 times—18 sts.
Rnd 5 [K1, ssk] 6 times—12 sts.
Rnd 7 [Ssk] 6 times—6 sts.
Stuff nose.
Cut yarn, draw end through sts twice, and pull tightly to close.
Sew nose to face.

Crown
With D, cast on 12 sts, and divide evenly over 3 dpn. Join, taking care not to twist sts, and pm for beg of rnd.
Rnds 1–13 Knit.
Rnd 14 *Cast on 2 sts, bind off 4 sts, sl st from RH needle to LH needle; rep from * to last 2 sts; cast on 2 sts, bind off rem sts. Fold cast-on edge up to the top of the crown at the bind-off edge (with picots showing for the crown) and seam in place for a doubled fabric crown.
Sew crown to top of head.

Gauge
24 sts and 34 rnds to 4"/10cm over St st using size 4 (3.5mm) dpn.
Take time to check gauge.

4,5
Royal Couple

Finishing for King
With F, embroider 4 tight satin sts for each eye and 2 for each eyebrow.
For mustache, cut ten 6"/15cm strands of E Tie one strand around others at middle to form a bundle and attach under nose. Separate the yarn plies to resemble hair and trim.

Finishing for Queen
With F, embroider 4 tight satin sts for each eye and 2 for each eyebrow.
For hair, cut thirty 6"/15cm strands of E. Divide evenly into 3 bundles.
For each bundle, take one strand and tie rem strands tog in middle to secure.
Secure around crown along back of head. Use 1 strand to knot around each of the bundles to create 4 ponytails that fall to the back.
Separate yarn plies to resemble hair, style, and trim, leave wisps for bangs at front.

6

Sleepy Bunny

Sleepy Bunny loves lullabies,
and is a gentle reminder that bedtime beckons.

DESIGNED BY CHERYL MURRAY

Knitted Measurements
Length Approx 16"/40.5cm
Width Approx 8½"/21.5cm

Materials
- 2 3½oz/100g hanks (each approx 150yd/138m) of Cascade Yarns *220 Superwash Aran* (superwash merino wool) in #201 Sesame (A) 【4】
- 1 hank in #894 Strawberry Cream (B)
- Small amount of yarn in black for face embroidery
- Two size 8 (5mm) circular needles, 24"/60cm long, *or size to obtain gauge*
- Stitch markers
- Embroidery needle
- Tapestry needle
- Polyester stuffing
- One ⅝"/45mm pompom maker

Notes
1) To work St st in rnds, k every rnd.
2) The sts are worked on 2 circular needles with sts slid around for easier working. If preferred, work on a set of (5) dpn.
3) Work four ear pieces back and forth in rows in St st.

Body
Beg at lower edge with A, cast on 12 sts on first circular needle and 12 sts on 2nd circular needle—24 sts. Join to work in rnds, taking care not to twist sts, and pm for beg of rnd. Knit 1 rnd.
Inc rnd On first needle, K1, M1, k to last st, M1, k1; on 2nd needle, k1, M1, k to last st, M1, k1—4 sts inc'd.
Rep inc rnd every rnd 13 times more—80 sts. Work even in St st (k every rnd) until piece measures 5½"/14cm from beg. With B, knit 4 rnds. With A, knit 4 rnds. With B, knit 4 rnds.

SHAPE TOP
Cont to work in stripe pat of 4 rnds A, 4 rnds B and work as foll:
Dec rnd On first needle, K1, ssk, k to last 3 sts, k2tog, k1; on 2nd needle, k1, ssk, k to last 3 sts, k2tog, k1—4 sts dec'd.
Next rnd Knit.
Rep the last 2 rnds 11 times more—32 sts. Using tip from one of the needles as the third needle, join the top using 3-needle bind-off (see page 182).

Head
With A, cast on 16 sts on first circular needle and 16 sts on 2nd circular needle—32 sts. Join to work in rnds, taking care not to twist sts, and pm for beg of rnd. Knit 1 rnd.
Inc rnd 1 K4, M1, k1, M1, k6, M1, k1, M1, k8, M1, k1, M1, k6, M1, k1, M1, k4—40 sts.
Knit 1 rnd.
Inc rnd 2 K5, M1, k1, M1, k8, M1, k1,

Gauge
18 sts and 25 rows/rnds to 4"/10cm over St st worked in rows/rnds using size 8 (5mm) needles.
Take time to check gauge.

Sleepy Bunny

M1, k10, M1, k1, M1, k8, M1, k1, M1, k5—48 sts.
Knit 15 rnds.

SHAPE TOP
Rnd 1 *K4, k2tog; rep from * around—40 sts.
Rnds 2, 4, and 6 Knit.
Rnd 3 *K3, k2tog; rep from * around—32 sts.
Rnd 5 *K2, k2tog; rep from * around—24 sts.
Rnd 7 *K1, k2tog; rep from * around—16 sts.
Rnd 8 [K2tog] 8 times—8 sts.
Cut yarn, leaving a long end. Thread end through rem sts twice to fasten off securely.

Arms and Legs (Make 4)
With A, cast on 14 sts on first circular needle and 14 sts on 2nd circular needle—28 sts. Join to work in rnds, taking care not to twist sts, and pm for beg of rnd. Knit 14 rnds.
Next rnd Purl.
Change to B and knit 4 rnds.
Dec rnd On first needle, *K1, k2tog, k to last 3 sts, ssk, k1*; on 2nd needle, rep between *'s once—4 sts dec'd.
Rep dec rnd 3 times more—12 sts.
Cut yarn, leaving long end to graft the rem 6 sts from each needle tog using Kitchener st (see page 182).

Ears
OUTER EARS (Make 2)
With A, cast on 9 sts and work in St st (k on RS, p on WS) for 16 rows.

Inc row 1 (RS) K1, M1, k7, M1, k1—11 sts.
Work even in St st for 9 rows.
Inc row 2 K1, M1, k9, M1, k1—13 sts.
Work even in St st for 11 rows.
Dec row (RS) K1, k2tog, k to last 3 sts, ssk, k1—2 sts dec'd.
Next row Purl.
Rep the last 2 rows 3 times more—5 sts.
Purl 1 row.
Next row K1, S2KP, k1—3 sts.
Cut yarn and draw through rem 3 sts tightly to fasten off.

INNER EARS (Make 2)
With B, work same as for outer ear.

Bow
With B, cast on 8 sts. Working back and forth in rows, knit 9 rows. Bind off. Cut an 8"/20.5cm length of B and wrap tightly around center to form the bow.

Tail
Using 1 strand of A and B held tog, work a pompom foll the pompom maker instructions.

Finishing
Foll the diagram, embroider face.
Sew head to body, leaving a small opening for stuffing. Stuff head, then sew rem seam.
Seam arms and legs to body, foll the photo, along angled body lines and stuff in same way.

Sew inner and outer ears tog, then attach to top of head.
Sew on tail approx 4"/10cm from lower edge on back.
Secure bow to center front.
Seam lower part of body. If desired, stuff body before sewing lower seam.
Note Sample is not stuffed. ■

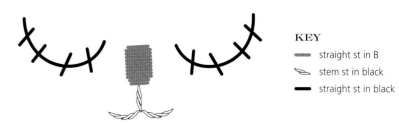

KEY
straight st in B
stem st in black
straight st in black

7,8,9

Hammer, Screwdriver & Saw Tool Set

Tots will love to "build" all kinds of projects.
Parents will love that the soft toys won't break things or make loud noises. Win-win!

DESIGNED BY LOIS S. YOUNG

Knitted Measurements
Hammer Approx 10"/25cm long
Saw Approx 10"/25.5cm long
Screwdriver Approx 8"/21cm long

Materials
▪ 1 3½oz/100g ball (each approx 220yd/200m) of Cascade Yarns *220 Superwash* (superwash wool) each in #907 Tangerine Heather (A), #892 Space Needle (B), and #848 Blueberry (C) (3)
▪ One pair size 5 (3.75mm) needles, *or size to obtain gauges*
▪ One set (4) size 5 (3.75mm) double-pointed needles (dpn)
▪ Stitch markers
▪ Polyester stuffing
▪ 10 straws, 10"/25cm long
▪ Tape

Stitch Glossary
M1R Insert LH needle from *back to front* under the strand between last st worked and next st on LH needle.
K into the *front* loop to twist the st.
M1L Insert LH needle from *front to back* under the strand between last st worked and next st on LH needle.
K into the *back* loop to twist the st.

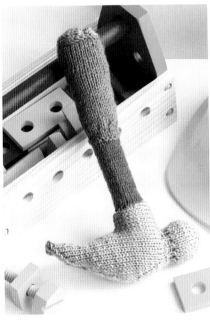

Note
The complete set of tools can be made from just one ball of each color.

Hammer
HANDLE
With C and dpn, cast on 28 sts. Join,

being careful not to twist sts, and pm for beg of rnd. Work in St st (k every rnd) until piece measures 3½"/9cm from beg.
Dec rnd [K1, k2tog] 8 times, [k2tog] twice—18 sts. Cut C.
With A, knit until piece measures 6"/15cm from beg. Bind off.

Base of handle
With B, cast on 4 sts. Purl 1 row.
Row 1 (RS) K1, M1L, k2, M1L, k1—6 sts.
Row 2 and all WS rows Purl.
Row 3 K1, M1L, k4, M1L, k1—8 sts.
Row 5 K1, M1L, k6, M1L, k1— 10 sts.
Work 5 rows in St st (k on RS, p on WS).
Row 11 Ssk, k6, k2tog—8 sts.
Row 13 Ssk, k4, k2tog—6 sts.
Row 15 Ssk, k2, k2tog—4 sts.
Purl 1 row. Bind off.

HEAD
With B and dpn, cast on 6 sts. Join, being careful not to twist sts, and pm for beg of rnd. Knit 1 rnd.
Inc rnd *K1, M1R; rep from * around—12 sts.
Knit 1 rnd. Rep inc rnd once more—24 sts.
Divide sts evenly over 3 dpn. Knit 7 rnds.
Next rnd [K2tog] 12 times around—12 sts.

Gauges
Hammer and Screwdriver 26 sts and 32 rows to 4"/10cm over St st using size 5 (3.75mm) needles.
Saw 26 sts and 44 rows to 4"/10cm over garter st using size 5 (3.75mm) needles.
Take time to check gauges

7,8,9
Hammer, Screwdriver & Saw Tool Set

Knit 2 rnds. Divide sts evenly over 2 dpn and beg working back and forth in rows in St st using a 3rd dpn.

Inc row (RS) *Dpn #1:* [k1, M1L] 5 times, k1; *Dpn #2:* [k1, M1L] 5 times, k1, cast on 6 sts—28 sts.

Next row *Dpn #2:* p17; *Dpn #1:* p11, cast on 6 sts—34 sts.

Knit 1 row. Purl 1 row.

Inc row (RS) *Dpn #1:* k to last 2 sts, M1R, k2; *Dpn #2:* k2, M1L, k to end —2 sts inc'd.

Cont in St st, rep inc row every other row 3 times more—42 sts.

Work 2 rows even.

Next row (WS) *Dpn #2:* bind off 6 sts, work to end; *Dpn #1:* purl.

Next row (RS) *Dpn #1:* bind off 6 sts, work to end; *Dpn #2:* knit—30 sts.

Join to work in rnds and pm for beg of rnd.

Next rnd K14, pm (marker 1), k2, pm (marker 2), k14.

Knit 1 rnd.

Inc rnd K to 2 sts before marker 1, ssk, sm, k2, sm, k2tog, k to end of rnd—2 sts dec'd.

Cont in St st, rep dec rnd every other rnd twice more—24 sts.

Keeping markers 1 and 2 in place, place last 12 sts of rnd on Dpn #3 for 2nd claw, place next 3 sts on Dpn #1, place rem 9 sts on dpn #2 for first claw. Join and place beg of rnd marker.

First Claw
Note Worked on Dpn #1 and #2
Dec rnd K3, k to 2 sts before marker 1, k2tog, k1—1 st dec'd.
Cont in St st, rep dec rnd every other rnd 6 times more—5 sts. Cut yarn, leaving a long tail. Thread tail through rem sts and pull tight.

Second Claw
Put 9 sts with marker on Dpn #1, put last 3 sts on Dpn #2. Join and pm for beg of rnd.
Dec rnd K1, ssk, k to end of rnd—1 st dec'd.
Cont in St st, rep dec rnd every other rnd 6 times more—5 sts. Cut yarn leaving a long tail. Thread yarn through rem sts and pull tight.

Finishing
Whipstitch base of handle to handle. Put thin layer of stuffing in base of handle. Tape together a bundle of 7 straws and insert into handle. Bundle should extend past top of handle. Sew sides of hammerhead tog. Stuff hammerhead and sew to handle (straws will extend into hammerhead). Darn hole between claws and in center of hammerhead. Pull all ends deep into stuffed part of hammer.

Saw
BLADE
With B, cast on 21 sts.
Row 1 (RS) Knit.
Row 2 K10, pm, p1, k to end.
Row 3 K1, M1L, k to last st, M1L, k1—2 sts inc'd.
Row 4 and all WS rows K to marker, sm, p1, k to end.
Rep rows 3 and 4 four times more—31 sts.
Dec row Ssk, k to last 2 sts, k2tog—2 sts dec'd.
Rep dec row every other row 6 times more—17 sts.
Rep row 4, then rep rows 3 and 4 five times—27 sts.
Rep dec row every other row 5 times more—17 sts.
Rep row 4, then rep rows 3 and 4 four times more—25 sts.
Rep dec row every other row 5 times more—15 sts.
Rep row 4, then rep rows 3 and 4 four times more—23 sts.
Rep dec row every other row 6 times more—11 sts.
Bind off in pat.

HANDLE
With A, cast on 36 sts. Work 2 rows in St st (k on RS, p on WS). Cont in St st, bind off 2 sts at beg of next 2 rows—32 sts.
Work 2 rows even.

Divide for hand opening
Next row (RS) K5, bind off 6 sts, k10, bind off 6 sts, k5.
Work 7 rows in St st on last 5 sts.
Cut yarn, leaving a tail 3"/8cm long.
Rejoin A to center 10 sts, ready to work a WS row. Work 3 rows even in St st.

ec row K2, k2tog, k2, ssk, k2—8 sts.
url 1 row.
ec row K1, k2tog, k2, ssk, k1—6 sts.
ut yarn leaving a tail 3"/8cm long.
ejoin A to rem 5 sts of row, ready to
work a WS row. Work 7 rows even.
oining row (RS) K5, cast on 3 sts, k2,
2tog, k2, cast on 3 sts, k5—21 sts.
Vork 3 rows even. Bind off.

inishing
old blade in half with WS held tog.
Vhipstitch teeth of saw tog. Tape two
traws tog, overlapping so 1"/3cm ex-
ends on either end to get proper length.
ghtly stuff teeth of saw and insert
traws at top with a small amount of
tuffing at end of blade for cushioning.
Vhipstitch sides and end of handle, pull-
g ends deep into stuffing. Lightly stuff
rea up to handle opening, then whip-
titch around edge. Stuff rest of handle
nd sew to blade. With C, embroider 4
rench knots on each side of handle to
esemble rivets, using photo as a guide.

Screwdriver
ASE OF HANDLE
Vith C and straight needles, cast on 4
ts. Purl 1 row.
Ic row K1, M1, k to last st, M1, k1—6 sts.
url 1 row. Rep inc row once more. Work
rows even in St st (k on RS, p on WS).
ec row Ssk, k to last 2 sts, k2tog—6 sts.
url 1 row. Rep inc row once more. Bind off.

ANDLE
Vith A and dpn, cast on 20 sts. Divide sts
venly over 3 dpn. Join, being careful not
o twist sts, and pm for beg of rnd.
ext rnd *K2, p2; rep from * around.

K the knit sts and p the purl sts for k2, p2 rib
until piece measures 2½"/7cm from beg.

Shape handle
Next rnd [P2tog, k2tog] 5 times—10 sts.
Next rnd Purl, dec 2 sts evenly
spaced—8 sts.
Cut A, leaving a tail 3"/8cm long.

SHAFT
Divide rem 8 sts evenly over 2 dpn.
With B, work in rnds of St st (k every rnd)
until shaft measures 4"/10cm.

BLADE
Rnd 1 [Sl 1, k3] twice.

Rnd 2 Knit.
Rep rnds 1 and 2 for an additional
1¼"/3cm. Bind off.

Finishing
Cut a 1"/3cm slit on each side of one
end of straw. Tape slit end flat together
to form blade. Tape small amount of
stuffing over end of blade to cushion it.
Whipstitch top of blade and insert straw.
Insert stuffing around straw in handle
of screwdriver.
Trim straw to proper length, if necessary.
Stuff handle.
Whipstitch base of handle in place. ∎

Woodstock Sisters

Fraternal twin dolls play by day
and snuggle up at night on their coordinating blanket bed.

DESIGNED BY CHERI ESPER

Knitted Measurements
Blanket Approx 20"/51cm in diameter
Dolls Approx 11"/28cm long and 7"/18cm at widest point

Materials
- 1 3½oz/100g hank (each approx 220yd/200m) of Cascade Yarns *220 Superwash Effects* (superwash wool) each in #09 Autumn (A), #08 Pinks (B), #07 Daffodil (C), and #01 Reds (D) (4)
- Small amount of red and black yarn
- One each size 10 (6mm) circular needle, 9"/23cm and 16"/40cm long, *or size to obtain gauges*
- One set (4) each sizes 4 and 10 (3.5 and 6mm) double-pointed needles (dpn)
- One size C/2 (2.25mm) crochet hook
- Stitch markers
- Tapestry needle
- Polyester stuffing

Notes
1) Work with 1 strand of yarn for the blanket and 2 strands of yarn held tog for the dolls.
2) The same size circular needle, size 10 (6mm) is used for both projects except for the doll's head.

Blanket
Beg at outer edge, with longer circular needle and 1 strand of A, cast on 200 sts. Join, taking care not to twist sts, and pm for beg of rnd. Cont to work in rnds as foll:
Rnds 1 and 3 *K1, p1; rep from * around.
Rnd 2 *P1, k1; rep from * around.
Rnd 4 Knit.
Rnds 5 and 6 With B, knit.

Dec rnd 7 [K18, k2tog] 10 times—190 sts.
Rnds 8 and 9 Knit.
Dec rnd 10 [K17, k2tog] 10 times—180 sts.
Rnds 11 and 12 With C, knit.
Dec rnd 13 [K16, k2tog] 10 times—170 sts.
Cont in this way to dec 10 sts every 3rd rnd, working 1 less st between dec every dec rnd, and working in stripes as foll: 6 rnds B, 3 rnds D, 6 rnds B, 3 rnds C, 6 rnds D, 3 rnds B, 6 rnds D, 3 rnds C. Change to larger dpn.
Rnds 50 and 51 With A, knit.
Dec rnd 52 [K3, k2tog] 10 times—40 sts.
Rnds 53 and 54 Knit.
Dec rnd 55 [K2, k2tog] 10 times—30 sts.
Rnds 56 and 57 With B, knit.
Dec rnd 58 [K1, k2tog] 10 times—20 sts.
Rnd 59 With A, knit.
Dec rnd 60 [K2tog] 10 times—10 sts.
Cut yarn, leaving a long end. Using tapestry needle, draw yarn through rem 10 sts twice and pull up tightly to finish the center. Block to finished measurements.

Striped-Skirt Sister
Beg at lower edge with shorter circular needle and D, cast on 52 sts. Join to work in rnds, taking care not to twist sts, and pm for beg of rnd. Cont to work in rnds as foll:

Gauges
15 sts and 26 rnds to 4"/10cm over St st worked in rnds, after blocking, using larger needles.
15 sts and 22 rnds to 4"/10cm over St st worked in rnds, after stuffing, using 2 strands of yarn held tog and larger needles.
Take time to check gauges.

Rnd 1 *K1, p1; rep from * around.
Rnd 2 With C, *p1, k1; rep from * around.
Rnd 3 With D, rep rnd 1.
Rnd 4 With C, knit.
Dec rnd 5 With D, k9, k2tog, k4, ssk, k18, k2tog, k4, ssk, k9—48 sts.
Rnd 6 With C, knit.
Rnd 7 With D, knit.
Dec rnd 8 With C, k8, k2tog, k4, ssk, k16, k2tog, k4, ssk, k8—44 sts.
Rnd 9 With D, knit.
Rnd 10 With C, knit.
Cont to dec 4 sts as established every 3rd rnd and alternate 1 rnd D with 1 rnd C, changing to dpn when there are too few sts to fit comfortably on circular needle,

until 24 sts remain. Cut C and cont with D only as foll:

BEGIN BODICE
Rnds 24–29 Knit.
Dec rnd 30 K2, k2tog, k4, ssk, k4, k2tog, k4, ssk, k2—20 sts.
Rnds 31 and 32 Knit.
Dec rnd 33 K1, k2tog, k4, ssk, k2, k2tog, k4, ssk, k1—16 sts.
Rnds 34 and 35 Knit.

DIVIDE FOR ARMHOLES
Place 8 sts for front on one dpn. The 2nd dpn sts will have beg of rnd marker in the center 8 sts for back. Work on the front dpn first.

FRONT
Next row (RS) K2, ssk, k2tog, k2, turn—6 sts.
Purl 1 row, knit 1 row, purl 1 row. Cut yarn.

BACK
Rejoin D and work the 4 rows as for front. Rejoin to work in the rnd again.

NECK
Rnds 1 and 3 *K1, p1; rep from * 5 times more.
Rnd 2 *P1, k1; rep from * 5 times more. Bind off.

ARMS (Make 2)
With dpn and C, pick up and k 8 sts around one of the armhole openings. Divide sts over 3 dpn (3 sts, 3 sts, 2 sts) and join to work in rnds. Knit 15 rnds.
Next rnd K2, M1, k4, M1, k2—10 sts. Knit 3 rnds. Divide sts evenly over 2 dpn and join using 3-needle bind-off (see page 182) from the RS. Rep for other arm.

HEAD
With B and smaller dpn, pick up and k 1. sts at the neck edge, dividing evenly over

dpn. Join and pm for beg of rnd.

Rnd 1 and all odd-numbered rnds
Knit.
Rnd 2 [K3, M1] 4 times—16 sts.
Rnd 4 [K4, M1] 4 times—20 sts.
Rnd 6 [K5, M1] 4 times—24 sts.
Rnd 8 [K6, M1] 4 times—28 sts.
Rnd 10 Knit.
Rnd 12 [K2, k2tog] 7 times—21 sts.
Rnd 14 [K1, k2tog] 7 times—14 sts.
Rnd 16 [K2tog] 7 times—7 sts.
Cut yarn, leaving a long end.
Draw yarn through rem sts twice and pull
tightly to finish.

HAIR
Cut desired number of 12"/30.5cm
lengths of color A. Fold in half and knot
in place, approx 16 locks around face.
Knot a 2nd set of hair locks behind the
first set, skipping one st in between.
Fill in with additional locks at back of head.
Style hair and trim as desired.

SHOES (Make 2)
Place markers at 3 sts to the right of the
center 6 sts on the front lower skirt and
again at 3 corresponding sts on the back
lower skirt. With larger dpn and A, pick
up and k the first 3 sts, M1, pick up and
k the back 3 sts, M1—8 sts. Divide sts
over 3 dpn (3 sts, 3 sts, 2 sts), join, and
pm for beg of rnd. Knit 4 rnds.
Next rnd *[K1, M1] 3 times, k1; rep
from * once more—14 sts.
Knit 3 rnds. Stuff lightly. Divide sts evenly
over 2 dpn and join using 3-needle
bind-off from the RS. Rep for other shoe
(after skipping the center 6 sts).

HEART
With smaller dpn and D, cast on 2 sts.
Work back and forth in rows as foll:
Row 1 Knit.

Row 2 K1, M1, k1—3 sts.
Rows 3, 5, 7, and 9 Knit.
Row 4 K1, M1, k1, M1, k1—5 sts.
Row 6 K2, M1, k1, M1, k2—7 sts.
Row 8 K3, M1, k4—8 sts.
Row 10 K4, turn (leave rem sts unworked).
Next 2 rows K4.
Next row [K2tog] twice.
Bind off. Cut yarn, leaving a long end,
and then rejoin yarn at center and work
2nd half of heart as for last 4 rows.
Sew heart to inside of right hand.

Finishing
With red and black yarn, embroider
mouth and eyes using chain stitch.
Stuff doll lightly. Seam lower skirt closed.

Color-Block Sister
Work as for striped-skirt sister only using
B for the skirt, A for the bodice, B for the
arms, C for the head, B for the hair,
A for the shoes, and C for the heart. ∎

11

Guitar

No need to read music or even to carry a tune
—this sweet stuffed guitar always plays the right song and is always in tune.

DESIGNED BY AMY BAHRT

Knitted Measurements
Approx 5"/12.5cm wide x14½"/37cm high

Materials
- 1 3½oz/100g ball (each approx 220yd/200m) of Cascade Yarns *220 Superwash* (superwash wool) each in #1952 Blaze (A), #877 Golden (B), #812 Turquoise (C), and #816 Gray (D) 📷
- One pair each sizes 5 and 7 (3.75 and 4.5mm) needles, *or size to obtain gauge*
- One size G/6 (4mm) crochet hook
- Polyester stuffing
- Foam board 1¼ x 14"/3 x 35cm
- Tapestry needle

Notes
1) For front, use a separate bobbin for each color section. Do *not* carry yarn across back of work.
2) For front, when changing colors, twist yarns on WS to prevent holes in work.

Front
With larger needles and A, cast on 15 sts. Work in St st (k on RS, p on WS) foll chart 1 for 58 rows. Bind off.

Back
Work as for front, but work only in A.

Gusset
With larger needles and B, cast on 9 sts. Work in St st for 21"/53.5cm. Bind off.

Neck
With larger needles and C, cast on 16 sts. Work in St st foll chart 2. Bind off.

Finishing
Sew one long edge of gusset along outer edge of back. Sew other long edge of gusset along outer edge of front, leaving an opening for stuffing at top. Stuff piece. Fold neck piece in half lengthwise and sew side and top seams. Slip over foam board, then insert rem foam board through opening at top of guitar. Sew bottom edge of neck piece to body of guitar.

SOUND HOLE
With tapestry needle and A, work chain st around circle on front.

GUITAR STRINGS (Make 3)
With crochet hook and D, chain 5"/13cm. Fasten off. Attach to neck and front as indicated on chart and in photo.

TUNING KNOBS (Make 4)
With smaller needles and B, cast on 6 sts. Work in St st for 7 rows.
Slip last 5 sts over first st and off needle. Fasten off last st, leaving a tail.
Stuff each knob. Use tail to sew to top of neck (see photo). ■

Gauge
20 sts and 26 rows to 4"/10cm over St st using larger needles.
Take time to check gauge.

Guitar

COLOR KEY

A   C

B   D

● = attach guitar string

CHART 1

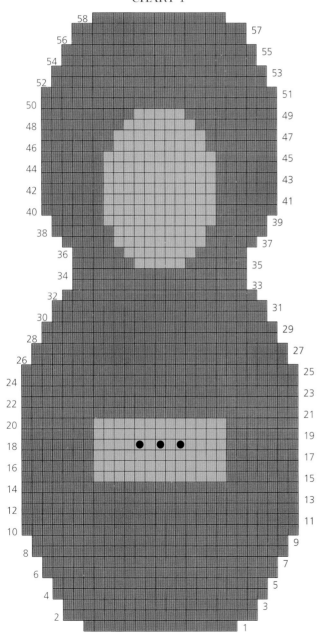

15 sts

CHART 2

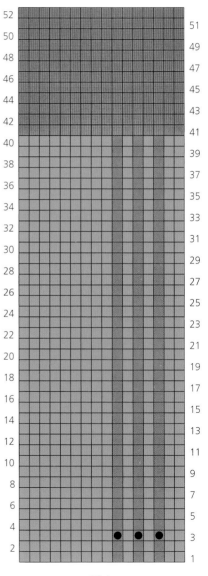

16 sts

32

Antelope Ring Toy

Whether you're home on the range or home in the city,
your wee one will love this adorable antelope, perched on an easy-to-hold ring.

DESIGNED BY CHRISTINA BEHNKE

◼◼◼◻

Knitted Measurements
Approx 9½"/24cm high

Materials
■ 1 3½oz/100g ball (each approx
220yd/200m) of Cascade Yarns *220
Superwash* (superwash wool) each in
#907 Tangerine Heather (A),
#815 Black (B), and #871 White (C) **3**
Note One ball of each color is enough
to make all 3 animal ring toys.
■ One set (5) size 3 (3.25mm)
double-pointed needles (dpn),
or size to obtain gauge
■ One size D/3 (3.25mm) crochet hook
■ Scrap yarn
■ Stitch marker
■ Polyester stuffing

Stitch Glossary
M1R Insert LH needle from back to front
under the strand between last st worked
and next st on LH needle. K into the
front loop to twist the st.
M1L Insert LH needle from front to back
under the strand between last st worked
and next st on LH needle. K
into the back loop to twist the st.

Ring
With A, cast on 28 sts using provisional
cast-on (see page 182). Divide sts over
3 dpn (9 sts, 9 sts, 10 sts). Join, being
careful not to twist sts, and pm for beg
of rnd. Work in St st (k every round),
stuffing tube as you go, until piece
measures 6"/15cm from beg.
Cut A. Knit 5 rnds B.
Cut B. With C cont in St st, stuffing as you
go until tube measures 12½"/31.5cm.

Cut C. Knit 4 rnds B.
Cut B, leaving a long tail. Gently shape ring,
placing beg of rnds at interior.
With tail, graft ends tog using Kitchener st
(see page 182).
Secure yarn and hide end inside ring.

Head
Note Antelope head is worked from top
of head down.
Beg with A, cast on 6 sts using
provisional cast-on method (see page
182). Knit 1 row A.
Divide sts evenly over 3 dpn. Join, being
careful not to twist sts, and pm for beg
of rnd.
Rnd 1 Kfb in each st—12 sts.
Rnd 2 and all even-numbered rnds
Knit.
Rnd 3 [K1, kfb] 6 times—18 sts.
Rnd 5 [K2, kfb] 6 times—24 sts.
Rnd 7 [K3, kfb] 6 times—30 sts.
Rnd 9 [K4, kfb] 6 times—36 sts.
Rnd 11 [K5, kfb] 6 times—42 sts.
Rnd 13 [K6, kfb] 6 times—48 sts.
Rnd 14 Knit.
Carefully remove provisional cast-on.
Draw through sts and pull tightly to

Gauge
28 sts and 38 rnds to 4"/10cm over St st using size 3 (3.25mm) needles.
Take time to check gauge.

Antelope Ring Toy

close. Stuff to a few rnds below the needles.

Rnd 15 K8, M1R, k8, ssk, k12, k2tog, k8, M1L, k8.

Rnd 17 K9, M1R, k8, ssk, k10, k2tog, k8, M1L, k9.

Rnd 19 K10, M1R, k8, ssk, k8, k2tog, k8, M1L, k10.

Rnd 21 K11, M1R, k8, ssk, k8, k2tog, k8, M1L, k11.

DIVIDE FOR NECK AND SNOUT

Rnd 22 *Dpn #1*: k9; *Dpn #2*: k3, cast on 4 sts using backwards loop, place next 24 sts on scrap yarn to hold for snout; cont with *Dpn #2*: k3; *Dpn #3*: k9—28 sts (9 sts each on Dpn #1 and #3, 10 sts on Dpn #2).

Neck

Note See page 183 for how to work short row wrapping (w&t).

Rnd 1 K21, w&t; p14, w&t; k to end of rnd, hiding first wrap.

Rnd 2 and all even-numbered rnds Knit, hiding any wraps.

Rnd 3 Purl.

Rnd 5 [K2, k2og] 7 times—21 sts.

Rnd 7 [K1, k2tog] 7 times—14 sts.

Rnd 9 [K2tog] 7 times—7 sts.

Complete stuffing. Cut yarn, leaving a long tail. Thread tail through rem sts. Fasten firmly and pull tail to inside. The rnds after the purl rnd should fall to the inside of the neck.

Snout

Set-up rnd With A and *Dpn #1*: pick up and k 4 sts along cast-on edge, k4 from scrap yarn; *Dpn #2*: k9 from scrap yarn; *Dpn #3*: k11 from scrap yarn; pm for beg of rnd—28 sts (8 sts on Dpn #1, 9 sts on Dpn #2, 11 sts on Dpn #3).

Rnd 1 K4, ssk, k6, ssk, k4, k2tog, k6, k2tog—24 sts.

Rnd 2 and all even-numbered rows Knit.

Rnd 3 K4, ssk, k4, k2tog, k4, ssk, k4, k2tog—20 sts.

Rnd 5 K8, k2tog, k4, ssk, k4—18 sts.

Rnd 6 Knit. Cut A.

Rnd 7 With C, [k2tog, k4] twice, ssk, k4—15 sts.

Rnd 9 K1, k2tog, k2, k2tog, k4, ssk, k2—12 sts.

Rnd 11 [K2tog] 6 times around—6 sts. Complete stuffing. Cut yarn, leaving a long tail. Thread tail through rem sts. Fasten firmly and pull tail to inside.

Finishing

Insert 2 markers at top center of ring, placing them 12 sts apart. Place neck between markers and using A, graft neck to ring along purl rnd.

Pull tails inside ring to fasten.

EARS (Make 2)

With A, cast on 8 sts and divide over 3 dpn (3 sts, 3 sts, 2 sts). Join, being careful not to twist sts, and pm for beg of rnd.

Rnd 1 and all odd-numbered rnds Knit

Rnd 2 *[Kfb] 3 times, k1; rep from * once more—14 sts.

Rnds 3–7 Knit.

Rnd 8 [K2, S2KP, k2] twice—10 sts.

Rnd 10 [K1, S2KP, k1] twice—6 sts.

Rnd 11 Knit.

Cut yarn, leaving a long tail.

Thread tail through rem sts.

Fasten firmly and pull tail to inside.

Sew ears to sides of head.

HORNS (Make 2)

With B, cast on 4 sts.

*Row 1 (RS) K4, slide sts to beg of needle to work next row from RS and bring yarn around from back. Rep from * for I-cord until piece measures 1"/2.5cm.

Next row (RS) K1, k2tog, k1.

Cont working I-cord on 3 sts until piece measures 1½"/4cm.

Cut yarn and pull through rem sts.

Fasten firmly and hide tail inside I-cord.

Sew horns to head.

With B, embroider French knots for eyes, straight sts for mouth and nose.

Add face markings using duplicate stitch.

Zebra Ring Toy

Baby will be fascinated by this darling zebra and its vivid stripes,
while the ring makes it easy-peasy for little fingers to grasp.

DESIGNED BY CHRISTINA BEHNKE

Knitted Measurements
Approx 8"/20.5cm high

Materials
▪ 1 3½oz/100g ball (each approx 220yd/200m) of Cascade Yarns *220 Superwash* (superwash wool) each in #871 White (A) and #815 Black (B) (3)
Note One ball of each color is enough to make all 3 animal ring toys.
▪ One set (5) size 3 (3.25mm) double-pointed needles (dpn), *or size to obtain gauge*
▪ One size D/3 (3.25mm) crochet hook
▪ Scrap yarn
▪ Stitch markers
▪ Polyester stuffing

Stitch Glossary
M1R Insert LH needle from back to front under the strand between last st worked and next st on LH needle.
K into the front loop to twist the st.
M1L Insert LH needle from front to back under the strand between last st worked and next st on LH needle.
K into the back loop to twist the st.

Zebra Stripe Pattern
In St st (k every rnd) work 2 rnds B, 2 rnds A. Rep these 4 rnds for zebra stripe pat.

Note
Carry yarn not in use by twisting it with the working yarn every few rnds.

Ring
Beg with A, cast on 28 sts using provisional cast-on method (see page 182). Divide sts over 3 dpn (9 sts, 9 sts, 10 sts). Join, being careful not to twist sts, and pm for beg of rnd.
Knit 1 rnd A. Rep 4 rnds of zebra stripe pat 30 times, stuffing tube as you go, until piece measures approx 12¾"/32.5cm. Cut A. With B, k 1 rnd. Cut B, leaving a long tail. Gently shape ring, placing beg of rnds at interior. With tail, graft ends tog using Kitchener st (see page 182). Secure yarn and hide end inside ring.

Head
Note Zebra head is worked from top of head down.
With A, cast on 6 sts using provisional cast-on (see page 182). Knit 1 row A. Divide sts evenly over 3 dpn. Join, being careful not to twist sts, and pm for beg of rnd.
Rnd 1 Kfb in each st—12 sts.
Rnd 2 and all even-numbered rnds Knit, keeping to stripe pat.
Cont in zebra stripe pat as foll:
Rnd 3 With B, [k1, kfb] 6 times—18 sts.
Rnd 5 [K2, kfb] 6 times—24 sts.
Rnd 7 [K3, kfb] 6 times—30 sts.
Rnd 9 [K4, kfb] 6 times—36 sts.

Gauge
28 sts and 38 rnds to 4"/10cm over zebra stripe pattern using size 3 (3.25mm) needles.
Take time to check gauge.

Zebra Ring Toy

Rnd 11 [K5, kfb] 6 times—42 sts.
Rnd 13 [K6, kfb] 6 times—48 sts.
Rnd 14 Knit.
Carefully remove provisional cast-on. Draw through sts and pull tightly to close. Stuff to a few rnds below the needles. Cont in zebra stripe pat as foll:
Rnd 15 K8, M1R, k12, M1L, k8, M1R, k12, M1L, k8—52 sts.
Rnd 17 K9, M1R, k12, M1L, k10, M1R, k12, M1L, k9—56 sts.
Rnd 19 K10, M1R, k11, ssk, k10, k2tog, k11, M1L, k10.
Rnd 21 K11, M1R, k11, ssk, k8, k2tog, k11, M1L, k11.

DIVIDE FOR NECK AND SNOUT
Rnd 22 *Dpn #1*: k9; *Dpn #2*: k3, cast on 4 sts using backwards loop method; place next 32 sts on scrap yarn to hold for snout; cont with *Dpn #2*: k3; *Dpn #3*: k9—28 sts (9 sts each on Dpn #1 and #3, 10 sts on Dpn #2).

Neck

Note See page 183 for how to work short row wrapping (w&t).
Rnd 1 With B, k21, w&t; p14, w&t; k to end of rnd, hiding first wrap. Cut B.
Rnd 2 and all even numbered rnds With A, knit, hiding any wraps.
Rnd 3 Purl.
Rnd 5 [K2, k2og] 7 times—21 sts.
Rnd 7 [K1, k2tog] 7 times—14 sts.

Rnd 9 [K2tog] 7 times—7 sts.
Complete stuffing. Cut yarn, leaving a long tail. Thread tail through rem sts. Fasten firmly and pull tail to inside. The rnds after the purl rnd should fall to the inside of the neck.

Snout

Set-up rnd With A and *Dpn #1*: pick up and k 4 sts along cast-on edge, k6 from scrap yarn; *Dpn #2*: k16 from scrap yarn; *Dpn #3*: k10 from scrap yarn; pm for beg of rnd—36 sts (10 sts each on Dpn #1 and #3, 16 sts on Dpn #2).
Rnd 1 With B, k4, ssk, k9, ssk, k6, k2tog, k9, k2tog—32 sts.
Rnd 2 and all even-numbered rnds Knit.
Rnd 3 With A, k14, ssk, k4, k2tog, k10—30 sts.
Rnd 5 With B, k13, k2tog, k4, ssk, k9—28 sts.
Rnd 7 With A, k12, k2tog, k4, ssk, k8—26 sts. Cut A.
Rnd 9 With B, k11, k2tog, k4, ssk, k7—24 sts.
Rnd 11 [K2, k2tog] 6 times—18 sts.
Knit 3 rnds.
Next rnd [K2tog] 9 times—9 sts.
Complete stuffing.
Cut yarn, leaving a long tail.
Thread tail through rem sts.
Fasten firmly and pull tail to inside.

Finishing

Insert 2 markers at top center of ring, placing them 12 sts apart.
Place neck between markers and using graft neck to ring along purl rnd.
Pull tails inside ring to fasten.

EARS (Make 2)
With A, cast on 8 sts and distribute over 3 dpn (3 sts, 3 sts, 2 sts). Join, being careful not to twist sts, and pm for beg of rnd. Work in zebra stripe pat as foll:
Rnd 1 and all odd-numbered rnds Knit
Rnd 2 *[Kfb] 3 times, k1; rep from * once more—14 sts.
Rnds 3–7 Knit.
Rnd 8 [K2, S2KP, k2] twice—10 sts.
Rnd 10 [K1, S2KP, k1] twice—6 sts.
Rnd 11 Knit.
Cut yarn, leaving a long tail.
Thread tail through rem sts.
Fasten firmly and pull tail to inside.
Sew ears to sides of head, using photo as a guide.

MANE
Cut 18 lengths of A and 20 lengths of B each 3"/7.5cm long for fringe.
With 2 strands of B held tog, fold fringe in half and using crochet hook, pull loop through a stitch at center of head between ears.
Pull ends of strands through loop.
Alternating A and B, add 18 more fringe along center back of head to beg of neck.
Trim mane to ¾"/2cm long.

EYES
With B, embroider French knots for eyes.

Tiger Ring Toy

Tiger, tiger, burning bright,
will charm your wee one, day or night!

DESIGNED BY CHRISTINA BEHNKE

Knitted Measurements
Approx 7½"/19cm high

Materials
1 3½oz/100g ball (each approx 20yd/200m) of Cascade Yarns *220 Superwash* (superwash wool) each in #907 Tangerine Heather (A), #815 Black (B), and #871 White (C) (3)

Note One ball of each color is enough to make all 3 animal ring toys.

One set (5) size 3 (3.25mm) double-pointed needles (dpn), *or size to obtain gauge*

One size D/3 (3.25mm) crochet hook

Scrap yarn

Stitch marker

Polyester stuffing

Stitch Glossary
M1R Insert LH needle from back to front under the strand between last st worked and next st on LH needle. K into the front loop to twist the st.
M1L Insert LH needle from front to back under the strand between last st worked and next st on LH needle. K into the back loop to twist the st.

Tiger Stripe Pattern
In St st (k every rnd) work 2 rnds B, 4 rnds A. Rep these 6 rnds for tiger stripe pat.

Belly Stripe Pattern
In St st work 4 rnds C, 2 rnds B. Rep these 6 rnds for belly stripe pat.

Note
Carry yarn not in use by twisting it with the working yarn every few rnds.

Ring
Beg with A, cast on 28 sts using provisional cast-on (see page 182). Divide sts over 3 dpn (9 sts, 9 sts, 10 sts). Join, being careful not to twist sts, and pm for beg of rnd. Knit 4 rnds A. Work 6 rnds of tiger stripe pat 13 times, stuffing tube as you go, until piece measures approx 8"/20.5cm from beg. Cut A. Cont to stuff as you go, work 6 rnds of belly stripe pat 6 times until piece measures approx 12½"/31.5cm from beg. Cut B. Knit 3 rnds C. Gently shape ring, placing beg of rnds at interior. With tail, graft ends tog using Kitchener st (see page 182).
Secure yarn and hide end inside ring.

Gauge
28 sts and 36 rnds to 4"/10cm over St st using size 3 (3.25mm) needles.
Take time to check gauge

Tiger Ring Toy

Head

Note Tiger head is worked from back of head to snout.

Beg with A, cast on 6 sts using provisional cast-on. With A, knit 1 row. Divide sts evenly over 3 dpn. Join, being careful not to twist sts, and pm for beg of rnd.

Rnd 1 With A, kfb in each st—12 sts.

Rnd 2 and all even-numbered rnds Knit.

Beg with 2 rnds B, work in tiger stripe pat as foll:

Rnd 3 [K1, kfb] 6 times—18 sts.

Rnd 5 [K2, kfb] 6 times—24 sts.

Rnd 7 [K3, kfb] 6 times—30 sts.

Rnd 9 [K4, kfb] 6 times—36 sts.

Rnd 11 [K5, kfb] 6 times— 42 sts.

Rnd 13 [K6, kfb] 6 times—48 sts.

Rnd 14 Knit.

Carefully remove provisional cast-on. Draw through sts and pull tightly to close. Stuff to a few rnds below the needles.

Rnds 15–20 Work even in tiger stripe pat.

Rnd 21 With B, k21, k2tog, k2, ssk, k21— 46 sts.

Rnd 22 Knit. Cut B.

Rnd 23 With A, [k2tog] 11 times, k2, ssk, [k2tog] 10 times—24 sts.

Rnd 25 K9, k2tog, k2, ssk, k9—22 sts.

Rnd 26 Knit. Cut A.

Rnd 27 With C, k8, k2tog, k2, ssk, k8—20 sts.

Rnd 29 K7, k2tog, k2, ssk, k7—18 sts.

Rnd 31 [K2tog] 9 times—9 sts.

Complete stuffing. Cut yarn, leaving a long tail. Thread tail through rem sts. Fasten firmly and pull tail to inside.

Finishing

Insert 2 markers at top center of ring, placing them 12 sts apart.

Place head between markers and graft to ring.

Pull tails inside ring to fasten.

EARS (Make 2)

With A and *Dpn #1*: pick up and k 3 sts in a diagonal line, going from front to back, near center top of head; with *Dpn #2*: pick up and k 2 sts in a diagonal line going in the opposite direction, forming a V shape; with *Dpn #3*: pick up and k 3 sts immediately behind Dpn #2; with *Dpn #4*: pick up and k 2 sts immediately behind Dpn #1; pm for beg of rnd—10 sts.

Knit 3 rnds.

Next rnd [K1, S2KP, k1] twice—6 sts.

Cut yarn, leaving a long tail.

Thread tail through rem sts.

Fasten firmly and pull tail to inside.

With C, duplicate stitch inside ears.

FACE

With C, embroider eye patches using duplicate st. With B, embroider French knots for eyes and straight sts for mouth and nose. ■

Color-Blocked Teddy Bear

Knit with six tonal shades ranging from periwinkle to cobalt,
this charming teddy bear gives a whole new meaning to "the blues."

DESIGNED BY KATHY NORTH

Knitted Measurements
Approx 14"/35.5cm tall

Materials
▓ 1 3½oz/100g ball (each approx 220yd/200m) of Cascade Yarns *220 Superwash* (superwash wool) each in #844 Periwinkle (A), #897 Baby Denim (B), #814 Hyacinth (C), #846 Blue (D), #848 Blueberry (E), and #1925 Cobalt Heather (F) **③**
▓ One pair size 4 (3.5mm) needles, *or size to obtain gauge*
▓ Stitch markers
▓ Stitch holders
▓ Bobbins
▓ Polyester stuffing

Notes
1) Bear is worked in St st (k on RS, p on WS).
2) Use a separate bobbin or ball of yarn for each block of color. When changing colors, twist yarns on WS to prevent holes in work.

Stitch Glossary
Dec 1 st K2tog on RS rows, p2tog on WS rows.
Inc 1 st Kfb on RS rows, pfb on WS rows.
2-st Dec Row Work across to 2 sts before marker, dec 1 st, sm, dec 1 st, work to end.
4-st Dec Row Dec 1 st at beg of row, work across to 2 sts before marker, dec 1 st, sm, dec 1 st, work across to last 2 sts, dec 1 st.
2-st Inc Row Work kfb before and after marker.
4-st Inc Row Inc 1 st at beg of row, work across and Inc 1 st before and after marker, work across and Inc 1 st in last s▮

Back
With E, cast on 2 sts, pm; with A, cast o▮ 2 sts— 4 sts.
Cont in St st, matching colors, as foll:
Row 1 (RS) Inc 1 st in each st—8 sts.
Row 2 (WS) Work 2-st Inc Row—10 sts.
Row 3 Work 4-st Inc Row—14 sts.
Rows 4–6 Work 2-st Inc Row—20 sts.
Row 7 Work 4-st Inc Row—24 sts.
Row 8 Purl.
Row 9 Work 2-st Inc Row.
Row 10 Purl.
Row 11 Work 4-st Inc Row.
Row 12 Purl.
Rep rows 9–12 twice—42 sts.
Work even for 2 rows in St st, then work 4-st Inc Row—46 sts.
Cont in St st, inc 1 st each side of every 4th row twice—50 sts.
Work even in St st for 5 rows.
Dec 1 st each side of every 4th row 4 times, end with a RS row—42 sts.

Gauge
24 sts and 34 rows to 4"/10cm over St st using size 4 (3.5mm) needles.
Take time to check gauge.

42

Color-Blocked Teddy Bear

Next 3 rows Work 2-st Dec Row—36 sts.
Next row Work 4-st Dec Row—32 sts.
Next 3 rows Work 2-st Dec row—26 sts.
Next 2 rows Work 4-st Dec Row.
Bind off rem 18 sts.

Front
With E, cast on 2 sts, pm; with A, cast on 2 sts—4 sts.
Cont in St st, matching colors, as foll: Knit 1 row, purl 1 row.
Next row (RS) Inc 1 St in each st across—8 sts.
Row 2 Purl.
Row 3 Work 2-st Inc Row.
Row 4 Purl.
Row 5 Work 4-st Inc Row.
Row 6 Purl.
Rep rows 3–6 six times more—50 sts.
Work even in St st for 2 rows.
Next row Inc 1 st each side of next row—52 sts.
Work even in St st for 7 rows.
Next row Work 4-st Dec Row—48 sts.
Next 3 rows Work even in St st.
Rep these 4 rows twice more—40 sts.
Next row Work 4-st Dec Row.
Next row Purl.
Next row Work 2-st Dec Row.
Next row Purl.
Rep these 4 rows once more—28 sts.
Next 2 rows Work 4-st Dec Row.
Bind off rem 20 sts.

Head
With C, cast on 18 sts for right side, pm; with E, cast on 18 sts for left side—36 sts.
Cont in St st, matching colors, as foll: Work even in St st for 2 rows.
Next row (RS) Inc 1 st each side—38 sts.
Purl 1 row.

Next row Work 4-st Inc Row—42 sts.
Purl 1 row.
*Next row (RS) Work 2-st Inc Row.
Next row (WS) Purl to 2 sts before marker, inc 1 st in next 2 sts, sm, inc 1 st in next 2 sts, p to end.
Knit 1 row.
Next row (WS) Purl to 2 sts before marker, inc 1 st in next 2 sts, sm, inc 1 st in next 2 sts, p to end.
Rep from * twice more—72 sts.
Next row Work 2-st Inc row—74 sts.
Purl 1 row.
Work left and right sides separately; gusset piece will fit into this area (see photo).

LEFT SIDE OF HEAD
Next row (RS) K to marker, turn, place sts for right side of head on holder.
Next row (WS) Bind off 2 sts, p to end—35 sts.
Dec 1 st at end of next 4 RS rows—31 sts.
Next row (WS) Purl.
Dec 1 st each side of next 2 RS rows, then every row until there are 9 sts. Bind off rem sts.

RIGHT SIDE OF HEAD
Sl sts from holder to needle, ready to work a RS row.
Next row With C, bind off 2 sts, k to end—35 sts.
Dec 1 st at beg of next 4 RS rows—31 sts.
Purl 1 row, then dec 1 st each side of next 2 RS rows, then every row until there are 9 sts. Bind off rem sts.

HEAD GUSSET
With B, cast on 7 sts.
Work in St st, inc 1 st each side of 5th row, and then every 6th row until there are 21 sts.

Work 5 rows even, then dec 1 st each side of next row, and then every 4th row until 7 sts rem.
Dec 1 st each side of every other row twice—3 sts.
Work 1 row even, then k1, k2tog, turn, p2tog, fasten off.

Right Ear
With D, cast on 18 sts. Work 8 rows in St st.
Dec 1 st at each side of next 3 RS rows, then dec 1 st at each side every row 3 times—6 sts.
Work 1 row even, then cut D.
Change to F, work 1 row even, then inc 1 st at each side of every row 3 times, then inc 1 st at each side of next 3 RS rows—18 sts.
Work 7 rows even. Bind off.

Left Ear
Work same as right ear, but cast on with F and change to D at the halfway point.

Right Arm
With C, cast on 2 sts, pm; with A, cast on 2 sts
Cont in St st, matching colors, as foll:
Work 2 rows even in St st.
Next row (RS) Inc 1 st in each st across—8 sts.
Next row Work 2-st Inc Row.
Next row Work 4-st Inc Row.
Rep these 2 rows twice more—26 sts.
Next row Work 2-st Inc Row.
Purl 1 row.
Rep last 2 rows twice more—32 sts.
Next row Inc 1 st in first st, work rest of row as 2-st Dec Row and inc 1 st in last st—32 sts.
Purl 1 row.
Rep these 2 rows 4 times more—32 sts.

Work 6 rows even.
Work 2-st Inc Row, then work 3 rows even.
Rep these 4 rows once—36 sts.
Next row K2tog, work rest of row as
2-st Inc Row and k2tog at end of row.
Work 3 rows even.
Rep these 3 rows 5 times more—36 sts.
Work 1 row even.
Next 5 rows Work 4-st Dec Row.
Bind off rem 8 sts.

Left Arm
With E, cast on 2 sts, pm; with D, cast on
sts. Work same as right arm.

Right Leg
With D, cast on 26 sts, pm; with E, cast on
6 sts. Cont in St st, matching colors, as foll:
Work 2 rows in St st. Work 2-st Dec Row
every row until 42 sts rem. Purl 1 row.
Work 2-st Dec Row on next 2 RS rows—
8 sts, then every 4th row twice—34 sts.
Work 5 rows even, then work 4-st Inc
Row—38 sts.
Work 7 rows even, then work 4-st Inc
Row—42 sts.
Work 7 rows even, then work 4-st Inc
Row—46 sts.
Work 5 rows even, then work 4-st Dec
Row—42 sts.
Work 3 rows even, then work 4-st Dec
Row on next row, then every RS row
twice more, then every row 5 times—10 sts.
Bind off rem sts.

Left Leg
With A, cast on 26 sts, pm; with C, cast
on 26 sts. Work same as right leg.

Right Sole
Beg at toe, with F, cast on 4 sts and work

2 rows in St st.
Cast on 2 sts at beg of next 2 rows—8 sts.
Inc 1 st each side of next 2 rows—12 sts.
Work even for 14 rows. Dec 1 st each
side of next 2 RS rows, then every row 3
times—2 sts. K2tog and fasten off last st.

Left Sole
Beg at toe, with B, cast on 4 sts and
work same as right sole.

Finishing
Sew arm seams, leaving ends open to stuff.
Sew gusset to right and left sides of head
(cast-on edge of gusset goes where right
and left sides separate at nose).
Sew back head seam, leaving neck open to
stuff. Sew front and back body pieces tog,
leaving open at bound-off edges for neck.
Firmly stuff head, body, and arms.
Sew leg seams, leaving bottoms of feet
open, stuff, then sew on soles.
Finish sewing arms shut.
Sew head to body at neck.
Fold ears in half and sew tog at side edges,
then sew to sides of head.
Arms and legs can be sewn individually onto
body, or attached by stitching each pair tog
through body so that arms and legs move.
With F, embroider face as shown in picture. ■

Bow-Wow and Meow-Meow Pillows

Cuddle up close with these playful pillows
for a restful nap or a relaxing afternoon.

DESIGNED BY LISA CRAIG

Knitted Measurements
Approx 14 x 16"/35.5 x 40.5cm

Materials
▦ 3 3½oz/100g hanks (each approx 150yd/138m) of Cascade Yarns *220 Superwash Aran* (superwash merino wool) in #1946 Silver Grey (MC)
▦ 1 hank in #815 Black (CC)
▦ One pair each sizes 7 and 8 (4.5 and 5mm) needles, *or size to obtain gauge*
▦ Polyester stuffing

Notes
1) Wind small balls of yarn for each section of CC.
2) When changing colors, twist yarns on WS to prevent holes in work.
3) 3 hanks of MC are required for each pillow.

Bow-Wow Pillow
BACK
With larger needles and MC, cast on 59 sts. Work in St st (k on RS, p on WS) for 48 rows Join CC and work 3 rows in St st.** Change to MC and work 47 rows more in St st. Bind off.

FRONT
Work as for back to **. Work 4 rows MC.

Gauge
17 sts and 24 rows to 4"/10cm over St st using larger needles.
Take time to check gauge

46

Bow-Wow and Meow-Meow Pillows

Begin chart 1
Work rows 1–32 of chart 1. Cont with MC only, work in St st for 11 rows. Bind off.

POCKET
With larger needles and MC, cast on 59 sts. Work in St st for 39 rows. Change to smaller needles. Work 6 rows in garter st (k every row). Bind off.

EARS (Make 2)
With smaller needles and CC, cast on 14 sts.
Work in garter st for 34 rows.
Dec row (RS) K2tog, k to last 2 sts, k2tog—2 sts dec'd.
Knit 1 row. Rep dec row once more.
Knit 1 row. Bind off.

Finishing
Sew pocket to front along side and lower edges. Sew front to back, leaving an opening for stuffing.
Stuff and sew closed.
Attach ears to sides of pillow, using photo as a guide.

Meow-Meow Pillow
BACK
With larger needles and MC, cast on 59 sts. Work in St st for 98 rows. Bind off.

FRONT
Work as for back for 60 rows.

Begin chart 2
Work rows 1–25 of chart 2.
Cont with MC only, work in St st for 13 rows. Bind off.

POCKET
With larger needles and MC, cast on 59 sts.
Work in St st for 39 rows.
Change to smaller needles.
Work 6 rows in garter st (k every row).
Bind off.

EARS (Make 2)
With smaller needles and CC, cast on 2 sts.
Inc row 1 (RS) [Kfb] twice—4 sts.
Row 2 Knit.
Inc row 3 Kfb, k to last st, kfb—2 sts inc'd.
Rep inc row 3 every other row 4 times more—14 sts.
Knit 1 row. Bind off.

Finishing
Sew pocket to front along side and lower edges.
Sew front to back, leaving an opening for stuffing. Stuff and sew closed.
Attach ears to top of pillow, using photo as a guide. ■

Chart 1

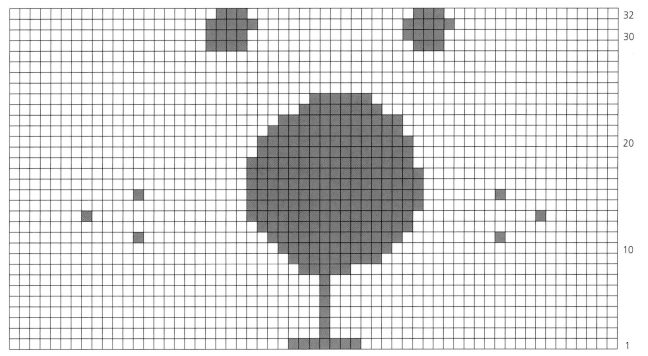

59 sts

Chart 2

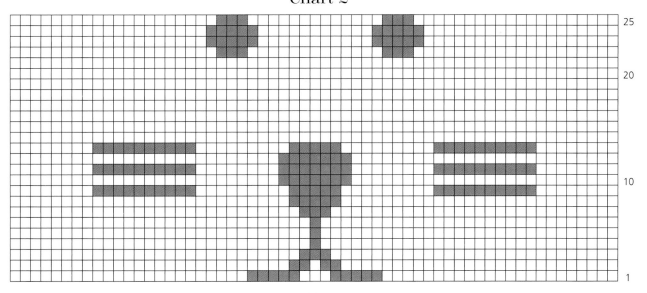

59 sts

COLOR KEY

☐ MC

■ CC

Fishing Game

No need to handle wiggly worms to go fishing!
This adorable playset has magnetized fish and fishing rod for a no-muss, no-fuss fishing trip.

DESIGNED BY LYNN M. WILSON

Knitted Measurements
Fish Approx 3¾"/9.5cm long, excluding tail

Materials
▪ 1 1¾oz/50g hank (each approx 137yd/125m) of Cascade Yarns *220 Superwash Sport* (superwash merino wool) each in #225 Classic Blue (A), #802 Green Apple (B), and #809 Really Red (C) (**3**)
▪ Two size 5 (3.75mm) double-pointed needles (dpn), *or size to obtain gauge*
▪ One size G/6 (4mm) crochet hook
▪ Six ¾"/19mm magnets
▪ ⁷/₁₆" wooden dowel, 12"/30.5cm long
▪ Polyester quilt batting 12½ x7"/31.5 x18cm
▪ Polyester stuffing
▪ Glue and tape

Stripe Pattern
2 rows A, 2 rows B.
Rep these 4 rows for stripe pat.

Notes
1) Carry yarn not in use by twisting it with the working yarn every few rnds.
2) To create an optional pond, take a 12"/30.5cm square piece of felt and either sew ends or sew in snaps to create sides (see photos).

Fish (Make 5)
SIDES (Make 2)
With A, cast on 3 sts.
Row 1 (RS) Knit.
Inc row 2 K1, M1, k to last st, M1, k1—2 sts inc'd.
Cont in garter st (k every row) and stripe pat, rep last 2 rows 4 times more—13 sts. Work 11 rows even in stripe pat.

Dec row (WS) K1, k2tog, k to last 3 sts, k2tog, k1—2 sts dec'd.
Rep dec row every other row 3 times more—5 sts.
Next row K1, S2KP, k1—3 sts.
Next row K2tog, k1, pass k2tog over k? Fasten off.
With C, embroider a French knot on each fish side, using photo for placement.
Glue 1 magnet to each of 5 fish sides.
When glue is dry, sew 2 fish sides tog.

FISH TAIL
With crochet hook, attach A with slip st to end of fish, [Ch 17, join to base with st] twice. Fasten off.

Fishing Pole
POLE
With C, cast on 8 sts. Knit 1 row.
Inc row [K1, M1] 7 times across, k1—15 sts. Knit 2 rows C, 2 rows A, 2 rows C. Cut C. With A, work 20 rows in St st (k on RS, p on WS). Join C and knit 4 rows. Cut C. Cont in St st and stripe pat until piece measures 12½"/31.5cm from beg.
Cut yarn, leaving a long tail.
Thread tail through sts to close.

Gauge
22 sts and 48 rows to 4"/10cm over garter st using size 5 (3.75mm) needles.
Take time to check gauge

Fishing Game

LINE

With C, cast on 3 sts. *Knit one row. Without turning work, slide the sts back to the opposite end of needle to work next row from RS.

Pull yarn tightly from the end of the row. Rep from * until I-cord measures 13"/28cm from beg.

Hook

Inc row (RS) [Kfb] twice, k to end—5 sts. Rep inc row every other row once more—7 sts.

Work 5 rows in St st.

Dec row (RS) K1, k2tog, k1, k2tog, k1—5 sts.

Purl 1 row.

Next row K1, S2KP—3 sts.

Rep from * once more.

Fold hook in half at center.

Whip stitch edges tog, leaving a space to insert magnet. Insert magnet. Sew closed.

Wrap batting around dowel and tape in place.

Wrap pole piece around dowel and sew seam.

Secure line to end of pole. ■

19, 20

Barnyard Buddy Balls

With an oink, oink here and a hop, hop there,
these cute critters are quick to knit and are sure to charm!

DESIGNED BY AMANDA KAFKA

Knitted Measurements
Circumference (at widest point)
Approx 11"/28cm

Materials
- 1 3½oz/100g hank (each approx 220yd/200m) of Cascade Yarns *220 Superwash Effects* (superwash wool) in #08 Pinks or #09 Autumn (4)
- Small amount of black and pink yarn
- One set (4) size 6 (4mm) double-pointed needles (dpn), *or size to obtain gauge*
- Polyester stuffing
- Stitch marker

Notes
1) Body is same for pigs and bunnies.
2) Ears are worked back and forth in rows with 2 strands of yarn held tog.

Body
Cast on 6 sts and divide evenly over 3 dpn. Join, taking care not to twist sts, and pm for beg of rnd.
Rnd 1 [Kfb] 6 times—12 sts.
Rnd 2 [K1, kfb] 6 times—18 sts.
Rnd 3 and all odd-numbered rnds through rnd 15 Knit.
Rnd 4 [K2, kfb] 6 times—24 sts.
Rnd 6 [K3, kfb] 6 times—30 sts.

Rnd 8 [K4, kfb] 6 times—36 sts.
Rnd 10 [K5, kfb] 6 times—42 sts.
Rnd 12 [K6, kfb] 6 times—48 sts.
Rnd 14 [K7, kfb] 6 times—54 sts.
Rnd 16 [K8, kfb] 6 times—60 sts.
Rnds 17—26 Knit.
Rnd 27 [K8, k2tog] 6 times—54 sts.
Rnd 28 and all even-numbered rnds through rnd 40 Knit.
Rnd 29 [K7, k2tog] 6 times—48 sts.
Rnd 31 [K6, k2tog] 6 times—42 sts.
Rnd 33 [K5, k2tog] 6 times—36 sts.
Rnd 35 [K4, k2tog] 6 times—30 sts.
Rnd 37 [K3, k2tog] 6 times—24 sts.
Stuff body, taking care not to overstuff.
Rnd 39 [K2, k2tog] 6 times—18 sts.
Rnd 41 [K1, k2tog] 6 times—12 sts.
Rnd 42 [K2tog] 6 times—6 sts.
Cut yarn and thread tail through rem sts to close.

PIG
SNOUT
Cast on 22 sts and divide over 3 dpn (7 sts, 8 sts, 7 sts). Join, taking care not to twist sts, and pm for beg of rnd.
Knit 3 rnds. Purl 1 rnd.
Next rnd [K2tog] 11 times—11 sts.
Lightly stuff snout.

Gauge
20 sts and 28 rnds to 4"/10cm over St st using size 6 (4mm) needles.
Take time to check gauge.

Barnyard Buddy Balls

Cut yarn, leaving a long tail.
Thread tail through rem 11 sts to close.

TAIL
Cast on 11 sts.
Next row [Kfb] 11 times—22 sts.
Bind off.

EARS (Make 2)
With 2 strands of yarn held tog, cast on 11 sts.
Knit 3 rows.
Shape Ear
Dec row (RS) K1, ssk, k to last 3 sts, k2tog, k1—2 sts dec'd.
Cont in garter st (k every row), rep dec row every other row twice more—5 sts.
Knit 1 row.
Next row Ssk, k1, k2tog—3 sts.
Knit 1 row.
Next row SK2P.
Fasten off rem st.

BUNNY
TAIL
Cast on 6 sts and divide evenly over 3 dpn. Join, taking care not to twist sts, and pm for beg of rnd.
Rnd 1 [Kfb] 6 times—12 sts.
Rnd 2 [K1, kfb] 6 times—18 sts.
Rnd 3 Knit.
Rnd 4 [K1, k2tog] 6 times—12 sts.
Lightly stuff tail.
Rnd 5 [K2tog] 6 times—6 sts.

Cut yarn, leaving a long tail.
Thread tail through rem sts to close.

EARS (Make 2)
With 2 strands of yarn held tog, cast on 9 sts. Knit 9 rows.
Dec row K1, ssk, k to last 3 sts, k2tog, k1—7 sts.
Cont in garter st, rep dec row every 6th row once more—5 sts.
Knit 6 rows.
Next row Ssk, k1, k2tog—3 sts.
Knit 3 rows.
Next row SK2P.
Fasten off rem st.

Finishing
PIG
Using photos as a guide, sew ears, snout and tail to body.
With small amount of black yarn, embroider face, using French knots for eyes and nostrils and straight sts for mouth.

BUNNY
Using photos as a guide, sew ears and tail to body. With small amount of black yarn, embroider face, using French knots for eyes and straight sts for mouth.
With small amount of pink yarn, embroider nose. ∎

Building Brick Pillow

After a busy day of building, your hard-working architect can snuggle up with this brick-shaped pillow and dream of new things to create!

DESIGNED BY AMY BAHRT

Knitted Measurements
Approx 7 x 12 x 4½"/18 x 30.5 x 11cm

Materials
- 2 3½oz/100g balls (each approx 220yd/200m) of Cascade Yarns *220 Superwash* (superwash wool) in #864 Christmas Green (3)
- One pair size 7 (4.5mm) needles, *or size to obtain gauge*
- One set (4) size 7 (4.5mm) double-pointed needles (dpn)
- Straight pins
- Polyester stuffing

Block
Cast on 60 sts. Work in St st (k on RS, p on WS) for 43 rows.
Turning row (WS) Knit.
Cont in St st for 27 rows more.
Turning row (WS) Knit.
Cont in St st for 43 rows more.
Turning row (WS) Knit.
Cont in St st for 27 rows more. Bind off.

End Panel (Make 2)
Cast on 34 sts. Work in St st for 27 rows. Bind off.

Knob (Make 6)
KNOB TOP
With A, cast on 5 sts. Working in St st, inc 1 st each side 3 times —11 sts. Work 1 row even. Inc 1 st each side once more —13 sts.

Work 7 rows even. Dec 1 st each side every other row twice, then every row twice more —5 sts. Bind off.

KNOB BASE
With dpn, cast on 33 sts. Join, being careful not to twist sts, and pm for beg of rnd. Knit 7 rnds. Bind off.

Finishing
With WS held tog, sew cast-on and bound-off edges of block together so seam is on RS. With RS tog, pin end panels to each end of block.
With WS facing, sew end panel seams, leaving an opening for stuffing
With RS facing, stuff to desired plumpness
Sew closed.

KNOBS
With RS tog, pin a knob top to each knob base and sew seams on WS.
Turn each to RS and place evenly spaced along top of block.
Sew knobs to block, stuffing each before closing. ■

Gauge
20 sts and 24 rows to 4"/10cm over St st using size 7 (4.5mm) needles.
Take time to check gauge.

Three Little Monkeys

One pattern times three color combinations
equals more fun than a barrel of . . . well, you know!

DESIGNED BY JACQUELINE VAN DILLEN

■◢■■▭

Knitted Measurements
Approx 12 x 14"/30.5 x 35.5cm, when stuffed

Materials
▪ 1 3½oz/100g ball (each approx 220yd/200m) of Cascade Yarns *220 Superwash* (superwash wool) each in #1949 Lavender (A), #881 Then There's Mauve (B), #811 Como Blue (C), and #1914 Alaska Sky (D) (▣)
▪ One set (4) size 4 (3.5mm) double-pointed needles (dpn), *or size to obtain gauge*
▪ One pair size 4 (3.5mm) needles
▪ Small amounts of red and dark gray yarn for embroidery
▪ Polyester stuffing
▪ Pellets
▪ Small bag for pellets when stuffing
▪ Stitch markers
▪ Stitch holders, scrap yarn
▪ Tapestry needle

Stripe Pattern 1
2 rnds B, 2 rnds A.
Rep these 4 rnds for stripe pat 1.

Stripe Pattern 2
2 rnds B, 2 rnds C.
Rep these 4 rnds for stripe pat 2.

Little Monkey #1
LEGS (MAKE 2)
With A and dpn, cast on 10 sts and divide over 3 dpn (3 sts, 4 sts, 3 sts). Join, taking care not to twist sts, and pm for beg of rnd. Work in St st (k every rnd) and inc as foll:
Rnd 1 *Dpn #1*: K to last st, M1, k1; *Dpn #2*: K1, M1, k to last st, M1, k1; *Dpn #3*: M1, k to end—4 sts inc'd.
Rnd 2 Knit.
Rep rnds 1 and 2 four times more—30 sts.
Cont in St st and stripe pat 1 for 9 rnds.
Dec rnd [K2tog, k13] twice—2 sts dec'd.
Knit 9 rnds.
Dec rnd [K2tog, k12] twice—2 sts dec'd.
Cont dec 2 sts every 10th rnd, working 1 less st between dec every dec rnd, 3 times more—20 sts.
Work even in St st until there are 19 A stripes.
Divide sts over 2 needles and *k1 st on front needle tog with 1 st on back needle; rep from * 9 times more.
Place rem 10 sts on a stitch holder.
Lightly stuff leg, then stuff toe with pellets.
Sew toe seam closed.

ARMS (Make 2)
With B and dpn, cast on 8 sts and divide

over 3 dpn (2 sts, 4 sts, 2 sts). Join, taking care not to twist sts, and pm for beg of rnd. Work in St st and inc as foll:
Rnd 1 *Dpn #1*: K to last st, M1, k1; *Dpn #2*: K1, M1, k to last st, M1, k1; *Dpn #3*: M1, k to end—4 sts inc'd.
Rnd 2 Knit.
Rep rnds 1 and 2 three times more—24 sts.
Cont in St st for 5 rnds.
Dec rnd [K2tog, k10] twice—2 sts dec'd.
Knit 5 rnds.
Dec rnd [K2tog, k9] twice—2 sts dec'd.
Cont in this way to dec 2 sts every 6th rnd, working 1 less st between dec every dec rnd, 3 times more—14 sts.
Work even in St st until there are 38 rnds from beg. Change to C and knit 10 rnds.
Divide sts over 2 needles and *k1 st on front needle tog with 1 st on back needle, rep from * 6 times more. Place rem 7 sts on a stitch holder. Stuff as for legs.

BODY
With C and straight needles, cast on 34 sts. Work back and forth in rows in St st (k on RS, p on WS) for 4 rows.
Next row (RS) K3, [M1, k3] 9 times, M1, k4—44 sts.
Purl 1 row.

Gauge
24 sts and 28 rows/rnds to 4"/10cm over St st using size 4 (3.5mm) needles.
Take time to check gauge.

Next row K9, [k 1 st from arm holder tog with next st on needle] 7 times, k12, [k 1 st from arm holder tog with next st on needle] 7 times, k9.
Purl 1 row.
Next row (RS) K10, M1, k1, M1, k22, M1, k1, M1, k10—4 sts inc'd.
Work 3 rows even.
Next row (RS) K11, M1, k1, M1, k24, M1, k1, M1, k11—4 sts inc'd.
Cont in this way to inc 4 sts every 4th row 3 times more, AT THE SAME TIME, when 16 rows of C have been worked, change to B.
After all incs have been worked and there are 64 sts on needle, divide sts evenly over 4 dpn, join, pm to mark beg of rnd, and cont in rnds as foll:
Work even in St st until body measures 7"/18cm from beg.

Attach legs as foll:
Next rnd K17, [k 1 st from leg holder tog with next st on needle] 10 times, k10, [k 1 st from leg holder tog with next st on needle] 10 times, k17.

Shape bottom as foll:
Knit 1 rnd.
Dec rnd [K6, k2tog] 8 times—56 sts.
Knit 1 rnd.
Dec rnd [K5, k2tog] 8 times—48 sts.
Knit 1 rnd.
Cont to dec 8 sts every other rnd, working 1 less st between dec every dec rnd, until there are 16 sts.
Next rnd [K2tog] 8 times—8 sts.
Cut yarn and draw through rem sts.
Pull tog tightly and secure end.

EARS (Make 2)
With A, cast on 12 sts and divide over 3 dpn (3 sts, 6 sts, 3 sts). Join, taking care not to twist sts, and pm for beg of rnd.
Rnd 1 *Dpn #1*: K to last st, M1, k1; *Dpn #2*: K1, M1, k to last sts, M1, k1; *Dpn #3*: M1, k to end—4 sts inc'd.
Rnd 2 Knit.
Rep rnds 1 and 2 twice more—24 sts.
Cont in St st (k every rnd) until piece measures 2"/5cm.
Divide sts over 2 needles and *k1 st on front needle tog with 1 st on back needle; rep from * 11 times more.
Place rem 12 sts on a stitch holder.

HEAD
With C and straight needles, cast on 30 sts.
Work in St st in rows as foll:
Beg with WS, purl 1 row.
Next row (RS) K14, M1, k2, M1, k14—2 sts inc'd.
Purl 1 row.
Next row (RS) K15, M1, k2, M1, k15—2 sts inc'd.
Purl 1 row.
Next row (RS) K16, M1, k2, M1, k16—36 sts.
Purl 1 row.

Attach ears as foll:
Next row (RS) K6, [k 1 st from ear holder tog with next st on needle] 12 times, M1, k2, M1, [k 1 st from ear holder tog with next st on needle] 12 times, k6—38 sts.
Purl 1 row.
Cont to inc 1 st at each side of center 2 sts every other row 9 times more—56 sts.
After all incs have been worked, work even for 1"/2.5cm, end with a WS row.
Divide sts evenly over 4 dpn, join, pm to mark beg of rnd, and work in rnds as foll:
Knit 10 rnds.

Nose
Next rnd [K6, k2tog] 7 times—49 sts.
Knit 1 rnd.
Next rnd [K5, k2tog] 7 times—42 sts.
Knit 1 rnd.
Cont in this way to dec 2 sts every other rnd, working 1 less st between dec, until 14 sts rem.
Knit 1 rnd.
Next rnd [K2tog] 7 times—7 sts.
Knit 1 rnd.
Cut yarn and draw through rem sts.
Pull tog tightly and secure end.

Finishing
Sew head seam. Attach head to front of body. Stuff head. Fill bottom of body with pellets, stuff rem of body, and sew back seam. Sew back of head to body. With red yarn, embroider chain st mouth with C, embroider duplicate st for eyes.

Little Monkey #2
Work as for little monkey #1, in colors as foll:
Legs With C only.
Arms 38 rnds with D, rem rnds with A.
Body 16 rows with A, rem body with D.
Head With A only.
Ears With C only.
Embroidery Red yarn for mouth, dark grey for eyes.

Little Monkey #3
Work as for little monkey #1, in colors as foll:
Legs With B only.
Arms 24 rnds in stripe pat 2, rem rnds with B.
Body Work in stripe pat 2 only.
Head With C only.
Ears With B only.
Embroidery Red yarn for mouth, dark grey for eyes. ■

Raccoon Puppet

This masked bandit is ready to steal your heart!
Knit this darling puppet in the round, and don't forget the striped tail.

DESIGNED BY PAT OLSKI

Knitted Measurements
Body circumference Approx 7"/18cm
Length Approx 8"/20.5cm

Materials
▓ 1 1¾oz/50g hank (each approx
137yd/125m) of Cascade Yarns
220 Superwash Sport (superwash merino
wool) each in #1946 Silver Grey (MC),
#1913 Jet (A), #900 Charcoal (B),
and #871 White (C) (3)
▓ One set (5) size 4 (3.5mm) double-pointed
needles (dpn), *or size to obtain gauge*
▓ Stitch markers
▓ Stitch holders
▓ Tapestry needle

Body
With A, cast on 48 sts and divide evenly
over 4 dpn. Join, taking care not to twist
sts, and pm for beg of rnd.
Work in garter st (k 1 rnd, p 1 rnd) for 6
rnds. Cont in St st (k every rnd) as foll:
With A, knit 4 rnds. With B, knit 10 rnds.
With MC, knit 13 rnds.

INCREASE FOR ARMS
Rnd 1 K12, pm, M1, pm, k24, pm, M1,
pm, k12—50 sts.

Rnds 2 and 3 Knit.
Rnd 4 K12, sm, M1, k1, M1, sm, k24,
sm, M1, k1, M1, sm, k12—54 sts.
Rnds 5–7 Knit.
Rnd 8 K12, sm, M1, k to next marker,
M1, sm, k24, sm, M1, k to next marker,
M1, sm, k12—58 sts.
Rnds 9 and 10 Knit.
Rnds 11–16 Rep rnds 8–10 twice—66 sts.
Rnd 17 Knit.

Rnd 18 K12, sm, place next 9 sts on
holder for arm, using backward loop,
cast on 5 sts onto RH needle, sm, k24,
sm, place next 9 sts on holder for arm,
using backward loop, cast on 5 sts onto
RH needle, sm, k12—58 sts.
Rnd 19 K10, k2tog, sm, k5, sm, k2tog
tbl, k20, k2tog, sm, k5, sm, k2tog tbl,
k10—54 sts.
Rnd 20 K9, k2tog, sm, k2tog tbl, k1,
k2tog, sm, k2tog tbl, k18, k2tog, sm,
k2tog tbl, k1, k2tog, sm, k2tog tbl,
k9—46 sts.
Rnd 20 K10, remove marker, k3tog,
remove marker, k20, remove marker,
k3tog, remove marker, k10—42 sts.

HEAD
With C, knit 8 rnds. With A, knit 1 rnd.
With B, knit 8 rnds. With A, knit 1 rnd.

Shape top of head
Change to MC.
Next rnd K11, pm, k20, pm, k11.
Dec rnd [K to 2 sts before marker, k2tog,
sm, ssk] twice, k to end—38 sts.
Rep dec rnd every rnd until 18 sts rem.
Bind off.

Gauge
26 sts and 36 rnds to 4"/10cm over St st using size 4 (3.5mm) needles.
Take time to check gauge.

Raccoon Puppet

Arms and Hands (Make 2)

With RS facing, MC and dpn, k 9 sts from holder, pick up and k 5 sts along cast-on edge—14 sts. Join, dividing sts over dpn as desired, pm for beg of rnd, and knit 9 rnds.

Change to A, knit 1 rnd, purl 1 rnd.

Next rnd [K2tog] 7 times—7 sts.

Purl 1 rnd; knit 1 rnd.

Cut yarn, thread tail through rem sts, and pull tightly to secure.

Ears (Make 2)

With RS facing and B, pick up and k 7 sts along angled edge at top of head.

Row 1 K6, sl 1 wyif.

Row 2 K1, ssk, k1, k2tog, sl 1 wyif—5 sts.

Rows 3–5 K4, sl 1 wyif.

Row 6 K1, SK2P, sl 1 wyif—3 sts.

Row 7 K2, sl 1 wyif.

Row 8 SK2P.

Cut yarn, thread tail through rem st, and pull tightly to secure.

Tail

With B, cast on 16 sts and divide evenly over 4 dpn. Join, taking care not to twist sts, and pm for beg of rnd. Knit 8 rnds. [Change to A and (knit 1 rnd, purl 1 rnd) 3 times. Change to B and knit 6 rnds] twice. Change to A and [knit 1 rnd, purl 1 rnd] 4 times.

DECREASE FOR TIP

Next rnd [K2, k2tog] 4 times—12 sts.

Purl 1 rnd.

Next rnd [K1, k2tog] 4 times—8 sts.

Purl 1 rnd, knit 1 rnd.

Cut yarn, thread tail through rem sts, and pull tightly to secure.

Finishing

Block lightly. Weave in all ends.

Attach tail to puppet.

With A, embroider 2 French knots for eyes, 1 French knot surrounded by 2 lazy daisy sts for nose, and back sts for mouth (see photo). ■

Baby Elephant

No one will mind this elephant in the room with its jaunty trunk and playful gait
—and it only takes one skein, too!

DESIGNED BY EMILY WHITTED

Knitted Measurements

Length Approx 16"/40.5cm, from trunk to hind legs

Body circumference Approx 11½"/29cm

Materials

- 1 3½oz/100g hank (each approx 150yd/138m) of Cascade Yarns *220 Superwash Aran Splatter* (superwash merino wool) in #04 Denim (4)
- Small amount of black yarn for eyes
- One pair size 9 (5.5mm) needles, *or size to obtain gauge*
- One size H/8 (5mm) crochet hook
- Stitch holders
- Stitch marker
- Polyester stuffing

First Back Leg

Cast on 14 sts. Work in St st (k on RS, p on WS) for 17 rows.

Next row (WS) Bind off 4 sts, p to end. Place sts on holder. Cut yarn and set aside.

Second Back Leg

Cast on 14 sts. Work in St st for 17 rows.

Next row (WS) P10, bind off rem 4 sts. Place sts on holder. Cut yarn and set aside.

Body

Move sts from holders to one needle with bound-off sts at ends to work next row from RS.

Joining row (RS) Knit.

Work in St st over these 20 sts for 3 rows more. Place marker in center of row.

Inc row (RS) K to 1 st before marker, kfb, sm, kfb, k to end—2 sts inc'd in center.

Next row (WS) Purl.

Rep last 2 rows 5 times more—32 sts. Work even in St st for 10 rows.

Dec row (RS) K to 2 sts before marker, k2tog, sm, ssk, k to end—2 sts dec'd in center.

Next row (WS) Purl.

Rep last 2 rows 5 times more—20 sts. Work 6 rows even.

DIVIDE FOR FRONT LEGS

Next row (RS) Cast on 4 sts, k10, place rem 10 sts on a holder.

Cont in St st on 14 sts for 17 rows more for first front leg. Bind off.

Slip 10 sts from holder to needle to work next row from RS.

Next row (RS) K10.

Next row (WS) Cast on 4 sts, p to end.

Cont in St st on these 14 sts for second front leg for 16 rows more. Bind off.

Tummy

Cast on 10 sts. Work in St st for 4"/10cm. Bind off.

Head and Trunk

Cast on 5 sts. Purl 1 row.

Next row (RS) K1, kfb, k1 (center st), kfb, k1.

Next row (WS) Purl.

Cont in St st, working kfb each side of center st every RS row 4 times more—15 sts.

Gauge

16 sts and 24 rows to 4"/10cm over St st using size 9 (5.5mm) needles.

Take time to check gauge

Baby Elephant

Bind off 3 sts at beg of next 2 rows—9 st
Work even in St st for 3½"/9cm. Bind of

Right Ear
Cast on 8 sts. Purl 1 row.
Next row (RS) K1, kfb, k to end—1 st inc'
Next row (WS) Purl.
Rep last 2 rows 5 times more—14 sts.
Work 2 rows even, then bind off.

Left Ear
Cast on 8 sts. Purl 1 row.
Next row (RS) K to last 2 sts, kfb,
k1—1 st inc'd.
Next row (WS) Purl.
Rep last 2 rows 5 times more—14 sts
Work 2 rows even, then bind off.

Feet and Tip of Trunk
(Make 5 Pieces)
With crochet hook, ch 3.
Join with sl st to first st to form a ring.
Work 6 dc in ring. Fasten off.

Finishing
Sew leg seams, stuff, and sew feet to
bottom of legs. Sew tummy to under
part of body, between front and back
legs and along one side of body.
Stuff body, then sew rem seam.
Gather center of tummy and tack a few
sts tog to make body curve a bit.
Sew head and trunk underseams,
stuffing as you go.
Sew head to body in center of decrease
section of body.
Sew ears to sides of head.
Tack ears to body, if desired.
With black yarn, embroider V for each eye.
For tail, make a braid approx 2"/5cm
long, knotting and trimming end,
and attach (see photo). ■

25 Happy, the Clown

Funhouse colors give this lovable circus star a bright style and insouciant charm.

DESIGNED BY IRINA POLUDNENKO

Knitted Measurements
18"/45.5cm tall and 8½"/21.5cm wide around body

Materials
■ 1 3½oz/100g ball (each approx 220yd/200m) of Cascade Yarns *220 Superwash* (superwash wool) each in #804 Amethyst (A), #812 Turquoise (B), #815 Black (C), #851 Lime (D), #228 Frosted Almond (E), #871 White (F), #808 Sunset Orange (G), and #820 Lemon (H) ■
■ One set (5) each sizes 3, 4, 7, and 10 (3.25, 3.5, 4.5 and 6mm) double-pointed needles (dpn), *or size to obtain gauge*
■ One size E/4 (3.5mm) crochet hook
■ Stitch holders
■ Stitch markers
■ Tapestry needle
■ Polyester stuffing

Legs (Make 2)
Beg at top edge with size 4 (3.5mm) dpn and A, cast on 16 sts. Divide sts evenly over 4 dpn. Join, taking care not to twist sts, and pm for beg of rnd.
Knit 4 rnds A, [knit 4 rows B, knit 4 rnds A] 4 times. Cut B and cont with A.
Dec rnd [K2tog, k2] 4 times.

Dec rnd [K2tog, k1] 4 times.
Dec rnd [K2tog] 4 times—4 sts.
Cut yarn, draw end through sts twice, pull tightly to close.

Shoes (Make 2)
SOLE
With 2 size 4 (3.5mm) dpn and C, cast on 6 sts. Knit 1 row.
Next row K1, kfb, k2, kfb, k1— 8 sts.

Knit 14 rows.
Next row K1, k2tog, k2, ssk, k1—6 sts.
Knit 13 rows.
Next row K1, k2tog, ssk, k1—4 sts.
Bind off.

SIDES
With size 4 (3.5mm) dpn and C, cast on 40 sts. Divide sts evenly over 4 dpn. Join, taking care not to twist sts, and pm for beg of rnd. [Knit 1 rnd, purl 1 rnd] 5 times.
Next rnd Bind off 34 sts, k rem sts—6 sts.

TOP
Work rem 6 sts in rows in St st (k on RS, p on WS) as foll:
Purl 1 row.
Next row K1, kfb, k2, kfb, k1— 8 sts.
Work 7 rows even.
Next row (RS) K1, ssk, k2, k2tog, k1—6 sts.
Purl 1 row.
Next row K1, ssk, k2tog, k1— 4 sts.

Work 5 rows even in St st. Bind off. Sew sides to sole. Sew top into shoe opening. Stuff leg and shoe. Put shoe into leg and sew in place. With tapestry needle and double strand D, work cross st for boot lacing effect (see photo).

Gauge
22 sts and 32 rnds to 4"/10cm over St st worked in rnds using size 4 (3.5mm) needles.
Take time to check gauge.

Happy, the Clown

Body

Beg at lower edge with size 4 (3.5mm) dpn and D, cast on 32 sts. Divide sts evenly over 4 dpn. Join, taking care not to twist sts, and pm for beg of rnd. Knit 1 rnd.

Next rnd [K1, M1, k14, M1, k1] twice—36 sts.
Knit 1 rnd.
Next rnd [K1, M1, k16, M1, k1] twice—40 sts.
Knit 1 rnd.
Next rnd [K1, M1, k18, M1, kl1] twice—44 sts.
Knit 30 rnds.

SHAPE ARMHOLES
Next row K22, leave rem sts on hold. Then work back and forth in St st on these 22 sts for 9 rows more.
Return to sts on hold. Rejoin D and work these 22 sts for 10 rows in St st. Join the 2 sets of sts, dividing evenly over 4 dpn, to cont in rnds. Knit 1 rnd. Cut D. Join E.

SHAPE SHOULDERS
Dec rnd *Dpn #1*: Ssk, k to end of needle; *Dpn #2*: k to last 2 sts, k2tog; *Dpn #3*: ssk, k to end of needle; *Dpn #4*: k to last 2 sts, k2tog—4 sts dec'd.
Rep the last dec rnd on the next 6 rnds —16 sts.
Knit 4 rnds.

Head

Cont on sts from body, work as foll:
Rnd 1 [K2, M1, k2] 4 times—20 sts.
Rnds 2, 4, and 6 Knit.
Rnd 3 [K1, M1, k3, M1, k1] 4 times—28 sts.
Rnd 5 [K3, M1, k1, M1, k3] 4 times—36 sts.
Rnd 7 [K3, M1, k3, M1, k3] 4 times—44 sts
Knit 14 rnds.

Next rnd [K3, ssk, k1, k2tog, k3] 4 times —36 sts.
Knit 1 rnd.
Next rnd [Ssk, k5, k2tog] 4 times—28 sts.
Knit 1 rnd.
Next rnd [Ssk, k3, k2tog] 4 times—20 sts.
Knit 1 rnd.
Next rnd [Ssk, k1, k2tog] 4 times—12 sts.
Knit 1 rnd.
Next rnd [K3tog] 4 times—4 sts.
Cut yarn, draw through sts twice, and pull tightly to close.

Stuff head and partially stuff body.
Sew legs to body after closing cast-on (lower) edge of body.

Arms (Make 2)
With size 4 (3.5mm) dpn and E, pick up and k 16 sts around one arm opening over 3 dpn (5 sts, 5 sts, 6 sts). Join to work in rnds and pm for beg of rnd. Knit 24 rnds.
Next rnd [Ssk, k4, k2tog] twice—12 sts.
Next rnd [Ssk, k2, k2tog] twice—8 sts.
Place sts onto 2 dpn. Stuff body as needed, then stuff arm. With tapestry needle, weave rem sts tog. Rep for 2nd arm.

Sleeves (Make 2)
With size 4 (3.5mm) dpn and F, cast on 20 sts. Divide sts over 3 dpn (7 sts, 7 sts, 5 sts). Join, taking care not to twist sts, and pm for beg of rnd. [Knit 2 rnds F, knit 2 rnds C] 3 times, knit 2 rnds F.
For right sleeve, with A, [knit 1 rnd, purl 1 rnd] twice, knit 1 rnd, and bind off.
For left sleeve, with B, [knit 1 rnd, purl 1 rnd] twice, knit 1 rnd, and bind off.
Sew sleeves in place where arms meet body.

PANTS
Beg at top edge with size 4 (3.5mm) dpn

and G, cast on 48 sts. Divide sts evenly over 4 dpn. Join, taking care not to twist sts, and pm for beg of rnd.
Knit 1 rnd, purl 1 rnd. Knit 14 rnds.

FIRST LEG
Next rnd K24, cast on 8 sts for leg—32 sts. Leave rem 24 sts unworked. Cont on the 32 leg sts for 14 rnds. Purl 1 rnd. Bind off.

SECOND LEG
Return to the 24 sts left unworked, join G, and pick up and k 8 sts in the cast-on sts of first leg—32 rows. Complete as for first leg.

STRAPS
With 2 dpn and A, beg at the center back, cast on 6 sts. Knit 16 rows.
Next row K3, leave rem sts on hold.
*Knit 48 rows.
Next row K1, (k1, yo, k1) into next st, k1—5 sts.
Next row K1, k3tog, k1.
Next row K3tog and fasten off last st.
Rep from * on rem sts for 2nd strap.
Sew straps to pants and fasten at fronts with tapestry needle and a French knot in H (see photo).

Collar
With size 4 (3.5mm) dpn and F, cast on 20 sts. Divide sts evenly over 4 dpn. Join, taking care not to twist sts, and pm for beg of rnd. Knit 1 rnd, purl 1 rnd. Change to size 7 (4.5mm) dpn.
Next rnd [K1, yo] around— 40 sts.
Next rnd [K1, yo] around— 80 sts.
Next rnd Knit, dropping yo's of previous rnd. Change to size 10 (6mm) dpn.
Next rnd [K1, yo] around— 80 sts.
Next rnd [K1, yo] around—160 sts.
Next rnd [P2tog] around— 80 sts.
Bind off knitwise. Sew in place.

Finishing
NOSE AND EYES
For nose, cast on 3 sts with size 4 (3.5mm) dpn and G.
Row 1 K1, [k1, yo, k1, yo, k1] in next st, k1—7 sts.
Purl 1 row, knit 1 row.
Next row (WS) K1, p2tog, p1, p2tog tbl, k1—5 sts. Knit 1 row.
Next row K1, p3tog, k1.
Cut yarn, draw through sts twice, and pull up tightly to close.
Sew nose to center of face.
With tapestry needle and C, embroider eyes with French knots.

MOUTH
With G, embroider mouth with several straight sts (see photo). With 2 dpn and F, cast on 13 sts. Knit 1 row. Bind off.
Sew to face under embroidered sts.

HAT AND HAIR
Beg at the brim with size 4 (3.5mm) dpn and C, cast on 48 sts. Divide sts evenly over 4 dpn. Join, taking care not to twist sts, and pm for beg of rnd. Knit 8 rnds.
With D, [knit 1 rnd, purl 1 rnd] twice.
Cut D and cont with C only, knit 11 rnds.
Next rnd [K8, pm] 6 times.
Dec rnd *K to marker, sm, k2tog; rep from * around—6 sts dec'd.
Rep dec rnd on the next 6 rnds—6 sts.
Cut yarn, draw tail through sts twice, and pull up tightly to close.
For hair, cut sixty 5"/12.5cm lengths of H. On WS of hat, working into hat band in D, fold each length in half and, using a crochet hook, knot 2 rows of hair around the back edge of the hat (see photo).
Sew hat to head. ∎

En-Pointe Pauline

Love of knitting meets love of dance
in this pretty ballerina doll with fanciful flourishes and clever details.

DESIGNED BY IRINA POLUDNENKO

Knitted Measurements
Approx 16"/40.5cm tall and 9"/23cm
around body, after stuffing

Materials
- 1 3½oz/100g ball (each approx 220yd/
200m) of Cascade Yarns *220 Superwash*
(superwash wool) each in #228 Frosted
Almond (A), #871 White (B), #815 Black (C),
and #901 Cotton Candy (D) (❸)
- One set (5) each sizes 4, 7, and 10
(3.5, 4.5, and 6mm) double-pointed
needles (dpn), *or size to obtain gauge*
- One crochet hook size F/5 (3.75mm)
- Stitch markers
- Stitch holders
- Safety pins
- Tapestry needle

Legs (Make 2)
With A and size 4 (3.5mm) dpn, cast on
15 sts and divide evenly over 3 needles.
Join, taking care not to twist sts, and pm
for beg of rnd. Knit 37 rnds.
Next rnd [K2tog, k3] 3 times—12 sts.
Next rnd [K2tog, k2] 3 times—9 sts.
Next rnd [K2tog, k1] 3 times—6 sts.
Next rnd [K2tog] 3 times—3 sts.
Cut yarn, draw end through rem sts
twice, and pull tightly to close. Stuff leg.

Body
With B and size 4 (3.5mm) dpn, cast on
32 sts and divide evenly over 4 needles.
Join, taking care not to twist sts, and pm
for beg of rnd.
Rnd 1 Knit.
Rnd 2 [Kfb, k to end of dpn] 4
times—36 sts.
Rnds 3–6 Rep the last 2 rnds twice
more—44 sts.
Knit 10 rnds. [Purl 1 rnd, knit 1 rnd] 3

times. Cut B. Join A and knit 16 rnds.

SEPARATE FOR ARMS
*Next row (RS) K22, turn.
Next row P22, turn.
Rep the last 2 rows 6 times more for front.
Cut yarn. Rejoin yarn to 2nd set of sts
and rep from * for back.

SHAPE SHOULDERS
Divide sts evenly over 4 dpn to work in
rnds as before.
Dec rnd *Dpn #1*: Ssk, k to end; *Dpn #2*:
k to last 2 sts, k2tog; *Dpn #3*: ssk, k to
end; *Dpn #4*: k to last 2 sts, k2tog—4 sts
dec'd.
Rep the last dec rnd on the next 6 rnds—
16 sts. Knit 4 rnds.

Head
Cont on sts from body, work as foll:
Inc rnd [K2, M1, k2] 4 times—20 sts.
Knit 1 rnd.
Inc rnd [K1, M1, k3, M1, k1] 4
times—28 sts.
Knit 1 rnd.
Inc rnd [K3, M1, k1, M1, k3] 4 times—36 sts.
Knit 14 rnds
Dec rnd [Ssk, k5, k2tog] 4 times—28 sts.
Knit 1 rnd.

Gauge
26 sts and 32 rnds to 4"/10cm over St st using size 4 (3.5mm) needles.
Take time to check gauge.

En-Pointe Pauline

Dec rnd [Ssk, k3, k2tog] 4 times—20 sts.
Knit 1 rnd.
Dec rnd [Ssk, k1, k2tog] 4 times—12 sts.
Knit 1 rnd.
Dec rnd [K3tog] 4 times—4 sts.
Cut yarn, draw end through sts twice, and pull tightly to finish.

Arms (Make 2)

With size 4 (3.5mm) dpn and A, pick up and k 14 sts around the arm opening, dividing sts evenly over 3 dpn (5 sts, 5 sts, 4 sts). Join, taking care not to twist sts, and pm for beg of rnd. Knit 24 rnds.
Next rnd [Ssk k3, k2tog] twice—10 sts.
Next rnd [Ssk, k1, k2tog] twice—6 sts.
Divide sts evenly over 2 dpn and graft using Kitchener stitch (see page 182). Before making 2nd arm, stuff first arm, head, and body. When working 2nd arm, stuff when 10 sts rem before completing.

Hair and Face

Cut approx eighty 10"/25cm lengths of C for hair. To create hairline around face and back of head, fold each length in half and use crochet hook to loop through the center of a different st. Work 1 or 2 more rows of hair, staggering behind first line to fill in. When all hair is in place, pull into ponytail and secure at top of head. With D, embroider mouth with several straight sts.
With C, embroider eyes with 2 French knots.

HEADBAND
With size 4 (3.5mm) dpn and D, cast on 12 sts.
Row 1 K2, bind off 8 sts, k rem sts.
Next row K2, then cast on 8 sts, k2.
Rep the last 2 rows 8 times more.
Bind off rem sts.
Fold the cast-on and bound-off edge tog to make flower.
For I-cord band, with size 4 (3.5mm) dpn

and B, cast on 2 sts.
*Row 1 K2, slide sts back to beg of row to work next row from the RS. Bring yarn around from back and rep from * until I-cord measures approx 5"/12.5cm. Bind off. Knot one end of the I-cord. Pull the other end of the I-cord through the center of the flower and around ponytail, knotting other end to secure in place (ends create 2 dots that appear in center of flower). Trim hair as desired.

Skirt

With crochet hook and B, working into top purl ridge on body, pull up loop and place on size 4 (3.5mm) dpn. Work evenly around body in this manner until there are 44 sts divided evenly over 4 needles. Join and pm for beg of rnd. Knit 4 rnds. Change to size 7 (4.5mm) dpn and work as foll:
Next rnd *K1, yo; rep from * around—88 sts.
Knit 1 rnd.
Next rnd *K1, yo; rep from * around—176 sts.
Change to size 10 (6mm) dpn.
Next rnd Knit, dropping yo's of previous rnd—88 sts.
Knit 1 rnd.
Next rnd *K1, yo; rep from * around—176 sts.
Purl 1 rnd. Bind off loosely.
Work 2 more skirt layers in same way into the other 2 purl ridges.

Camisole Top

With size 4 (3.5mm) dpn and B, cast on 44 sts. Divide sts evenly over 4 dpn.
Join, taking care not to twist sts, and pm for beg of rnd. Purl 1 rnd, knit 14 rnds, purl 1 rnd. Bind off 22 sts. Cont to work bodice back and forth in rows as foll:
Next row (RS) Sl 1, k1, ssk, k to last 4

sts, k2tog, k1, p1.
Next row (WS) Sl 1, k1, p to last 2 sts, k1, p1.
Rep the last 2 rows 3 times more—14 sts.
Next 2 rows Sl 1, k to last st, p1.
Next row K2 and sl these sts to a safety pin (for strap), bind off next 10 sts—2 sts rem.
Next row (RS) Bring yarn around from back to work next row from the RS and k2, do *not* turn.
Rep last row for I-cord for 4"/10cm.
Bind off. Sl other 2 strap sts to dpn and work a 4"/10cm I-cord in same way.
Cross I-cords at back and sew ends in place.
Dress doll with camisole.

Slippers (Make 2)

With size 4 (3.5mm) dpn and D, cast on 4 sts. Work back and forth in rows as foll:
Row 1 (WS) Sl 1, k2, p1.
Row 2 (RS) Sl 1, [kfb] twice, p1—6 sts.
Row 3 Sl 1, k1, p2, k1, p1.
Row 4 Sl 1, k1, M1, k2, M1, k1, p1—8 sts.
Row 5 Sl 1, k1, p4, k1, p1.
Row 6 Sl 1, k1, M1, k4, M1, k1, p1—10 sts.
Row 7 Sl 1, k1, p6, k1, p1.
Row 8 Sl 1, k1, M1, k6, M1, k1, p1—12 sts.
Row 9 Sl 1, k1, p8, k1, p1.
Divide 12 sts evenly over 3 dpn, then cast on 4 sts onto 4th dpn—16 sts.
Join and pm for beg of rnd. Knit 5 rnds.
Next rnd [K2tog, k2] 4 times—12 sts.
Next rnd [K2tog, k1] 4 times—8 sts.
Next rnd [K2tog] 4 times—4 sts.
Cut yarn, draw through sts twice, and pull tightly to finish.

I-CORD STRAPS
Beg at the cast-on edge of shoes, with 2 size 4 (3.5mm) dpn and D, pick up and k2 sts. Work an I-cord for 4"/10cm. Bind off. Work a 2nd strap beside the first.
Place slipper on foot then crossover and knot straps at back. ∎

Some Bunny to Love

Everybody needs some bunny to love,
like this roguish rabbit dapperly dressed in a spiffy sweater.

DESIGNED BY LINDA MEDINA

◼◼◼▢

Knitted Measurements
Approx 13½"/34.5cm high

Materials
1 3½oz/100g ball (each approx 220yd/200m) of Cascade Yarns *220 Superwash* (superwash wool) each in #1946 Silver Gray (MC), #904 Colonial Blue Heather (A), #902 Soft Pink (B), #229 Ash Rose (C), #1914 Alaska Sky (D), #1944 Westpoint Blue Heather (E), #826 Tangerine (F), and #905 Celery (G) (4)
One pair size 4 (3.5mm) needles, *or size to obtain gauge*
One set (5) size 4 (3.5mm) double-pointed needles (dpn)
Two 12mm solid black safety eyes
Note As animal eyes are a choking hazard, embroider eyes if making for a child.
Stitch markers
Stitch holders
Polyester stuffing

Notes
1) Bunny is knit on smaller needles to make a firmer fabric so stuffing does not show through.
2) Bunny body is knit from top of the head down. Arms and legs are made separately and sewn on.

Head
With MC, cast on 16 sts using provisional cast-on (see page 182) and divide evenly over 4 dpn. Join, taking care not to twist sts, and pm for beg of rnd.
Rnd 1 Knit.
Rnd 2 *Kfb in each st—32 sts.
Rnd 3 Knit.
Rnd 4 [K1, kfb] 16 times—48 sts.
Rnd 5 Knit.
Rnd 6 [K5, kfb] 8 times—56 sts.
Rnd 7 Knit.
Rnd 8 [K7, kfb, k5] 4 times—60 sts.
Rnds 9 and 10 Knit.

Face
Divide sts over 4 dpn (12 sts, 16 sts, 16 sts, 16 sts). Cont to work back and forth in rows *on Dpn #1 only* to beg shaping (in same manner as knitting sock heel flap).
Row 1 (RS) Knit.
Row 2 Sl 1 st purlwise, p11.
Row 3 Sl 1, k11.
Rep rows 2 and 3 three times more.

Shape nose
Row 1 (WS) Sl 1, p6, p2tog, p1.
Row 2 Sl 1, k3, ssk, k1—10 sts.
Row 3 Sl 1, p4, p2tog, p1.
Row 4 (RS) Sl 1, k5, ssk, k1—8 sts. Do *not* turn.

Nose gusset
Note Nose gusset is created in same manner as sock gusset.
Next rnd (RS) *Dpn #1*: Pick up and k 5 sts along nose edge; *Dpn #2, #3, and #4*: Knit; pick up and k 5 sts along other side of nose edge and sl these 5 sts to end of Dpn #1. There are 18 sts on Dpn #1 and 16 sts each on Dpn #2, #3, and #4—66 sts in total.

Gauge
23 sts and 26 rows/rnds to 4"/10cm over St st using size 4 (3.5mm) needles.
Take time to check gauge.

Some Bunny to Love

Cont in rnds as foll:

Next rnd Knit, pm for new beg of rnd.

Rnd 2 *Dpn #1*: K1, ssk, k to last 3 sts, k2tog, k1; *Dpn #2, #3, and #4*: Knit.

Rnd 3 Knit.

Rnds 4–7 Rep rnds 2 and 3 twice more—60 sts.

Lower face

Rnd 1 *Dpn #1*: K1, ssk, k to last 3 sts, k2tog, k1; *Dpn #2, #3 and #4*: K5, k2tog, k1, ssk, k6—52 sts.

Rnds 2 and 4 Knit.

Rnd 3 *Dpn #1*: K1, ssk, k to last 3 sts, k2tog, k1; *Dpn #2, #3 and #4*: K4, k2tog, k1, ssk, k5—44 sts.

Rnd 5 *Dpn #1*: K1, ssk, k to last 3 sts, k2tog, k1; *Dpn #2, #3 and #4*: K1, [k2tog] twice, k1, ssk, k1, k2tog, k1 (6 sts on Dpn #1 and 8 sts each on Dpn #2, #3, and #4)—30 sts in total.

Carefully remove scrap yarn from pro-visional cast-on, draw tail end through open sts, pull tog tightly and secure end.

Neck

Knit 7 rnds. With work on needles, lightly stuff head. Mark placement for eyes. Remove stuffing. Install (or embroider) eyes. Restuff head. Stuffing should hold features, but still be soft.

Body

Rnd 1 *Dpn #1*: K1, kfb, k2, kfb, k1 (8 sts); *Dpn #2*: K1, kfb, k1, [kfb] twice, k1, kfb, k1 (12 sts); *Dpn #3* K1, kfb, k4, kfb, k1 (10 sts); *Dpn #4*: Same as Dpn #2 (12 sts)—42 sts in total.

Rnd 2 and all even-numbered rnds Knit.

Rnd 3 *Dpn #1*: K2, kfb, k to last 3 sts, kfb, k2 (10 sts); *Dpn #2*: K2, kfb, k2, [kfb] twice, k2, kfb, k2 (16 sts); *Dpn #3*: K2, kfb, k1, [kfb] twice, k1, kfb, k2 (14 sts); *Dpn #4*: Same as Dpn #2 (16 sts)—56 sts.

Rnd 5 *Dpn #1*: K2, kfb, k to last 3 sts, kfb, k2 (12 sts); *Dpn #2*: K2, kfb, k4, [kfb] twice, k4, kfb, k2 (20 sts); *Dpn #3*: K14; *Dpn #4*: Same as Dpn #2 (20 sts) —66 sts.

Rnd 7 *Dpn #1*: K12; *Dpn #2*: K8, kfb, k2, kfb, k8 (22 sts); *Dpn #3*: K14; *Dpn #4*: Same as Dpn #2 (22 sts)—70 sts.

Rnds 9–27 Knit.

Pants

Cut MC, join A.

Next rnd *K2, kfb; rep from * to last st, kfb—94 sts.

Redistribute sts as foll: Dpn #1 and #3: 24 sts each; Dpn #2 and #4: 23 sts.

Note Place center front marker between sts 12 and 13 on Dpn #1, this also counts as beg of rnd marker.

Rnd 1 *P1, k1; rep from * around.

Rnd 2 *Sl 1 wyib, k1; rep from * around.

Rep rnds 1 and 2 for mock rib for 17 rnds more.

Cont in mock rib as foll:

Rnd 20 *Dpn #1*: Work rib over 12 sts; *Dpn #2*: Rib 9 sts, ssk, k1, k2tog, rib to end (21 sts); *Dpn #3*: Rib 5 sts, ssk, rib 3, ssk, k1, k2tog, rib 2, rib to end (20 sts); *Dpn #4*: Rib 8 sts, ssk, k1, k2tog, rib to end (21 sts); *Dpn #1*: rib to end of rnd—86 sts.

Rnd 21 *Dpn #1*: Rib 12 sts; *Dpn #2*: Rib 9, k3tog, rib to end (19 sts); *Dpn #3*: Rib 4, k2tog, rib 3, k3tog, sl 1, k2tog, rib to end (16 sts); *Dpn #4*: Rib 8, k3tog, rib to end (19 sts); *Dpn #1*: rib to end of rnd—78 sts.

Rnds 22 and 23 Work even in rib.

Rnd 24 *Dpn #1*: Rib 8, p2tog, k2tog (10 sts); *Dpn #2*: [P2tog, k2tog] twice, p1, k1, p1, [k2tog, p2tog] twice (11 sts); *Dpn #3*: K1, p1, [k2tog, p2tog] 3 times, k1, p1 (10 sts); *Dpn #4*: [K2tog, p2tog] twice, k1, p1, k1, [p2tog, k2tog] twice (11 sts); *Dpn #1*: P2tog, k2tog, rib to end

of rnd (10 sts)—52 sts.

Stuff body.

Slip first 3 sts of Dpn #2 to Dpn #1 (13 sts on half of needle). Slip first 5 sts of Dpn #3 to Dpn #2 (13 sts on needle). Slip 8 sts from Dpn #4 to Dpn #3 (13 sts on needle). Slip last 10 sts from 2nd half of Dpn #1 to Dpn #4 (13 sts on needle). There are now 13 sts on each needle; yarn is now between Dpn #1 and #4. Work across Dpn #1 *only* as foll: [Sl 1, k1] 6 times, sl 1.

Yarn is now between Dpn #1 and #2.

Slip sts from Dpn #3 to Needle 2 (26 sts on needle).

Slip sts from Dpn #4 to Dpn #1 (26 sts on needle).

Bind off sts using 3-needle bind off (see page 182). Weave in tail.

With B, embroider heart on upper chest with duplicate stitch (see photo).

Legs (Make 2)

With A, cast on 30 sts and divide evenly over 3 dpn. Join, taking care not to twist sts, and pm for beg of rnd. Rep rnds 1 and 2 of mock rib as on pants for 5"/12.5cm. Cut A, join MC.

FEET

Set-up rnd *Dpn #1*: K2tog, k1, [k2tog] twice, k1, k2tog (6 sts); *Dpn #2 and #3*: Same as Dpn #1—18 sts.

Rnd 1 Knit.

Rnd 2 *Dpn #1*: K6; *Dpn #2*: K3, [kfb] 3 times (9 sts); *Dpn #3*: [Kfb] 3 times, k3 (9 sts)—24 st

Rnds 3–5 Knit.

Rnd 6 *Dpn #1*: K6; *Dpn #2*: K4, kfb, [k1 kfb] twice (12 sts); *Dpn #3*: [K1, kfb] 3 times, k3 (12 sts)—30 sts.

Rnds 7–10 Knit.

Rnd 11 *Dpn #1*: [K2tog, k1] twice (4 sts); *Dpn #2 and #3*: K2tog, k8, k2tog (10 sts each)—24 sts.

Rnd 12 *Dpn #1*: [K2tog] twice; *Dpn #2*

and #3: K2tog, k6, k2tog—18 sts. Sl 1 st from Dpn #1 to Dpn #3, sl 1 st from Dpn #1 to Dpn #2—9 sts on each needle. Graft sts together using Kitchener Stitch (see page 182).
Stuff legs, leaving top ½"/1.5cm unstuffed.
Whipstitch top opening closed.
Whipstitch legs to body.

Arms (Make 2)
With MC, cast on 2 sts.
Note First 7 rows of arms are worked back and forth in rows.
Row 1 and all WS rows Purl.
Row 2 (RS) [Kfb] twice—4 sts.
Row 4 K1, [kfb] twice, k1—6 sts.
Row 6 K1, kfb, k2, kfb, k1—8 sts.
Row 7 Purl.
Cont working in rnds with dpn as foll:
Next rnd (RS) Cast on 10 sts, *k6 of these sts onto a dpn; k4 rem cast-on sts onto another dpn along with k2 arm sts; knit last 6 arm sts onto 3rd dpn—18 sts. Join, taking care not to twist sts.
Rnds 1–34 Knit.
Rnd 35 [K2tog] 9 times—9 sts.
Cut yarn, leaving a 10"/25.5cm tail, and pull tightly through rem sts twice to secure.
Stuff arm, leaving about ½"/1.5cm below beg of work in the round unstuffed.
Whipstitch top opening closed. Sew to body.

Ears (Make 2)
Note Ears are made in 2 pieces and sewn together. Sl first st of every row knitwise.

EAR FRONTS (Make 2)
With MC, cast on 9 sts.
Row 1 (WS) Purl.
Row 2 (RS) Sl 1 knitwise, kfb, k to last 2 sts, kfb, k1—11 sts.
Rows 3 and 5 Sl 1, p to last st, k1.
Row 4 Rep row 2—13 sts.

Row 6 Sl 1, kfb, k1; join B, k7; join 2nd small ball of MC, k1, kfb, k1—15 sts.
Row 7 With MC, sl 1, p3; with B, p7; with MC, p4.
Row 8 With MC, sl 1, kfb, k1; with B, k9; with MC, k1, kfb, k1—17 sts.
Row 9 With MC, sl 1, p3; with B, p9; with MC, p2, k1.
Row 10 With MC, sl 1, k3; with B, k9; with MC, k4.
Rows 11–23 Rep rows 9 and 10.
Row 24 With MC, sl 1, k3; with B, ssk, k5, k2tog; with MC, k4—15 sts.
Row 25 With MC, sl 1, p3; with B, p7; with MC, p3, k1.
Rows 26 With MC, sl 1, k3; with B, ssk, k3, k2tog; with MC, k4—13 sts.
Row 27 With MC, sl 1, p3; with B, p5; with MC, p3, k1.
Row 28 With MC, sl 1, k3; with B, ssk, k1, k2tog; with MC, k4—11 sts.
Row 29 With MC, sl 1, p3; with B, p2tog, p1; with MC, p3, k1—10 sts. Cut B. Cont with 1 ball of MC only.
Row 30 Sl 1, k2, ssk, k5—9 sts.
Row 31 Sl 1, p7, k1.
Row 32 Sl 1, ssk, [k2tog, k1] twice—6 sts.
Row 33 Sl 1, p to last st, k1.
Row 34 Sl 1, ssk, k2tog, k1—4 sts.
Row 35 [P2tog] twice.
Row 36 K2tog. Fasten off last st.

EAR BACKS (Make 2)
With MC, cast on 9 sts.

Rows 1–23 Rep rows 1–23 of ear front, working with MC only.
Row 24 (RS) Sl 1, ssk, k to last 3 sts, k2tog, k1—15 sts.
Row 25 and all WS rows Sl 1, p to last st, k1
Rows 26, 28, and 30 Rep row 24—9 sts.
Row 32 Sl 1, ssk, [k2tog, k1] twice—6 sts.
Row 34 Sl 1, ssk, k2tog, k1—4 sts.
Row 35 [P2tog] twice.
Row 36 K2tog. Fasten off, leaving a tail long enough to sew front & back together.
Pin front and back pieces together with WS held tog, whipstitch to join. Make a small pleat in each lower front ear to shape and tack into place. Sew ears to head.

Finishing
Embroider nose and mouth with B (see photo). For tail, make small pompom with MC and attach. With C, embroider heart using duplicate st on chest (see photo opposite page).

Sweater
FRONT
With straight needles and C, cast on 51 sts.
Row 1 (RS) K1, *p1, k1, rep from * to end.
Row 2 (WS) K the knit sts and p the purl sts.
Rep rows 1 and 2 twice more. Cut C.
Join D and knit 1 row, then purl 1 row.

BEGIN SLIP-STITCH STRIPE PATTERN
Note Slip all sts purlwise wyib on RS rows and wyif on WS rows.

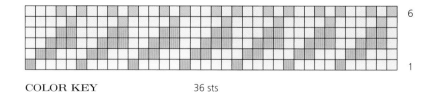

COLOR KEY   36 sts

□ D   ▨ F   ▨ G

Row 1 (RS) With E, k1, *sl 1, k1; rep from * to end.

Row 2 With E, p1,*sl 1, p1; rep from * to end.

Row 3 With D, k2, sl 1, *k1, sl 1; rep from * to last 2 sts, k2.

Row 4 With D, p2, sl 1, *p1, sl 1; rep from * to last 2 sts, p2.

Rows 5–12 Rep rows 1–4 twice.

Row 13 and 14 With D, knit 1 row, purl row. Join C.

Row 15 *With E, k1; with C, k1; rep from * to last st; with E, k1.

Row 16 *With C, p1; with E, p1; rep from * to last st; with C, p1.

Rows 17 and 18 With D, knit. Mark each side of last row for sleeve placement.

Row 19 *With C, k1; with E, k1; rep from * to last st; with C, k1.

Row 20 *With E, p1; with C, p1; rep from * to last st; with E, p1.

Rows 21 and 22 With D, knit 1 row, purl 1 row.

BEGIN CHART

Row 23 With D, k7; work row 1 of chart over 36 sts; with D, k8.

Rows 24–28 Cont in St st (k on RS, p on WS), working 36 sts in chart as established and working edge sts with D.

Rows 29 and 30 With D, knit 1 row, purl 1 row.

Rows 31 and 32 Rep rows 15 and 16. Cut C and E.

Neck shaping

Row 33 With D, k14, join 2nd ball of D and bind off center 23 sts, k to end. Working both sides at once, cont as foll:

Row 34 With D, k all sts on each side. Dec 1 st at each neck edge on next row, then every other row twice more, then *very* row once, AND AT THE SAME TIME,

rep rows 19 and 20 for color pat, then cont in D only to end of piece. Cut E and place rem 10 sts each side on holders.

BACK

Work same as front, but replace chart sts with slip-st stripe pat.

Sew front and back shoulder seams.

TURTLENECK

With RS facing, dpn and C, pick up and k 68 sts evenly around neck edge. Join and pm for beg of rnd. Work in k1, p1 rib for 17 rnds. Bind off loosely in pat.

SLEEVES

Note Sleeves are worked back and forth in rows and seamed at underarm.

With RS facing and D, pick up 42 sts

along armhole edge between markers.

Next row (WS) Purl.

Row 1 (RS) *With C, k1; with E, k1; rep from * to end.

Row 2 With E p2tog, *with C p1, with E p1; rep from * to last 2 sts, with C p2tog—40 sts.

With D, knit 1 row, purl 1 row.

Work in slip-st stripes as before, dec 1 st each side on next row, then every 3rd row twice more—34 sts.

Work even in slip-st stripe pat for 5 rows more, end with a WS row.

With D, knit 1 row, purl 1 row.

Cut D, join C.

Next row K2tog, k to end—33 sts.

Work in k1, p1 rib for 5 rows.

Bind off in pat.

Sew side and sleeve seams. ■

28

Shaggy Sheep

It's never too early to cultivate a love of sheep; this adorable ovine has loopy textured "fleece" and features short-row shaping on its woolly head.

DESIGNED BY SANDI PROSSER

Knitted Measurements
Approx 14"/35.5cm tall

Materials
- 4 3½oz/100g hanks (each approx 137yd/125m) of Cascade Yarns *220 Superwash Aran* (superwash merino wool) in #871 White (MC) **(4)**
- 1 hank in #900 Charcoal (CC)
- One pair size 7 (4.5mm) needles, *or size to obtain gauge*
- ½yd/.5m of ¼"/6mm wide ribbon (optional)
- Stitch markers
- Polyester stuffing

Stitch Glossary
Loop St K1 but do not drop st from LH needle, bring yarn to front between needles and wrap it clockwise around thumb, bring yarn to back and k into same st on LH needle, sl st off needle; sl 2 sts from RH needle back to LH needle and k them tog through back loops.

Loop Stitch Pattern
(over an even number of sts)
Rows 1 and 3 (WS) Knit.
Row 2 K1, *loop st, k1; rep from * to last st, k1.
Row 4 K2, *loop st, k1; rep from * to end.
Rep rows 1–4 for loop st pat.

Loop Stitch Pattern
(over an odd number of sts)
Rows 1 and 3 (WS) Knit.
Row 2 K1, *loop st, k1; rep from * to end
Row 4 K2, *loop st, k1; rep from * to last st, k1.
Rep rows 1–4 for loop st pat.

Upper Body
With MC, cast on 48 sts and mark center of row.
Knit 1 row on WS.

SHAPE BACK LEGS
Next row (RS) Cast on 7 sts, k2, *loop st, k1; rep from * to last st, k1.
Next row (WS) Cast on 7 sts, k to end.
Rep last 2 rows once more—76 sts.
Beg with row 2, work 10 rows in loop st pat (over an even number of sts).
Cont in pat, bind off 10 sts at beg of next 2 rows. Dec 1 st each side on next 3 rows —50 sts. Work even in pat for 45 rows.

SHAPE FRONT LEGS
Cast on 6 sts at beg of next 2 rows, then 5 sts at beg of next 2 rows—72 sts.
Work 12 rows even.

Gauge
18 sts and 28 rows to 4"/10cm over St st using size 7 (4.5mm) needles.
Take time to check gauge.

Shaggy Sheep

Bind off 5 sts at beg of next 2 rows, then 4 sts at beg of next 2 rows—54 sts. Dec 1 st each side on next row, then every other row 3 times more—46 sts. Dec 1 st each side on next 6 rows—34 sts. Work 3 rows even. Bind off.

Inner Legs and Tummy

With MC, cast on 5 sts and mark center st. Knit 1 row on WS.
Next row (RS) K1, *loop st, k1; rep from * to end.
Next row (WS) K1, M1, k to last st, M1, k1—7 sts.
Rep last 2 rows once more—9 sts. Beg with row 2, work loop st pat (over an odd number of sts), and inc 1 st each side on 8th row, then every 6th row twice more—15 sts. Work 8 rows even in pat.

SHAPE BACK LEGS
Next row (RS) Cast on 7 sts, k1, *loop st, k1; rep from * to last st, k1.
Next row (WS) Cast on 7 sts, k to end—29 sts.
Rep last 2 rows once more—43 sts. Knit 1 row.
Next row (WS) K14, k2tog, k11, ssk, k14. Knit 1 row.
Next row (WS) K13, k2tog, k11, ssk, k13—39 sts.
Cont to dec 2 sts every other row (working 1 less st before first dec and after 2nd dec) twice more—35 sts. Work 1 row even.
Bind off 10 sts at beg of next 2 rows. Dec 1 st each side on next 3 rows—9 sts. Beg with row 2, work 10 rows in loop st pat (over an odd number of sts). Work even in pat for 44 rows.

SHAPE FRONT LEGS
Next row (RS) Cast on 6 sts, then k2, *loop st, k1; rep from * to last st, k1.
Next row Cast on 6 sts, k to end—21 sts.
Next row (RS) Cast on 5 sts, then k2, *loop st, k1; rep from * to last st, k1.
Next row Cast on 5 sts, k to end—31 sts. Work 12 rows even in pat.
Bind off 5 sts at beg of next 2 rows, then bind off 4 sts at beg of next 2 rows—13 sts. Dec 1 st each side on next row, then every 6th row once more—9 sts. Work 15 rows even. Bind off.

Head

With MC, cast on 43 sts.

BEGIN SHORT ROW SHAPING
Note See page 183 for instructions on short row wrapping (w&t).
Next row (RS) K41, w&t.
Next row (WS) K39, w&t.
Next row (RS) K37, w&t.
Next row (WS) K35, w&t.
Next 14 rows K to 2 sts before last wrapped st, w&t.
Next 3 rows K to end of row. Cut MC.

NOSE
Row 1 With CC, k1, [k2tog] 10 times, k1, [ssk] 10 times, k1—23 sts.
Row 2 and all WS rows Knit.
Row 3 K4, k2tog, k2, k2tog, k3, ssk, k2, ssk, k4—19 sts.
Row 5 K6, k2tog, k3, ssk, k6—17 sts.
Row 7 K3, [k2tog] twice, k3, [ssk] twice, k3—13 sts.
Row 9 K4, k2tog, k1, ssk, k4—11 sts.
Row 11 K1, [k2tog] twice, k1, [ssk] twice, k1—7 sts.

Cut yarn, leaving a long tail. Thread yarn through rem sts and pull tog tightly. Sew nose seam. Sew upper body to inner legs; sew tummy front neck to bottom of front legs (do not sew across bottom of legs).

Front Feet (Make 2)

Open front legs flat. With RS facing and CC, pick up and k 16 sts along bottom edge of front leg. Knit 9 rows.
Next row K1, [ssk] 3 times, k2, [k2tog] 3 times, k1—10 sts.
Next row K1, [ssk] 4 times, k1—6 sts.
Cut yarn, leaving a long tail. Thread yarn through rem sts and pull tog tightly. Sew seam in foot and cont sewing from front across tummy and down front of back legs.

Back Feet (Make 2)

Work same as front feet. Match marked sts. Sew foot seam, then cont sewing to marked sts and down other side to other back foot.

Ears (Make 2)

With CC, cast on 4 sts. Knit 1 row.
Next row Kfb, k1, kfb, k1—6 sts.
Knit 3 rows.
Next row K2tog, k2, ssk—4 sts.
Knit 1 row.
Next row K2tog, ssk—2 sts.
Next row K2tog. Fasten off last st.

Tail

With MC, cast on 16 sts. Knit 2 rows. Bind off.

Finishing

Stuff head and body. Sew head to body. Sew ears and tail in position. Tie ribbon around neck, if desired. ∎

29

Pinkie Pig

This little piggy may not go to market,
but he'll go wee-wee-wee all the way into your heart.

DESIGNED BY JACQUELINE VAN DILLEN

Knitted Measurements
Approx 12 x 14"/30.5 x 35.5cm, when stuffed

Materials
1   3½oz/100g ball (each approx 220yd/200m) of Cascade Yarns *220 Superwash* (superwash wool) in #838 Rose Petal (3)

One set (5) size 4 (3.5mm) double-pointed needles (dpn), *or size to obtain gauge*
One extra size 4 (3.5mm) dpn
Small amount of charcoal yarn
Polyester stuffing
Pellets and plastic baggie
Stitch markers
Scrap yarn

Nose
Cast on 4 sts.
Next row (RS) Knit.
Cont in St st (k on RS, p on WS), cast on 2 sts at beg of next 4 rows—12 sts.
Work 4 rows even.
Bind off 2 sts at beg of next 4 rows.
Bind off 4 sts.

Snout
Pick up and k 36 sts around entire edge of nose. Divide sts evenly over 4 dpn

and pm for beg of rnd (center bottom of nose). Work 12 rnds in garter st (knit 1 rnd, purl 1 rnd).

BEGIN SHAPING
Rnd 1 K8, M1, [k2, M1, K7, M1] twice, k2, M1, k8—42 sts.
Rnd 2 and all even-numbered rnds Purl.
Rnd 3 K9, M1, [k2, M1, K9, M1] twice,

k2, M1, k9—48 sts.
Rnd 5 K10, M1, [k2, M1, K11, M1] twice, k2, M1, k10—54 sts.
Rnd 7 K11, M1, [k2, M1, K13, M1] twice, k2, M1, k11—60 sts.
Rnd 9 K12, M1, [k2, M1, K15, M1] twice, k2, M1, k12—66 sts.
Rnd 11 K13, M1, [k2, M1, K17, M1] twice, k2, M1, k13—72 sts.
Rnd 13 K14, M1, [k2, M1, K19, M1] twice, k2, M1, k14—78 sts. Cut yarn.
Place first 6 sts on scrap yarn to hold for neck. Place next 20 sts on Dpn #4, place next 9 sts on Dpn #2, place next 8 sts on Dpn #1 for crown of head, place next 9 sts on Dpn #3, place next 20 sts on Dpn #5, and place rem 6 sts on scrap yarn with first 6 sts for neck.

Head
Row 1 (RS) Beg with *Dpn #1*: k8; *Dpn #2*: k1; turn.
Row 2 *Dpn #2 and #1*: k9; *Dpn #3*: k1; turn.
Cont in this manner until all sts from Dpn #1, #2, and #3 are worked.
Next row (RS) K25, k2tog with first st from Dpn #4, turn.
Next row K25, k2tog with first st from Dpn #5, turn.

Gauge
22 sts and 40 rnds to 4"/10cm over garter st using size 4 (3.5mm) needles.
Take time to check gauge.

Pinkie Pig

Next row K26, k2tog with first st from Dpn #4, turn.
Next row K26, k2tog with first st from Dpn #5, turn.
Cont in this manner until 10 sts each rem on Dpn #4 and #5—46 sts.

SHAPE BACK OF HEAD
Dec row (RS) K10, k2tog tbl, pm, k2, k2tog, k9, k2tog tbl, pm, k2, k2tog, k9, k next st tog with next st from Dpn #4, turn.
Next row (WS) K to last st, k last st tog with next st from Dpn #5.
Dec row (RS) K to 2 sts before marker, k2tog tbl, sm, k2, k2tog, k to 2 sts before marker, k2tog tbl, sm, k2, k2 tog, k to last st, k last st tog with next st from Dpn #4.
Rep last 2 rnds until 12 sts rem.
Next row K12, k6 neck sts from scrap yarn, pm for beg of rnd, place rem 6 neck sts on a dpn—24 sts. Divide sts evenly over 4 dpn with beg of rnd at center back. Purl 1 rnd.

Body
Rnd 1 [K4, M1] twice, k3, M1, k2, M1, K3, [M1, k4] twice—30 sts.
Rnd 2 and all even-numbered rnds Purl.
Rnd 3 K4, pm, M1, k6, M1, pm, k4, M1, pm, k2, pm, M1, k4, pm, M1, k6, M1, pm, k4—36 sts.
Inc rnd 5 K to marker, sm, M1, k to marker, M1, sm, k to marker, M1, sm, k2, sm, M1, k to marker, sm, M1, k to marker, M1, sm, k to end—6 sts inc'd.
Cont in garter st, rep inc rnd 5 every other rnd twice more—54 sts.
Purl 1 rnd, removing markers.
Inc rnd K4, M1, k14, M1, k18, M1, k14, M1, k4—58 sts. Purl 1 rnd.

Next rnd K18, place last 14 sts just worked on scrap yarn for arm, k36, place last 14 sts just worked on scrap yarn for arm, k4.
Next rnd P4, pm, p2, pm, p18, pm, p2, pm, p4.
Inc rnd K to marker, M1, sm, k2, sm, M1, k to marker, M1, sm, k2, sm, M1, k to end—4 sts inc'd.
Next rnd Purl.
Rep inc rnd every other rnd 3 times more, then every 4th rnd twice—54 sts.
Cont in garter st, working back and forth in rows to create opening at center back for stuffing, and rep inc row every other row 9 times more—90 sts.
Knit 1 row, removing markers.
Next row (RS) K33, M1, k24, M1, k33—92 sts.

SHAPE BOTTOM
Keeping opening at center back, divide work over 4 dpn as follows: 23 back sts on Dpn #1, 23 front sts each on Dpn #2 and #3, 23 back sts on Dpn #4.
Work to center front.
Next row (RS) K6 front sts, place next 16 sts on scrap yarn for leg, cast on 1 st, turn, k13, place next 16 sts on scrap yarn for leg, cast on 1 st, turn.
Short row 1 K13, sl 1 purlwise wyif, turn.
Short row 2 Sl 1 purlwise, k14, sl 1 purlwise wyif, turn.
Cont in this manner until all front sts are worked into the short rows.
Next row K to the last 3 front sts, k2tog, k1, sl 1 back st, turn.
Next row K2tog, k to the last 3 front sts, k2tog, k1, sl 1 back st, turn.
Cont in this manner until 12 sts rem each for front and back. Bind off.

Legs (Make 2)
Divide 16 sts from scrap yarn over 3 dpn, inc 2 sts at center back of leg—18 sts. Place marker for beg of rnd. Work 4 rnds garter s[t]
Next rnd (RS) K8, M1, pm, k2, pm, M1, k to end.
Next rnd P20.
Inc rnd K to marker, M1, sm, k2, sm, M1, k to end—2 sts inc'd.
Rep inc rnd every other rnd 5 times more—32 sts.
Work 3 rnds even in garter st.
Dec rnd (RS) K2tog, k to 2 sts before marker, k2tog, sm, k2, sm, k2tog, k to last 2 sts, k2tog—4 sts dec'd.
Rep dec rnd every other rnd once more—24 sts.
Purl 1 rnd. Divide sts evenly over 2 dpn and graft foot closed.
Work same for 2nd leg on other set of 16 st[s]

Arms (Make 2)
Place the 14 sts from scrap yarn on 3 dp[n] and pm for beg of rnd. Work 50 rnds in garter st. Divide sts evenly over 2 dpn and graft closed. Work same for 2nd arm on other set of 14 sts.

Ears (Make 2)
Cast on 14 sts. Work 12 rows even.
Dec row K1, k2tog, k to end—1 st dec'[d]
Rep this row every row until 3 sts rem.
Next row SK2P. Fasten off.
Work same for 2nd ear.

Finishing
Stuff head. Sew ears to head, using photo as guide. Stuff arms lightly. Place pellets in bag, seal, and place in pig's bottom. Stuff body and legs, and sew back seam. Embroider eyes and nostrils, using photo as guide. ∎

Jumbo Tic-Tac-Toe

Teach your tots how to play "tic-tac-toe, three in a row," with this handy game.
Then you can show them how Xs and Os stand for hugs and kisses.

DESIGNED BY JACOB SEIFERT

■■■◻

Knitted Measurements
Game board Approx 30 x 30"/76 x 76cm
X pieces Approx 5 x 6"/12.5 x 15cm
O pieces Approx 6 x 6"/15 x 15cm

Materials
2 3 1/2oz/100g hanks (each approx 150yd/138m) of Cascade Yarns *220 Superwash Aran* (superwash merino wool) in #240 Jasmine Green (A) ④
3 hanks in #1946 Silver Grey (B)
4 hanks in #900 Charcoal (C)
One set (5) size 8 (5mm) double-pointed needles (dpn), *or size to obtain gauge*
One extra size 8 (5mm) dpn
One size 8 (5mm) circular needle, 32"/81cm long
Bobbins
Stitch markers
Stitch holder
Polyester stuffing
Scrap yarn

Notes
1) For X pieces, always divide sts currently being worked evenly over 2 dpn.
2) For game board, circular needle is used to accommodate large number of stitches. Do *not* join.

3) When changing colors for squares on game board, twist yarns on WS to prevent holes in work. Use a separate bobbin of yarn for each block of color.
4) When working game board, it may be helpful to weave in ends along the way to avoid tangling.
5) The main game board is worked in St st (k on RS, p on WS) throughout. All borders are worked in garter st (k every row).

X Pieces (Make 5)
BOTTOM LEGS (Make 2)
With A, cast on 6 sts and divide evenly over 2 dpn. Join, taking care not to twist sts, and pm for beg of rnd.
Rnd 1 and all odd rnds Knit.
Rnd 2 Kfb into each st—12 sts.
Rnds 4 and 6 [K1, kfb, k to last 2 sts on needle, kfb, k1] twice—20 sts.
Rnds 8, 10, and 12 K1, kfb, k5, k2tog, k2, ssk, k5, kfb, k1.
Rnds 14 and 16 K to last 3 sts on first needle, k2tog, k2, ssk, k to end—16 sts.
Rnd 17 Knit.
Cut yarn and set aside, leaving first bottom leg on 2 dpn to work later.
Use additional dpn to make 2nd bottom leg. Cut yarn.

JOIN BOTTOM LEGS
Slide 2nd bottom leg onto dpn with first bottom leg so that legs lean towards each other, forming the bottom of the X—32 sts.
Tie cut ends tog and tuck inside one leg. Make sure only one marker is in place for beg of rnd.
Rnd 18 [K1, ssk, k4, k2tog, k4, k2tog, k1] twice—26 sts.

Gauge
18 sts and 26 rows/rnds to 4"/10cm over St st using size 8 (5mm) needles.
Take time to check gauge.

86

Jumbo Tic-Tac-Toe

Rnd 20 [K1, ssk, k7, k2tog, k1] twice — 22 sts.
Rnd 22 [K1, kfb, k7, kfb, k1] twice — 26 sts.
Rnd 24 [K1, kfb, k4, kfb, k4, kfb, k1] twice — 32 sts.
Rnd 25 Knit.

FIRST TOP LEG
With working yarn at right edge of X, slide left half of X (leftmost 8 sts from each dpn) to st holder to work first top leg — 16 sts. Place marker for beg of rnd.
Rnds 26 and 28 K1, kfb, k to last 2 sts on 2nd needle, kfb, k1 — 20 sts.
Rnds 30, 32, and 34 K1, kfb, k5, k2tog, k2, ssk, k5, kfb, k1.
Rnds 36 and 38 [K1, k2tog, k to last 3 sts on needle, k2tog, k1] twice — 12 sts.
Rnd 40 K2tog around — 6 sts.
Cut yarn, leaving long tail. Use tapestry needle to thread tail through rem sts and gather to close.

SECOND TOP LEG
Work same as first top leg on other half of sts from body, stuffing entire X before rnd 40. Weave in all ends, using ends to close up gaps where legs join body of X, as necessary.

O Pieces (Make 5)
With A and using provisional cast-on (see page 182), cast on 42 sts onto 1 dpn. Knit 1 row. Divide sts evenly over 3 dpn. Join to work in rnds, taking care not to twist sts, and pm for beg of rnd.
Rnd 1 Knit.
Rnd 2 K2, [M1, k4] 10 times — 52 sts.
Rnds 3 and 4 Knit.
Rnd 5 K2, [M1, k5] 10 times — 62 sts.

Rnds 6 and 7 Knit.
Rnd 8 K2, [M1, k6] 10 times — 72 sts.
Rnds 9 and 10 Knit.
Rnd 11 K2, [M1, k7] 10 times — 82 sts.
Rnds 12 and 13 Knit.
Rnd 14 K2, [k2tog, k6] 10 times — 72 sts.
Rnds 15 and 16 Knit.
Rnd 17 K2, [k2tog, k5] 10 times — 62 sts.
Rnds 18 and 19 Knit.
Rnd 20 K2, [k2tog, k4] 10 times — 52 sts.
Rnds 21 and 22 Knit.
Rnd 23 K2, [k2tog, k3] 10 times — 42 sts.
Rnd 24 Knit.
Remove scrap yarn from provisional cast-on and divide cast-on sts evenly over 3 dpn. Bring these dpn up through the middle of the O so that RS shows. Stuff and graft with Kitchener stitch (see page 182), working one third of O at a time. Check and adjust tension of grafted sts as necessary.

Game Board
With circular needle and C, cast on 128 sts Do *not* join. Knit 12 rows for bottom border. Cut C.
With B, work approx 2"/5cm in St st, enc with a WS row.

END ROW OF SQUARES
Next row (RS) K10 with first ball of B; k36 with first ball of C; k36 with 2nd ba of B; k36 with 2nd ball of C; k10 with 3rd ball of B.
Next row (WS) P10 with 3rd ball of B; p36 with 2nd ball of C; p36 with 2nd ba of B; p36 with first ball of C; p10 with first ball of B.
Rep last two rows for approx 8"/20.5cm, end with WS row.
Cut all yarns except first ball of B.

MIDDLE ROW OF SQUARES
Next row (RS) K46 with first ball of B; k36 with C; k46 with 2nd ball of B.
New row (WS) P46 with 2nd ball of B; p36 with C; p46 with first ball of B.
Rep last two rows for approx 8"/20.25cm, end with WS row.
Cut all yarns except first ball of B.

Work a 2nd end row of squares. Cut C.
With B, work approx 2"/5cm in St st.
Cut B. With C, work 12 rows in garter st for top border. Bind off.

SIDE BORDERS
With RS facing and circular needle, pick up and k 7 sts along side of top border, 128 sts along side of board, and 7 sts along side of bottom border. Knit 11 rows.
Bind off. Repeat for other side border. ■

Friendly Lobster

This stripey lobster is good enough to eat but so cute, you'll want to keep him around forever.

DESIGNED BY AMY BAHRT

Knitted Measurements

Approx 8½"/21.5cm long and 3¼"/8cm wide

Materials

- 1 1¾oz/50g hank (each approx 137yd/125m) of Cascade Yarns *220 Superwash Sport Multis* (superwash merino wool) in #113 Fire (**3**)
- One pair size 5 (3.75mm) needles, or size to obtain gauge
- Two size 5 (3.75mm) double-pointed needles (dpn)
- One size G/6 (4mm) crochet hook
- Embroidery needle
- Two ³⁄₈"/12mm white buttons for eyes

Note As small buttons are a choking hazard, embroider eyes if making for a child.

- Black thread
- Polyester stuffing

Body (Make 2)

Note Foll chart for body pieces.
Cast on 19 sts. Work 8 rows in St st (k on RS, p on WS).
Row 9 (RS) K2tog, k to last 2 sts, k2tog—17 sts.
Row 10 (WS) Purl.
Rep rows 9 and 10—15 sts.
Row 13 (RS) P2tog, p to last 2 sts, p2tog—13 sts.

Rows 14 Knit.
Rows 15–18 Work even in St st.
Row 19 Kfb, k to last st, kfb—15 sts.
Rows 20 and 21 Purl.
Row 22 Knit.
Row 23 Kfb, k to last st, kfb—17 sts.
Row 24 Purl.
Rep rows 23 and 24—19 sts.
Rows 27–48 Work even, foll chart.
Row 49 K2tog, k to last 2 sts, k2tog—17 sts.
Row 50 Purl.
Row 51 P2tog, p to last 2 sts, p2tog—15 sts.
Row 52 Knit.
Row 53 K2tog, k to last 2 sts, k2tog—13 sts.
Rows 54–62 Work even foll chart.
Row 63 K2tog, k to last 2 sts, k2tog—11 sts.
Row 64 Purl.
Rows 65 and 66 Rep rows 63 and 64—9 sts.
Row 67 K2tog, k to last 2 sts, k2tog.
Row 68 P2tog, p to last 2 sts, p2tog.
Row 69 Rep row 67—3 sts.
Cut yarn, pull end through rem sts and fasten off lightly.

Claws (Make 2)

Cast on 11 sts. Knit 1 row, purl 1 row.
Row 3 (RS) [K3, kfb] twice, k3—13 sts.
Row 4 and all WS rows Purl.
Row 5 K4, kfb, [k3, kfb] twice—16 sts.
Row 7 K5, kfb, [k3, kfb] twice, k2— 19 sts.
Rows 8–10 Work even.
Row 11 K4, k2tog, [k3, k2tog] twice, k3.
Row 13 K3, k2tog, [k2, k2tog] twice, k3.
Row 15 K2, k2tog, [k1, k2tog] twice, k3.
Row 17 K1, [k2tog] 4 times, k1—6 sts.
Row 19 [K2tog] 3 times.
Row 20 K3tog. Bind off.

Arms (Make 2)

With dpn, cast on 5 sts and work I-cord as foll: *K3, do *not* turn. Slide sts to work

Gauge

24 sts and 28 rows to 4"/10 cm over St st using size 5 (3.75 mm) needles.
Take time to check gauge.

31 Friendly Lobster

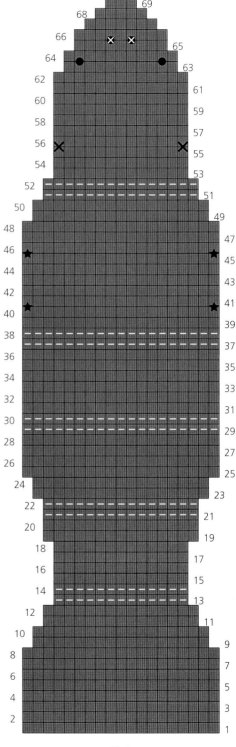

next row from RS. Rep from * for 3"/7.5cm. Cut yarn, leaving a long tail, and draw through sts on needle. Pull tail to cinch off.

Legs (Make 4)
With dpn, cast on 4 sts and work I-cord as for arms for 3"/7.5cm. Cut yarn, leaving a long tail, and draw through sts on needle. Pull tail to cinch off.

Finishing
Embroider or sew eyes to body, foll chart. Stuff claws and sew each to an arm. Pin claws and legs in place, foll chart. Sew body pieces tog on WS with arms and legs in place, leaving lower edge open.
Turn inside out, stuff, and sew closed.

ANTENNAE
For large antennae, with crochet hook, make an 8"/20.5cm chain, knot the end, and trim. Weave through stitches in head, see chart and photo.
For small antennae, with crochet hook, make a 2"/5cm chain, knot the end, and trim. Weave through a stitch at tip of the head (see photo). ■

KEY

▨	k on RS, p on WS
▤	p on RS, k on WS
⊙	= antennae placement
⊠	= eye placement
✕	= claw placement
★	= leg placement

19 sts

32

The Peace Van

C'mon, get happy in this totally hip van. Thoughtful details like windows
knit intarsia-style, tires with hubcabs, and a tiny hood ornament make this toy van-tastic.

DESIGNED BY AUDREY DRYSDALE

Knitted Measurements

Approx 17"/43cm wide x 10"/25.5cm
high x 6"/15cm deep, when stuffed

Materials

■ 2 3½oz/100g balls (each approx
220yd/200m) of Cascade Yarns *220
Superwash* (superwash wool) in #809
Really Red (A) **3**
■ 1 ball each in #871 White (B), #892
Space Needle (C), and #816 Gray (D)
■ One pair size 5 (3.75mm) needles,
or size to obtain gauge
■ Polyester stuffing
■ Tapestry needle
■ Bobbins

Note

1) Use a separate bobbin for each color section.
Do *not* carry yarn across back of work.
2) When changing colors, twist yarns on
WS to prevent holes in work.

Sides (Make 2)

With A, cast on 62 sts. Knit 1 row.
Working in St st (k on RS, p on WS), inc 1
st each side every row 4 times, then every
other row 3 times more—76 sts. Work
even until a total of 38 rows are complete.

WINDOWS
Change to B and knit 4 rows. Work 2
rows more in St st.
Window row (RS) [With C, k16; with B,
k4] 3 times; with C, k16.
Cont in St st, working colors as set until
10 window rows are complete.
Dec 1 st each side in the foll row and
every other row once more—72 sts.
Work 1 row even, matching colors.
Next row (RS) With B, knit, dec 1 st
each side—70 sts.

With B, purl 1 row.
Next row (RS) With C, knit. Cut C.
With B, cont in St st, dec 1 st each side
every row 4 times—62 sts. Bind off.
With D, embroider door outline with
back using chart 1 and back st, reversing
placement of door on 2nd side (for mirror
image).

Front

With A, cast on 22 sts. Work chart 2
through row 64. With B, bind off all sts.
With D, embroider peace sign as charted
(see photo).

Back

With A, cast on 22 sts. Work chart 3
through row 64. With B, bind off all sts.

Base

With A, cast on 22 sts. Work
11¼"/28.5cm in St st, end with a RS row.
Bind off.

Top

With B, work as for base.

Front Wheel (Make 4)

With D, cast on 5 sts. Work chart 4
through row 22. With D, bind off rem 5 sts.

Gauge

22 sts and 30 rows to 4"/10cm over St st using size 5 (3.75mm) needles.
Take time to check gauge.

The Peace Van

Back Wheel (Make 4)

With D, cast on 5 sts. Work as for front with D only.

Finishing

Sew straight edges of sides to base and top pieces. Sew front and back pieces to sides, base, and top pieces, leaving an opening at back to insert stuffing. Stuff. Sew opening closed.

Sew front and back wheel pieces tog, leaving an opening to insert stuffing. Stuff lightly. Sew opening closed.

Sew wheels in place as shown in photo. ■

CHART 4

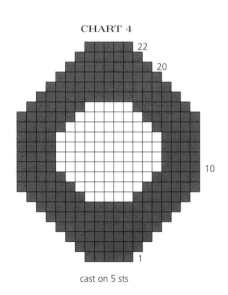

cast on 5 sts

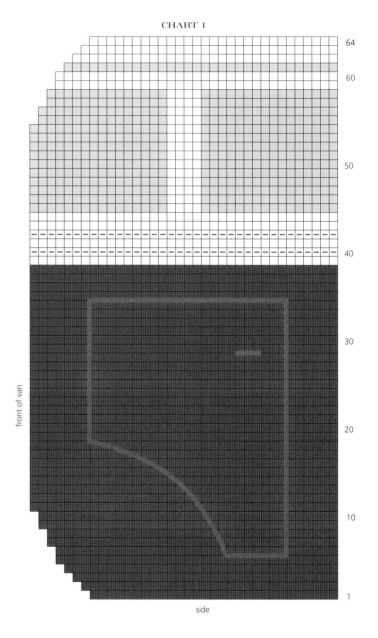

CHART 1

front of van

side

COLOR KEY

▨	A	⊟	p on RS, k on WS
☐	B	▬	embroider with D
▨	C	☑	duplicate stitch in D
▨	D		

94

CHART 2

CHART 3

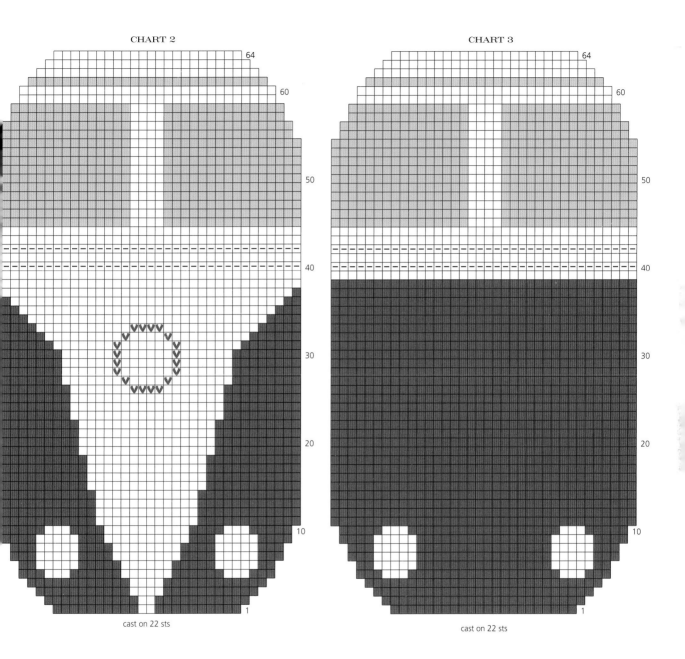

64

60

50

40

30

20

10

1

cast on 22 sts

64

60

50

40

30

20

10

1

cast on 22 sts

33

Whale Puppet

You'll have a whale of a time knitting this puppet;
your tot will have just as much fun playing with it.

DESIGNED BY ANN FAITH

Knitted Measurements
Approx 12"/30.5cm long, when worn

Materials
▓ 1 3½oz/100g hank (each approx 150yd/138m) of Cascade Yarns *220 Superwash Aran Splatter* (superwash merino wool) in #06 Tempest (MC) (4)
▓ 1 3½oz/100g hank (each approx 150yd/138m) of Cascade Yarns *220 Superwash Aran* (superwash merino wool) in #871 White (CC) (4)
▓ One pair size 8 (5mm) needles, *or size to obtain gauge*
▓ Small black shank button
Note As small buttons are a choking hazard, embroider eyes if making for a child.
▓ Scrap yarn
▓ 2½"/6.5cm square of cardboard
▓ Stitch markers

WHALE
With MC, cast on 34 sts.
Row 1 (RS) *K2, p2; rep from *, end k2.
Row 2 K the knit sts and p the purl sts.
Rep row 2 for k2, p2 rib until piece measures 1"/2.5cm from beg.
Cont in St st (k on RS, p on WS) until piece measures 3"/7.5cm from beg, end with a WS row.

SHAPE GUSSET
Next row (RS) K16, pm, [kfb] twice, pm, k to end—36 sts.
Purl 1 row.
Inc row K to marker, sm, kfb, k to 1 st before marker, kfb, sm, k to end—2 sts inc'd.
Rep inc row every other row 3 times more—44 sts, 12 sts between markers.
Purl 1 row.
Next row (RS) K to marker, remove marker, k to next marker and place the 12 sts just worked on scrap yarn to hold, remove 2nd marker, cast on 2 sts, k to end—34 sts.
Purl 1 row.
Spout row (RS) K7, yo, k2tog, k to end.
Cont in St st until piece measures 7½"/19cm from beg, end with a WS row.

SHAPE HEAD
Row 1 (RS) K2, [k2tog, k2] 8 times—26 sts.
Row 2 Purl.
Row 3 K2, [k2tog, k2] 6 times—20 sts.
Row 4 Purl.
Row 5 K1, [k2tog, k1] 6 times—14 sts.
Row 6 [P2tog] 7 times—7 sts.
Row 7 K1, [k2tog] 3 times.
Cut yarn, leaving a long tail.
Thread tail through rem sts to close.

THUMB
Place sts from scrap yarn on needle.
Join yarn, ready to work a WS row.
Work 9 rows in St st.
Row 10 (RS) [K2tog] 6 times—6 sts.
Row 11 Purl.
Row 12 [K2tog] 3 times—3 sts.
Cut yarn, leaving a long tail.
Thread tail through rem sts to close.

Finishing
Working 2 rows above thumb and 1 st to the right of the thumb, with CC, duplicate st 3 rows of 3 sts.
Sew black button in center or embroider

TASSEL SPOUT
Wrap CC yarn around cardboard 12 times. Cut ends of yarn along one edge. Cut a 6"/15cm length of CC and tie kno around center of yarn lengths. Fold tasse in half and wrap a 6"/15cm length of CC ½"/1.5cm up from base and tie knot Thread yarn ends from knots through bas Trim tassel ends to uniform length. Secure tassel to yarn over hole by weavir in ends from knots.
Sew side and thumb seams. ∎

Gauge
18 sts and 24 rows to 4"/10cm over St st using size 8 (5mm) needles.
Take time to check gauge.

Multi-Colored Balls

A classic, these soft balls can be rolled, tossed, or flung without any damage to baby or nursery. The perfect project for using up small amounts of yarn!

DESIGNED BY AUDREY DRYSDALE

◼◼◼◻

Knitted Measurements
Smaller Ball Approx 6½"/16.5cm diameter
Larger Ball Approx 8½"/21.5cm diameter

Materials
- 1 1¾oz/50g hank (each approx 136yd/125m) of Cascade Yarns *220 Superwash Sport* (superwash merino wool) each in #875 Feather Gray, #812 Turquoise, #1952 Blaze, #240 Jasmine Green, and #219 Moon Rock (3)
- One set (5) size 5 (3.75mm) double-pointed needles (dpn), *or size to obtain gauge*
- Stitch marker
- Polyester stuffing

Note
Each ball is worked in four different stripe combinations. Choose colors as desired.

Stripe Pattern for Large Ball
12 rnds color 1, 20 rnds color 2, 8 rnds color 3, work to end with color 4.

Stripe Pattern for Small Ball
8 rnds color 1, 10 rnds color 2, 14 rnds color 3, work to end with color 4.

Large Ball
**With color 1, cast on 5 sts.
Row 1 (RS) [Kfb] 4 times, k1—9 sts.
Divide sts evenly over 3 dpn. Join, taking care not to twists sts, and pm for beg of rnd.

BEGIN STRIPE PATTERN
Note Add 4th dpn and divide sts evenly, when necessary, to fit extra sts.
Work in St st (k every rnd) and stripe pat for large ball, as foll:
Rnds 1 and 2 Kfb in every st—36 sts.
Rnd 3 *K3, M1; rep from * around—48 sts.
Rnd 4 and every even-numbered rnd Knit.
Rnd 5 *K6, M1; rep from * around—56 sts.
Rnd 7 *K7, M1; rep from * around— 64 sts.
Rnd 9 *K8, M1; rep from * around—72 sts.**
Rnd 11 *K9, M1; rep from * around—80 sts.
Rnd 13 *K10, M1; rep from * around—88 sts.
Rnd 15 *K11, M1; rep from * around—96 sts.
Work even for 27 rnds, keeping in stripe pat.

SHAPE TOP
Cont in St st and stripe pat as foll:
Rnd 1 and all odd-numbered rnds Knit.
Rnd 2 *K10, k2tog; rep from * around—88 sts.
Rnd 4 *K9, k2tog; rep from *

around—80 sts.
Rnd 6 *K8, k2tog; rep from * around—72 sts.
Rnd 8 *K7, k2tog; rep from * around—64 sts.
Rnd 10 *K6, k2tog; rep from * around—56 sts.
Rnd 12 *K5, k2tog; rep from * around—48 sts.
Stuff ball.
Rnd 14 *K4, k2tog; rep from * around—40 sts.
Rnd 16 *K3, k2tog; rep from * around—32 sts.
Rnd 18 *K2, k2tog; rep from * around—24 sts.
Rnd 20 *K1, k2tog; rep from * around—16 sts.
Cut yarn. Draw end through rem sts and fasten securely.

Small Ball
Work from ** to ** as for large ball—72 st
Work even for 21 rnds, keeping in stripe pa
SHAPE TOP
Cont in St st and stripe pat as foll:
Rnd 1 and all odd-numbered rnds Knit. Beg with dec rnd 8, complete as fo large ball. ◼

Gauge
24 sts and 32 rnds to 4"/10cm over St st using size 5 (3.75mm) needles.
Take time to check gauge.

Fancy Cat

Knit in two pieces, this striped gray tabby
is dressed to impress in a spiffy vest and bowtie.

DESIGNED BY LORI STEINBERG

Knitted Measurements
Approx 21"/53.5cm high, from top
of head to foot

Materials
■ 2 3½oz/100g hanks (each approx
150yd/138m) of Cascade Yarns *220
Superwash Aran* (superwash merino wool)
each in #817 Aran (A), #1946 Silver Gray
(B), and #240 Jasmine Green (C) (4)
■ 1 hank in #1987 Magenta (D)
■ Small amounts in #836 Pink Ice (E)
and #815 Black (F)
■ One pair size 9 (5.5mm) needles,
or size to obtain gauge
■ Size J/10 (6mm) crochet hook
■ Bobbins
■ 3 buttons to match D
■ Polyester stuffing

Note
1) When working front vest pat, use a
separate bobbin for each block of color.
2) When changing colors, twist yarns on
WS row to prevent holes in work.

Stripe Pattern
Working in St st (k on RS, p on WS),
work 4 rows A, 4 rows B.
Rep these 8 rows for stripe pat.

Vest Pattern
(over an even number of sts)
Row 1 (RS) Knit.
Row 2 Purl.
Row 3 *K1, p1; rep from * to end.
Row 4 K the purl sts and p the knit sts.
Rep rows 1–4 for vest pat.

Back
FIRST LEG
Note Each leg is worked separately in St
st and then joined to continue working
the back of the cat.
With A, cast on 12 sts. Work 4 rows in St st.

Shape foot
Next row (RS) Bind off 2 sts, k to end.
Next row P to last 2 sts, p2tog tbl.
Next row SKP, k to end—8 sts.
Purl 1 row with A. Join B.

Begin stripes and shaping
Work 2 rows B.
Inc row 1 (RS) K1, kfb, k to end—9 sts.
Purl 1 row B. Change to A.
Inc row 2 K to last 2 sts, kfb, k1—10 sts.
Cont in stripe pat and rep inc row 1 every
other row 3 times more, AT THE SAME
TIME, rep inc row 2 every 4th row twice
more—15 sts.
Purl 1 row. Set work aside.

SECOND LEG
With A, cast on 12 sts. Work 5 rows in St st

Shape foot
Next row (WS) Bind off 2 sts, work to end
Next row K to last 2 sts, k2tog.
Next row P2tog, p to end—8 sts.

Begin stripes and shaping
Join B. Work 2 rows B.
Inc row 1 (RS) K to last 2 sts, kfb, k1—9 sts.
Purl 1 row B. Change to A.
Inc row 2 K1, kfb, k to end—10 sts.
Cont in stripe pat and rep inc row 1 ever
other row 3 times more, AT THE SAME
TIME, rep inc row 2 every 4th row twice
more—15 sts. Purl 1 row.

BODY
Joining row (RS) Cont in stripe pat, k15
sts of first leg, cast on 4 sts, k15 sts of
2nd leg—34 sts.
Work 3 rows even.
Inc row (RS) K1, kfb, k to last 2 sts, kfb,
k1—2 sts inc'd.
Work 3 rows. Cut A and B. Join C and
beg vest pat, AT THE SAME TIME, rep inc
row every 6th row 4 times more, then
every other row twice more—48 sts.
When all incs are complete, work even unti
piece measures 10"/25.5cm from joining.

Gauge
16 sts and 24 rows to 4"/10cm over St st using size 9 (5.5mm) needles.
Take time to check gauge.

Fancy Cat

Shape shoulders
Dec 1 st each side. Work 1 row even.
Bind off 3 sts at beg of next 6 rows—28 sts.
Cut C.

Head
Join B and work in St st, inc 1 st each
side *every* row 8 times—44 sts. Work
4"/10cm even. Bind off 3 sts at beg of
next 2 rows, then 4 sts at beg of next 2
rows, then 5 sts at beg of next 2 rows.
Bind off rem 20 sts.

Front
Work as for back until 5 rows have been
worked after joining legs.

BEGIN VEST PATTERN
Next row (RS) With C, k1, kfb, cont in
stripe pat to last 2 sts, join 2nd ball of C,
kfb, k1—2 sts inc'd.
Cont in stripe pat as established and
shaping as for back, AT THE SAME TIME,
work 4 sts less in stripe pat at center (2
sts more in C each side) every other row,
incorporating C sts into vest pat, until all
sts are in C and vest pat. Cont shaping as
for back through shoulder shaping—28 sts.

HEAD
Work shaping as for back of head to
end, AT THE SAME TIME, work in St st in
colors as foll: 4 rows A.
Next row (RS) With B, k3; with A, work to
last 3 sts; add 2nd bobbin of B, k to end.
Cont to shape as for back, work 2 less sts
in A at center (1 st more in B each side)
every other row until all sts are being
worked in B.
Complete as for back of head.

Arms (Make 4 Pieces)
With B, cast on 12 sts. Work in St st, [4
rows B, 4 rows A] 5 times. Cut B and
cont with A only.
Next row (RS) K1, SKP, k to last 3 sts,
k2tog, k1.
Next row P1, p2tog, p to last 3 sts,
p2tog tbl, p1.
Next row [SKP] twice, [k2tog] twice—4 sts.
Bind off.
Sew two pieces tog to form each arm,
leaving cast-on edges unsewn.

Tail
With B, cast on 20 sts. Work in St st and
stripe pat (4 rows B, 4 rows A) for 48
rows. Cut B and cont with A only.
Next row (RS) [K2tog] 10 times.
Next row (WS) [P2tog] 5 times. Cut yarn,
leaving an end for sewing and draw through
rem 5 sts. Pull tog and sew side seam.

Pocket
With D, cast on 14 sts. Work rows 1–4
in vest pat 3 times. Rep rows 3 and 4.
Bind off.

Ears (Make 2)
With E, cast on 1 st.
Next row (RS) Knit into front, back, and
front of st—3 sts.
Next row Purl.
Next row Kfb, k to last st, kfb—5 sts.
Rep last 2 rows twice more. Bind off 9 sts.

Bowtie
With D, cast on 25 sts.
Next row *K1, p1; rep from * to end.
Next row K the knit sts and p the purl
sts for k1, p1 rib.
Rep last row for rib until piece measures
2"/5cm from beg. Bind off.
Wrap strand of D several times around
center of strip to cinch.

Finishing
With crochet hook and E, slip stitch along
lower front edge of vest and up the
center front (see photo). Sew buttons and
pocket to front (see photo).
Sew front to back, leaving an opening at
head. Stuff legs and body lightly to creat
a flat appearance. Sew head closed.
Stuff arms lightly, sew closed, and sew to
body. Sew tail to center of back, leaving
unstuffed, beg at bottom of last gray
stripe and ending at first few rows of vest
With E, use duplicate stitch to create nose.
With E, embroider mouth (see photo).
With C and F, embroider eyes (see photo)
For whiskers, cut 3 strands of F approx
6"/15cm and thread under nose.
Trim whiskers as desired.
Sew ears and bowtie in place. ■

Colorful Owl Pillow

An ancient symbol of wisdom, the owl has become a modern symbol of cute.
Big eyes, feather-like fringe, and a bright-red mouth will help this little owl fly right into your heart.

DESIGNED BY JACQUELINE VAN DILLEN

Knitted Measurements
Body Approx 12 x 14"/30.5 x 35.5cm

Materials
- 1 3½oz/100g ball (each approx 220yd/200m) of Cascade Yarns *220 Superwash* (superwash wool) each in #901 Cotton Candy (A), #850 Lime Sherbet (B), #900 Charcoal (C), #821 Daffodil (D), #849 Dark Aqua (E), and #809 Really Red (F) (3️⃣)
- Small amount #1914 Alaska Sky (G)
- Size 6 (4mm) circular needle, 24"/60cm long, *or size to obtain gauge*
- One set (4) size 6 (4mm) double-pointed needles (dpn)
- Polyester stuffing
- Stitch markers

Notes
1) Circular needle is used to accommodate large number of sts. Do *not* join.
2) When working eyes, wind small balls of yarn for each block of color. When changing colors, twist yarns on WS to prevent holes in work.

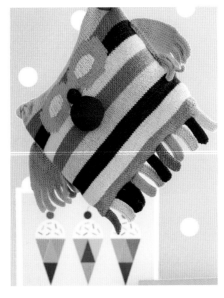

Stripe Pattern
Work in St st as foll: 10 rows each A, B, C, D, A, B, C, A, D—90 rows in total.

Body
With A, cast on 144 sts. Work in St st (k on RS, p on WS) for 56 rows, end after 6 rows on 2nd B stripe. Cont in stripe pat as foll:

BEGIN CHART
Place marker on each side of center 44 sts.
Row 1 (RS) With B, k to marker, sm, work row 1 of chart pat, sm, with B, k to end.
Cont in pat as established, working center 44 sts in chart pat and rem sts in stripe pat, until all chart rows have been worked. Remove markers. Then cont St st and stripe pat until 90 rows of stripe pat have been worked *in total*. Cont with D only as foll:

SHAPE HORNS
Next row (RS) Bind off 6 sts, work until there are 66 sts from bind-off, turn, keep rem 72 sts on hold.
Next row (WS) Bind off 6 sts, work to end.
Bind off 4 sts at beg of next 4 rows, 3 sts at beg of next 2 rows, 2 sts at beg of each row until 8 sts rem. Work even for 16 rows. Bind off.
Work 2nd side in same way.

Finishing
With G, using photo as guide, duplicate stitch center of eyes. Sew sides of body together to form tube with seam as center back.

Gauge
20 sts and 28 rows to 4"/10cm over St st using size 6 (4mm) needle.
Take time to check gauge.

Colorful Owl Pillow

NOSE

With C, cast on 4 sts. Work 2 rows in St st.
Cast on 2 sts at beg of next 2 rows—8 sts.
Inc 1 st each side every other row
twice—12 sts.
Work 3 rows even.
Dec 1 st each side every other row
twice—8 sts.
Bind off 2 sts at beg of next 2 rows—4 sts.
Work 2 rows even. Bind off.
Sew nose to front of owl, using photo as
guide, leaving small opening for stuffing.
Stuff firmly and close.

MOUTH

With F, cast on 8 sts. Work 2 rows in St st.

Cast on 2 sts at beg of next 8 rows—24 sts.
Inc 1 st each side every other row 3
times—30 sts.
Work 7 rows even.
Dec 1 st each side every other row 3
times—24 sts.
Bind off 2 sts at beg of next 8 rows—8 sts.
Work 2 rows even. Bind off.
Sew mouth to front of owl, using photo
as guide, leaving a small opening for
stuffing. Stuff firmly and close.

FEATHERS (Make 2 each in A, B, C, D, E,
and F)
Cast on 14 sts. Knit 16 rows. Bind off.
Pin feathers to one side of lower edge.

Sew lower edge seam, sewing feathers
into seam.
Stuff body lightly. Sew upper edge seam.
Tie knot in each horn.

WINGS (Make 2)
With E, cast on 24 sts. Knit 2 rows.
Row 1 (RS) Cast on 11 sts, k to last 3 sts,
SKP, k1—1 st dec'd.
Row 2 Knit.
Row 3 K to last 3 sts, SKP, k1—1 st dec'd.
Row 4 Rep row 2.
Row 5 Rep row 3.
Row 6 Bind off 11 sts, k to end.
Rep rows 1–6 six times more. Bind off all sts.
Sew wings to sides of owl (see photo). ∎

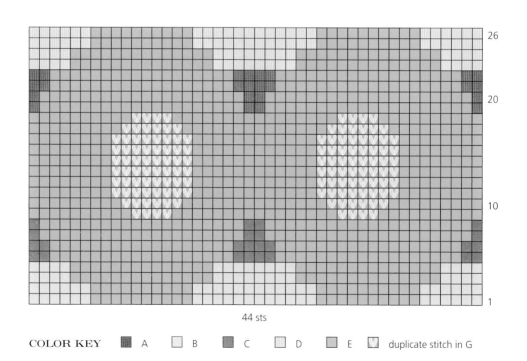

26
20
10
1

44 sts

COLOR KEY   ■ A   □ B   ■ C   □ D   ■ E   ∨ duplicate stitch in G

37

Flamingo Rattle

Start your little one's pink flamingo collection early
with this darling rattle, a perfect gift for any little one.

DESIGNED BY AMY BAHRT

Knitted Measurements
Approx 7½"/19cm long and 5½"/14cm wide

Materials
▦ 1 3½oz/100g ball (each approx 220yd/
200m) of Cascade Yarns *220 Superwash*
(superwash wool) each in #827 Coral (A)
and #808 Sunset Orange (B) (③)
▦ Small amount in blue yarn for eyes
▦ One pair size 7 (4.5mm) needles,
or size to obtain gauge
▦ Two size 7 (4.5mm) double-pointed
needles (dpn)
▦ Small plastic capsule (taped closed)
with plastic beads for head rattle
▦ Polyester stuffing
▦ Embroidery needle

Body (Make 2)
Note Foll chart 1 for body pieces.
With A, cast on 11 sts.
Row 1 (RS) Knit.
Row 2 [Pfb] twice, p to last 2 sts, [pfb]
twice—15 sts.
Row 3 Knit.
Row 4 With A, pfb; [with B, p1; with A,
p5] twice; with B, p1; with A, pfb—17 sts.

Row 5 Knit.
Row 6 Pfb, p to last st, pfb—19 sts.
Row 7 Knit, foll chart.
Rep rows 6 and 7 twice more—23 sts.
Row 12 (WS) Pfb, p8, with 2nd ball of
yarn, bind off center 5 sts, p to last st, pfb.
Row 13 (RS) Knit, foll chart to last 2 sts
on first side, k2tog; on 2nd side, k2tog,
foll chart to end.
Rows 14–24 Work each side separately,
foll chart.
Row 25 Knit, foll chart to last st on first
side, kfb; on 2nd side, kfb, k to end.
Row 26 P2tog, p to end of first side, cast

on 5 sts to join the 2 pieces, p to last 2
sts, p2tog—23 sts.
Row 27 Knit, foll chart.
Row 28 P2tog, p to last 2 sts foll chart,
p2tog.
Rows 29–34 Rep rows 27 and 28 three
times more—15 sts.
Row 35 Knit, foll chart.
Row 36 P3tog, p to last 3 sts foll chart,
p3tog—11 sts. Bind off.

Head
Note Foll chart 2 for head pieces.
FIRST HALF
With A, cast on 8 sts for neck. Work in St s
(k on RS, p on WS) for 12 rows. Set aside.
With B, cast on 2 sts for beak.
Row 1 (WS) Purl.
Row 2 (RS) K to last st, kfb.
Rep rows 1 and 2—4 sts.
Row 5 Purl.
Row 6 K2tog, k1, kfb—4 sts.
(Purl 1 row, knit 1 row) twice. Change to
A and purl 1 row.
Joining row 12 (RS) With A, k8 sts of
neck, cast on 2 sts, k4 sts of beak—14 sts
Purl 1 row, knit 1 row, purl 1 row.
Row 16 (RS) K2tog, k to end.
Row 17 Purl.

Gauge
20 sts and 26 rows to 4"/10cm over St st using size 7 (4.5mm) needles.
Take time to check gauge

Flamingo Rattle

Row 18 K2tog, k to last 2 sts, k2tog.
Row 19 Purl.
Rows 20 and 21 Rep rows 18 and 19—9 sts. Bind off.

SECOND HALF
Note This half is a mirror image of first half.
With A, cast on 8 sts for neck.
Work in St st for 12 rows. Set aside.
With B, cast on 2 sts for beak.
Row 1 (WS) Purl.
Row 2 (RS) Kfb, k to end.
Rep rows 1 and 2—4 sts.
Row 5 Purl.
Row 6 Kfb, k1, k2tog—4 sts.
[Purl 1 row, knit 1 row] twice.
Change to A and purl 1 row.
Joining row 12 (RS) With A, k4 sts of beak, cast on 2 sts, k8 sts of neck—14 sts.
Purl 1 row, knit 1 row, purl 1 row.
Row 16 (RS) K to last 2 sts, k2tog.
Row 17 Purl.
Row 18 K2tog, k to last 2 sts, k2tog.
Row 19 Purl.
Rows 20 and 21 Rep rows 18 and 19—9 sts. Bind off.

Wings (Make 2)

With A, cast on 3 sts. Knit 1 row, purl 1 row.
Row 3 Kfb, k1, kfb—5 sts.
Row 4 Purl.
Row 5 Kfb, k3, kfb—7 sts.
Rows 6–12 Work even in St st.
Bind off.

Legs (Make 2)

With dpn and B, cast on 4 sts. Work I-cord as foll:
*K3, do *not* turn. Slide sts back to beg of needle to work next row from RS; rep from * 4 times more.
Change to A and cont I-cord until piece measures 3½"/9cm. Bind off.

Finishing

With blue yarn, embroider French knots for eyes on both sides of head, then sew pieces together. With B, work ch-st embroidery around the outer 3 edges of the wings, evening edges. Pin body tog with wings in place, foll chart for placement, and sew, leaving opening for head. Stuff body. Stuff head, including rattle, and sew head in place, foll chart. Sew legs in place.
With B, tie bows on feet (see photo). ■

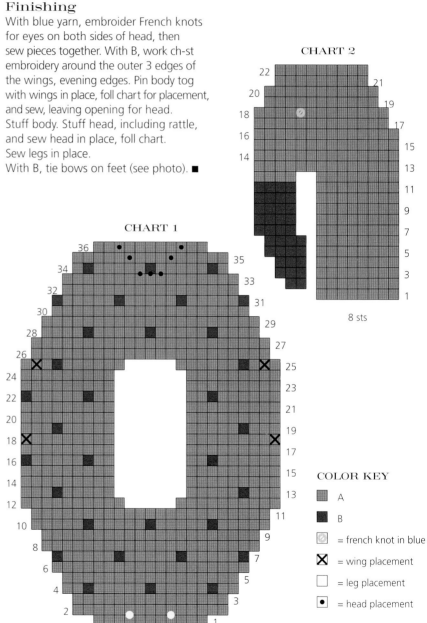

CHART 2

8 sts

CHART 1

11 sts

COLOR KEY

▨ A

■ B

⊘ = french knot in blue

✕ = wing placement

☐ = leg placement

● = head placement

Duck Rattle

Don't go quackers: use charts or step-by-step instructions to create this sweet duck-shaped rattle for your little duckling.

DESIGNED BY AMY BAHRT

Knitted Measurements
Approx 6"/15cm long and 5"/12.5cm wide

Materials
- 1 3½oz/100g ball (each approx 220yd/200m) of Cascade Yarns *220 superwash* (superwash wool) each in #871 White (A), #821 Daffodil (B), #848 Blueberry (C), #825 Orange (D), and #827 Coral (E) **(3)**
- One pair size 7 (4.5mm) needles, or size to obtain gauge
- Small plastic capsule (taped closed) with plastic beads for head rattle
- Polyester stuffing
- Embroidery needle

Note
1) Wind small balls of yarn for each block of color.
2) When changing colors, twist yarns on WS to prevent holes in work.
3) For the 2nd body piece, switch to an E stripe on the right side and a D stripe on the left side to match the first piece when sewn tog

Body (Make 2)
Note Foll chart 1 for body pieces.
With A, cast on 11 sts.
Row 1 (RS) With A, k4; with C, k3; with A, k4.
Row 2 Foll chart, [pfb] twice, p to last 2 sts, [pfb] twice—15 sts.
Row 3 Work even in colors, foll chart.
Row 4 Pfb, p to last st, pfb—17 sts.
Row 5 Work even in colors, foll chart.
Rep rows 4 and 5 three times more—23 sts.
Row 12 Pfb, p8, join 2nd ball of A and bind off center 5 sts, p8, pfb—10 sts each side.

Gauge
20 sts and 26 rows to 4"/10cm over St st using size 7 (4.5mm) needles.
Take time to check gauge.

Row 13 K8, k2tog; on 2nd side, k2tog, k to end—9 sts each side.
Rows 14–16 Working both sides at once, work even with A.
Rows 17–20 Working both sides at once, work even with D stripe on right side and E stripe on left side.
Rows 21–24 Work even with A.
Joining row 25 (RS) With A, k8, kfb, cast on 5 sts, kfb, k to end—25 sts.
Row 26 With A, p2tog, p9; with C, p3; with A, p9, p2tog—23 sts.
Row 27 Work even in colors, foll chart.
Row 28 P2tog, p to last 2 sts, p2tog—21 sts.
Rep rows 27 and 28 three times more—15 sts.
Row 35 Work even in colors, foll chart.
Row 36 P3tog, p to last 3 sts, p3tog.
Bind off.

Head
Note Foll chart 2 for head pieces.

FIRST HALF
With B, cast on 8 sts.
Work 4 rows in St st (k on RS, p on WS).
Row 5 (RS) With B, K7, k in front of last st; with D, k in back of last st.

Duck Rattle

Row 6 With D, pfb; with B, p8.
Row 7 With B, k8; with D, [kfb] twice.
Row 8 With D, [pfb] twice, p2; with B, p8.
Row 9 With B, k8; with D, k5, kfb—15 sts.
Row 10 Work even in colors, foll chart.
Row 11 K to last 2 sts, k2tog.
Row 12 Bind off 2 sts, p to end.
Row 13 K to last 3 sts, k3tog.
Row 14 Bind off 2 sts, p to end.
With B only, dec 1 st each side of the last 2 rows—4 sts. Bind off.

SECOND HALF
This half (which is a mirror image of the first half) is worked foll chart 2 through row 4, then the beak section in color A is worked on the opposite side of the piece using chart and previous instructions as a guide.

Wings (Make 2)
With B, cast on 3 sts. Knit 1 row, purl 1 row.
Row 3 Kfb, k to last st, kfb—5 sts.
Row 4 Purl.
Row 5 Rep row 3—7 sts.
Rows 6–12 Work even in St st. Bind off.

Feet (Make 2)
Note Foll chart 3 for feet.
With D, cast on 2 sts. Knit 1 row, purl 1 row.
Row 3 Kfb, k to last st, kfb—4 sts.
Row 4 Purl.
Rep rows 3 and 4 twice more—8 sts.
Knit 1 row, purl 1 row. Bind off.

Finishing
With B, work ch-st embroidery on each foot, foll chart 3. Join feet to front of body, using chart and photo as a guide.

With B, work ch-st around outer edges of wings. Pin wings in place, foll chart 1, and sew body pieces, leaving an opening for head. Stuff the body. With C, embroider French knots on head pieces for eyes, foll chart 2. Sew head pieces tog, stuff, then sew in place on body, foll chart 1. ■

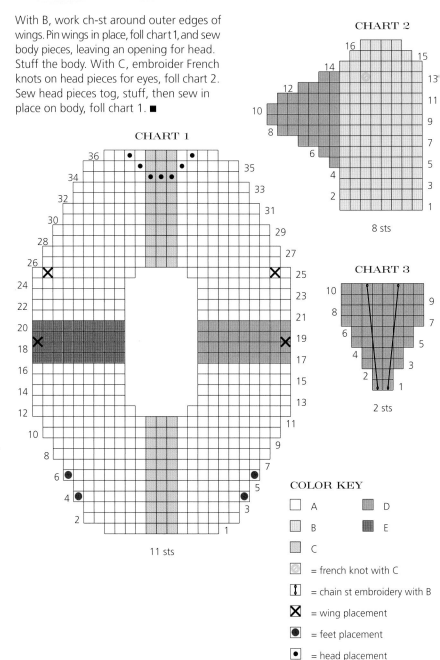

CHART 1

CHART 2

CHART 3

COLOR KEY

☐ A   ▨ D
☐ B   ▨ E
☐ C

⊘ = french knot with C
🔋 = chain st embroidery with B
✖ = wing placement
● = feet placement
▪ = head placement

110

Naptime Elf

A simple striped shape is embellished with a face,
making a quick toy guaranteed to bring sweet dreams!

DESIGNED BY ERIN SLONAKER

Knitted Measurements
Approx 11"/28cm high

Materials
- 1 1¾oz/50g hank (each approx 137yd/125m) of Cascade Yarns *220 Superwash Sport* (superwash merino wool) each in #871 White (A), #827 Coral (B), and #1940 Peach (C) (3)
- Small amount in #815 Black (D)
- One set (5) size 5 (3.75mm) double-pointed needles (dpn), `or size to obtain gauge`
- One size F/5 crochet hook
- Scrap yarn
- Stitch markers
- Tapestry needle
- Polyester stuffing

Stitch Glossary
M1R Insert LH needle from back to front under the strand between last st worked and next st on LH needle. K into the front loop to twist the st.

M1L Insert LH needle from front to back under the strand between last st worked and next st on LH needle. K into the back loop to twist the st.

Stripe Pattern
In St st (k every rnd), work 10 rnds B, 10 rnds C. Rep these 20 rnds for stripe pat.

Face
With A, cast on 6 sts and divide over 4 dpn. Join, being careful not to twist sts, and pm for beg of rnd.
Rnd 1 [Kfb] 6 times—12 sts.
Rnd 2 and all even-numbered rnds Knit.
Rnd 3 [M1L, k2] 6 times—18 sts.
Rnd 5 [M1L, k2] 9 times—27 sts.
Rnd 7 [M1L, k3] 9 times—36 sts.
Rnd 9 [M1L, k4] 9 times—45 sts.
Rnd 11 [M1L, k5] 9 times—54 sts.
Rnd 13 [M1L, k6] 9 times—63 sts.
Rnd 15 [M1L, k7] 9 times—72 sts.
Rnd 17 [M1L, k8] 9 times—81 sts.
Rnd 19 [M1L, k9] 9 times—90 sts.
Rnd 21 [M1L, k10] 9 times—99 sts.
Rnd 23 [M1L, k11] 9 times—108 sts.
Bind off.

Body
With B, cast on 20 sts using provisional cast-on (see page 182).
Knit 1 row.
Carefully remove scrap yarn, placing open sts onto 2nd dpn—40 sts.

Place marker for beg of rnd and divide sts evenly over 4 dpn.
Cont in stripe pat for body as foll:
Next rnd K20, pm, k20.
Inc rnd [K2, M1R, k to 2 sts before marker, M1L, k to marker] twice—4 sts inc'd.
Rep inc rnd every other rnd 12 times more—92 sts. Knit 10 rnds.
Dec rnd [K2, k2tog, k to 4 sts before marker, ssk, k to marker] twice—4 sts dec'd.
Rep dec rnd every 4th rnd 14 times more—32 sts. Knit 3 rnds. Do *not* cut yarn.

ATTACH AND EMBELLISH THE FACE
Note Stuff firmly for a flat appearance. Center face on side of body, sew down with running sts and A. With D, embroider mouth and eyes with chain st (see photo). Weave in ends, stuff body.

COMPLETE BODY
Stuffing every few rnds, cont as foll:
Rep dec rnd every 4th rnd 5 times more—12 sts. Knit 3 rnds.
Next rnd [K1, k2tog, ssk, k1] twice—8 sts.
Knit 2 rnds.
Next rnd [K2tog, ssk] twice—4 sts.
Knit 1 rnd.
Cut yarn, leaving a long tail. Thread tail through rem sts, and pull tight to close.

Gauge
26 sts and 36 rnds to 4"/10cm over St st using size 5 (3.75mm) needles.
Take time to check gauge.

40

Cuddly Triceratops

Dino-lovers will flip for this toy triceratops,
adorable from the tip of its horn to the last bump on its tail.

DESIGNED BY VIOLET

Knitted Measurements
Approx 18"/46cm high when sitting

Materials
▪ 2 3½oz/100g hanks (each approx 150yd/138m) of Cascade Yarns *220 Superwash Aran* (superwash merino wool) in #849 Dark Aqua (A) (4️⃣)
▪ 1 hank each in #871 White (B) and #802 Green Apple (C)
▪ Small amount of black yarn for face embroidery
▪ One pair size 7 (4.5mm) needles, *or size to obtain gauge*
▪ Stitch markers and holders
▪ White felt
▪ Craft glue
▪ Polyester stuffing

Notes
1) Gauge is worked tighter than recommended for a firmer fabric.
2) When changing colors, twist yarns on WS to prevent holes in work.
3) When binding off, the last st on RH needle counts as the first st of the stitch count that directly follows.

Left Foot and Leg
SOLE
**With A, cast on 5 sts.
Row 1 (RS) Knit.
Cont in garter st (k every row) and inc 1 st each side every row 3 times, then every other row 3 times—17 sts.
Work even until piece measures 4"/10cm from beg, end with a WS row.
Change to B and work in St st (k on RS,

p on WS), AT THE SAME TIME, dec 1 st each side on the 3rd row, then every other row 3 times more, then *every* row once. Bind off rem 7 sts.

TOP OF FOOT
With A, cast on 26 sts, with B cast on 28 sts, with A cast on 26—80 sts total.
Knit 1 row, purl 1 row, matching colors.

TOES
Row 3 (RS) With A, k26; [with B, k8; with A, k2] 3 times; with A, k24.
Row 4 With A, p26; [with B, p2tog, p4, p2tog tbl; with A, p2] 3 times; with A, p24—74 sts.
Row 5 (RS) With A, k25, M1, k1; [with B, k6; with A, k1, M1, k1] 3 times; with A, k24—78 sts.
Row 6 With A, p27; [with B, p2tog, p2, p2tog tbl; with A, p3] 3 times; with A, p24—72 sts.
Row 7 (RS) With A, k25, [M1, k1] twice, with B, SKP, k2tog; with A, k1, M1, k2; with B, SKP, k2tog; with A, k2, M1, k1; with B, SKP, k2tog; with A, [k1, M1] twice, k25—72 sts.
Cut B. With A, work in St st for 5 rows.

Gauge
18 sts and 28 rows to 4"/10cm over St st using size 7 (4.5mm) needles.
Take time to check gauge.

Cuddly Triceratops

SHAPE ANKLE
Next row (RS) K21, [k3tog] 10 times,
k21—52 sts.**
Work 16 rows even.
Next row Bind off 26 sts, p to end—26 sts.

SHAPE THIGH AND TAIL OPENING
Row 1 (RS) Bind off 3 sts, k2, [M1, k6] 3
times, k3—26 sts.
Row 2 and all WS rows Purl.
Row 3 Bind off 2 sts, k8, M1, k7, M1,
k6, M1, k3—27 sts.
Row 5 Bind off 2 sts, k7, M1, k8, M1,
k7, M1, k3—28 sts.
Row 7 Bind off 2 sts, k6, M1, k9, M1,
k11—28 sts.
Work 7 rows even. Cast on 2 sts at beg
of next 2 RS rows—32 sts.
Next row (WS) Bind off 6 sts, p to
end—26 sts.
Next row Cast on 2 sts, k to end—28 sts.
Next row Bind off 6 sts, p to end—22 sts.
Next row Cast on 3 sts, k to end—25 sts.
Cont in St st, bind off 6 sts at beg of
every WS row 3 times. Work 1 row even.
Bind off rem 7 sts.

Right Foot and Leg
Work as for left leg from ** to **.
Work 17 rows even.

SHAPE THIGH AND TAIL OPENING
Row 1 (RS) Bind off 26 sts, k9, [M1, k6]
twice, M1, k5—29 sts.
Row 2 Bind off 3 sts, p to end—26 sts.
Row 3 K3, M1, k6, M1, k7, M1, k10—29 sts.
Row 4 Bind off 2 sts, p to end—27 sts.
Row 5 K3, M1, k7, M1, k8, M1, k9—30sts.
Row 6 Rep row 4—28 sts.
Row 7 K11, M1, k9, M1, k8—30 sts.
Row 8 Rep row 4—28 sts.
Work 5 rows even. Cast on 2 sts at beg
of next 2 WS rows—32 sts.
Next row (RS) Bind off 6 sts, k to
end—26 sts.

Next row Cast on 2 sts, p to end—28 sts.
Next row Bind off 6 sts, k to end—22 sts.
Next row Cast on 3 sts, p to end—25 sts.
Cont in St st, bind off 6 sts at beg of
every RS row 3 times. Work 1 row even.
Bind off rem 7 sts.

Arms (Make 2)
With B, cast on 18 sts. Purl 1 row, pm in
center of row.
Next row Kfb in each st—36 sts.
Next row Purl.
Cut B. With A, work in St st for 14 rows,
pm in center of 8th row.
Next row K4, [k2tog, k1] 10 times,
k2—26 sts.
Inc 1 st each side every other row 8
times—42 sts. Work 11 rows even.

SHAPE UPPER ARM
Bind off 4 sts at beg of next 2 rows—34
sts. Dec 1 st each side every other row
twice, then *every* row 5 times—20 sts.
Bind off.

Tail and Gusset
With A, cast on 12 sts. Work in St st for
6 rows.
Next row (RS) K3, M1, k1, M1, k4, M1,
k1, M1, k3—16 sts. Work 3 rows even.
Next row K4, M1, k1, M1, k6, M1, k1,
M1, k4—20 sts. Work 3 rows even.
Next row K5, M1, k1, M1, k8, M1, k1,
M1, k5—24 sts.
Work 3 rows even.
Next row K6, M1, k1, M1, k10, M1, k1,
M1, k6—28 sts.
Work 3 rows even.
Cont in St st, inc 4 sts every 4th row as
established 8 times more, then every other
row 4 times—76 sts. Work 3 rows even.

SHAPE TOP OF TAIL
Bind off 6 sts at beg of next 10 rows—
16 sts. Work 2 rows even.

SHAPE GUSSET
Dec 1 st each side every other row 4
times, then every 4th row once—6 sts.
Work 5 rows even.
Inc 1 st each side every 4th row 6
times—18 sts.
Inc 1 st each side every other row 7
times—32 sts.
Work 3 rows even. Place sts on a holder.

Upper Body
With RS facing and MC, pick up and k 37
sts evenly along top of left leg, k32 from
gusset, then pick up and k 37 sts evenly
along top of right leg—106 sts. Beg with
a WS row, work in St st for 3 rows.
Next row (RS) K35, k2tog, SKP, k28,
k2tog, SKP, k35—102 sts.
Work 3 rows even.
Next row K34, k2tog, SKP, k26, k2tog,
SKP, k34—98 sts.
Work 3 rows even.
Next row K33, k2tog, SKP, k24, k2tog,
SKP, k33—94 sts.
Work 3 rows even.
Cont in St st, dec 4 sts every 4th row as
established 5 times more—74 sts. Then,
dec 4 st every other row 4 times—58 sts.
Work 5 rows even.

NECK
Next row (RS) K29, turn and cont on
these 29 sts as foll: Work in St st for 3
rows, AT THE SAME TIME, bind off 4 sts
at beg of next 2 WS rows—21 sts.
Next row Knit.
Next row (WS) Bind off 4 sts, pm for
position of head frill, p to end—17 sts.
Work even for 14 rows.
Dec 1 st at beg of next row and every RS
row until 13 sts rem, then dec 1 st from
same edge every row 5 times—8 sts.
Bind off. Join yarn to rem sts, bind off next
4 sts, k to end—25 sts. Work 1 row even.
Work in St st for 3 rows, AT THE SAME

...ME, bind off 4 sts at beg of every RS
row twice—17 sts.
Work 1 row, pm for head frill. Work even
for 14 rows. Dec 1 st at end of every RS
row until 13 sts rem, then dec 1 st from
same edge *every* row 5 times—8 sts. Bind
off.

Head
With A, cast on 40 sts. Work in St st for
rows, pm at each end of first row for
head frill position.
Cast on 5 sts at beg of next 6 rows—70
sts. Work even for 20 rows.

SHAPE NOSE
Next row (RS) [K3tog] 5 times, k40,
[k3tog] 5 times—50 sts.
Next row Purl.
Next row K10, [k3tog] 10 times, k10—
30 sts.
Next row Purl.
Bind off 8 sts at beg of next 2 rows—14 sts.
Dec 1 st each side *every* row until 4 sts rem.
Next row P4tog. Fasten off.

Frill
FRONT AND BACK PIECES (Make 2)
With A, cast on 12 sts. Work in St st for 2
rows. Cast on 4 sts at beg of next 2 rows,
then 3 sts at beg of next 2 rows—26 sts.
Cast on 2 sts at beg of next 2 rows—30 sts.
Dec 1 st each side of next row, then every
other row twice more, then every 4th
row once—38 sts. Work 3 rows even.

Divide for Head
Next row (RS) K13, turn and cont on
these 13 sts as foll: Dec 1 st at beg of
next row, then at same edge on next 3
rows—9 sts.
Work 1 row even. Dec 1 st at end of next
row—8 sts. Work 13 rows even, pm on
1st st of last row. Bind off.
Join yarn to rem sts, bind off next 12

sts, k to end—13 sts. Dec 1 st at end of
next row, then at same edge on next 3
rows—9 sts. Work 1 row even.
Dec 1 st at beg of next row—8 sts. Work
13 rows even, pm on first st of last row.
Bind off.

FRILL BORDER
With RS facing and A, beg at 2nd marker
of one frill piece, pick up and k 46 sts
evenly down side edge to center of cast-
on edge, 1 st from center of cast-on
edge, then 46 sts to first marker—93 sts.
Row 1 (WS) Purl.
Row 2 Bind off 4 sts, *k5, bind off 3 sts;
rep from * to last st. Place sts on holder.

HORNS
With RS facing and B, knit across first set
of 5 sts.
**Next row P5, turn.
Next row K5, turn.
Next row P5, turn.
Next row SKP, k1, k2tog, turn.
Next row P3, turn.
Next row SKP. Cut B and pull end
through sts to secure.***
With RS facing, join B to next set of 5 sts.**
Rep between **'s 9 times more, then work
from ** to *** once more—11 horns.
Rep frill border and horns on 2nd frill piece.

Head Horns (Make 2)
With A, cast on 18 sts. Knit 1 row on
WS. With B, work in St st, dec 1 st each
side of 3rd row then every other row 7
times more—2 sts.
Next row K2tog, cut yarn and pull end
through sts to secure.

Nose Horn
With A, cast on 20 sts. Knit 1 row on WS.
With B, work in St st, dec 1 st each side
of 3rd row, then every other row twice
more—14 sts.

Dec 1 st each side *every* row 6 times—2 sts.
Next row K2tog. Fasten off.

Tail Bumps (Make 5)
With C, cast on 7 sts. Work in garter st
for 3 rows, dec 1 st each side on 2nd and
3rd rows. Bind off rem 3 sts.

Finishing
FRILL
With RS tog, back stitch frill pieces tog,
leaving an opening at center of bound-
off edge. Turn frill to RS. Stuff each horn,
secure with a small stitch on inside.
Stuff rest of frill lightly and close opening.

HEAD
Join straight under seam of head. Place
a point at each end of nose to end of
underseam, then sew shaped edges to
bound-off sts at end of nose. Join bound-
off sts at top of neck shaping on upper
body. Align frill markers on head will frill
marker on neck shaping of upper body.
Pin frill between markers. Sew frill in
place, working through all 4 thicknesses.
Sew rest of head in place to neck shaping.

LEGS AND FEET
Join back seam of each leg. Sew soles
of feet to base of legs, matching top of
soles to toes of feet. Sew side edges of
gusset to side edge of thighs. Sew rem
edges of gusset to bound-off sts of legs.

TAIL
Sew tail into tail opening. Join tail seam.
Join back seam of toy, leaving an opening
at base. Stuff toy and close opening.

HORNS AND TAIL BUMPS
Join side edges of head and nose horns
and stuff. Sew horns to top of head and
nose (see photo). Sew cast-on edge of
tail bumps evenly spaced along tail seam.

Cuddly Triceratops

With black yarn, stem st nostrils to each side of nose and embroider mouth. Cut out different size circles from felt and glue to tail, front of frill, and each thigh (see photo).

SWEATER

BACK
With C, cast on 61 sts.
Row 1 K2, *p1, k1; rep from * to last st, k1.
Row 2 K1, *p1, k1; rep from * to end.
Rep rows 1 and 2 once more, dec 1 st in center of last row—60 sts.
Work in St st, dec 1 st each side, alternating dec rows between every 3rd and 4th row (therefore 4 sts dec'd every 7 rows) until 48 sts rem.
Dec 1 st each side every other row 8 times—32 sts.
Work 1 row even. Place sts on holder.

FRONT
Work same as back.

SLEEVES (Make 2)
With C, cast on 35 sts.
Work 4 rows rib as on back.
Work in St st, inc 1 st each side of 3rd row then every other row until there are 45 sts. Work 9 rows even. Bind off.

Finishing

With RS facing and C, k across 32 sts on front holder and 32 sts on back holder, inc 1 st in center—65 sts.
Work 11 rows rib as on back, beg with a row 2. Bind off loosely in rib.
Sew neckband seam, reversing seam halfway for turn back.
Fold down and sew in place.
Sew in sleeves.
Sew side and sleeve seams. ∎

ARMS AND HANDS
Join arm seams. Join cast-on edge of arms, matching marker at cast-on edge to arm seams. Stuff arms. Sew a tight running stitch through both thicknesses of arm between marker at cast-on edge and 2nd marker. Sew tight running st halfway between first running st and each edge of hand, to form 4 fingers. Sew top of arms to body.

EMBELLISHMENTS
With B and black yarn, using stem and satin st, embroider eyes to sides of head.

41

Baby's Blocks

Baby's blocks are cleverly built one square at a time.
Bonus: each square is picked up and knit from the one before to minimize seaming.

DESIGNED BY GINGER LUTERS

◀■■▢

Knitted Measurements
Each block approx 3"/7.5cm cubed

Materials
1 1¾oz/50g hank (each approx 137yd/125m) of Cascade Yarns *220 Superwash Sport* (superwash merino wool) each in #877 Golden (A), #224 Methyl Blue (B), and #240 Jasmine Green (C) **3**
One pair size 5 (3.75mm) needles, *or size to obtain gauge*
Removable stitch markers
Five 3 x 3 x 3"/7.5 x 7.5 x 7.5cm foam blocks

Note
Instructions are given for 2 blocks: Solid Block, which has single-colored squares, and Mitered Block, which has 4 two-colored mitered squares. Each block is made up of 6 squares and worked in 1 piece by picking up stitches along previously made squares. Approx 24yd/22m of each color is needed for each block.

Solid Block
SQUARE 1
With A, cast on 16 sts.
Row 1 (WS) K1 tbl, k14, sl 1 wyif.
Place removable marker to indicate RS of square. Rep row 1 thirty times more.
Bind off.

SQUARE 2
With RS facing and B, pick up and k 16 sts along LH edge of square 1.
Complete as for square 1.

SQUARE 3
With RS facing and C, pick up and k 16 sts along LH edge of square 2.
Row 1 (WS) K1 tbl, k14, sl 1 wyif.
Place removable marker to indicate RS of square.
Row 2 (RS) K1 tbl, k14, sl 1 wyif, pick up and k 1 st purlwise in cast-on edge of square 1, pass slip stitch over picked up st (psso).
Row 3 Sl 1 knitwise, k14, sl 1 wyif.
Rep rows 2 and 3 fourteen times more.
Bind off.

SQUARE 4
With RS facing and A, pick up and k 16 sts along RH edge of square 3.
Row 1 (WS) K1 tbl, k14, sl 1 wyif, pick up and k 1 st knitwise in bound-off edge of square 2, psso.
Row 2 Sl 1 wyif, move yarn to back between needles, k14, sl1 wyif.
Row 3 Rep row 1.
Rep rows 2 and 3 fourteen times more.
Bind off.

SQUARE 5
With RS facing and B, pick up and k 16 sts along LH edge of square 4.
Row 1 (WS) K1 tbl, k14, sl 1 wyif.
Row 2 K1 tbl, k14, sl 1 wyif, pick up and k 1 st purlwise in bound-off edge of square 3, psso.
Row 3 Sl 1 knitwise, k14, sl 1 wyif.

Gauge
20 sts and 40 rows to 4"/10cm over garter st using size 5 (3.75mm) needles.
Take time to check gauge.

Rep rows 2 and 3 fourteen times more. Bind off. Sew bound-off edge of square 5 to RH edge of square 1.

SQUARE 6
With RS facing and C, pick up and k 16 sts along RH edge of square 5.
Row 1 (WS) K1 tbl, k14, sl 1 wyif, pick up and k 1 st knitwise in bound-off edge of square 4, psso.
Row 2 Sl 1 wyif, move yarn to back between needles, k14, sl1 wyif.
Row 3 Rep row 1.
Rep rows 2 and 3 fourteen times more. Bind off.

Finishing
Insert styrofoam cube through openings of un-joined sides of square 6.
Align edges of squares with edges of cubes and sew all rem sides closed.

Mitered Block
Note Twist yarns when changing colors to prevent holes in work.

SQUARE 1
With C, cast on 16 sts, pm; with A, cast on 16 sts—32 sts.
Row 1 (WS) With A, k1 tbl, k to marker, sm; with C, k15, sl 1 wyif.
Row 2 With C, k1 tbl, k to 2 sts before marker, k2tog, sm; with A, ssk, k to last st, sl 1 wyif—2 sts dec'd.
Row 3 Rep row 1.
Rep rows 2 and 3 until 4 sts rem.
Next row With C, k2tog, remove marker; with A, ssk.
Next row With C, k2tog.
Cut yarn. Fasten off.

SQUARE 2
With RS facing and B, pick up and k16 sts along LH edge (A edge) of square 1.
Row 1 (WS) K1 tbl, k14, sl 1 wyif.
Place removable marker to indicate RS of square. Rep row 1 thirty times more.
Bind off.

SQUARE 3
With RS facing and C, pick up and k 16

sts along LH edge of square 2, pm; with B, pick up and k 16 sts along cast-on A sts of square 1.
Complete as for square 1, using appropriate colors.

SQUARE 4
With RS facing and A, pick up and k 16 sts along bound-off edge of square 2, pm; with B, pick up and k 16 sts along RH edge (C edge) of square 3.
Complete as for square 1, using appropriate colors.

SQUARE 5
With RS facing and A, pick up and k 16 sts along LH edge (B edge) of square 4.
Row 1 (WS) K1 tbl, k14, sl 1 wyif.
Row 2 K1 tbl, k14, sl 1 wyif, pick up and k 1 st purlwise in rem edge of B sts of square 3, psso.
Row 3 Sl 1 knitwise, k14, sl 1 wyif.
Rep rows 2 and 3 fourteen times more. Bind off. Sew bound-off edge of square to cast-on edge of C sts of square 1.

SQUARE 6
With RS facing and C, pick up and k 16 sts along A sts of rem edge of square 4, pm; with B, pick up and k 16 sts along rem edge of square 5.
Complete as for square 1, using appropriate colors.

Finishing
Insert styrofoam cube through openings of un-joined sides of square 6.
Align edges of squares with edges of cubes and sew all rem sides closed. ■

SOLID BLOCK

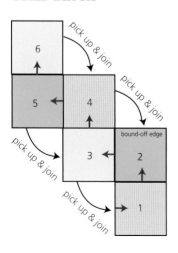

MITERED BLOCK

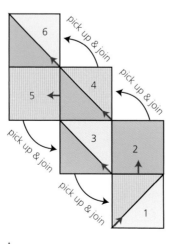

direction of work

120

Twist-Stitch Hippo

Knit with the subtle texture of twisted Stockinette stitch,
this happy hippo is ready to become pals with the tiny hipster in your life.

DESIGNED BY JEANNIE CHIN

Knitted Measurements
Length 12"/30.5cm
Height 5¾"/14.5cm

Materials
- 2 3½oz/100g hanks (each approx 220yd/200m) of Cascade Yarns *220 Superwash Aran Splatter* (superwash merino wool) in #06 Tempest (4)
- Small amount of black yarn for eyes
- One pair size 9 (5.5mm) needles, *or size to obtain gauge*
- Polyester stuffing
- Stitch holder

Twisted Stockinette Stitch
(over any number of sts)
Row 1 (RS) K1 tbl in every st.
Row 2 (WS) Purl.
Rep rows 1 and 2 for twisted St st.

Stitch Glossary
1 selv (selvage st) P1 tbl (RS), k1 tbl (WS).

Notes
1) Hippo is worked with smaller needles for tighter gauge.
2) Each piece is worked in twisted St st with 1 selvage st each side.

Ears (Make 2)
Cast on 4 sts. Work in twisted St st with 1 selv each side as foll:
Row 1 (RS) 1 selv, [kfb] 2 times, 1 selv—6 sts.
Row 2 (WS) 1 selv, p1, M1 p-st, p2, M1 p-st, 1 selv—8 sts.
Row 3 1 selv, k1 tbl, M1, k4 tbl, M1, k1 tbl, 1 selv—10 sts.
Row 4 Work even.
Row 5 1 selv, k1 tbl, M1, k6 tbl, M1, k1 tbl, 1 selv—12 sts.

Row 6 1 selv, p3, p2tog, p2tog tbl, p3, selv—10 sts.
Rows 7 and 8 Work even.
Row 9 1 selv, k2 tbl, ssk, k2tog, k2 tbl, selv—8 sts.
Rows 10 and 12 Work even.
Row 11 1 selv, k1 tbl, ssk, k2tog, k1 tbl, 1 selv — 6 sts.
Bind off in pat.

Underbelly
Note Underbelly is worked in 2 sections, from center to legs on right side, then center to legs on left side.

RIGHT SIDE
Cast on 41 sts. Work in twisted St st with 1 selv each side as foll:
Row 1 (WS) 1 selv, work to last 3 sts, p2tog tbl, 1 selv.
Row 2 (RS) 1 selv, work to last 3 sts, k2tog, 1 selv—39 sts.
Row 3 Rep row 1.
Row 4 Work even.
Row 5 1 selv, p1, M1 p-st, work to end—39 sts.
Row 6 1 selv, ssk, work to end—38 sts.
Rows 7 and 9 Rep row 5.
Rows 8 and 10 Work even.

Gauge
16 sts and 24 rows to 4"/10cm over twisted St st using size 9 (5.5mm) needles.
Take time to check gauge.

122

Twist-Stitch Hippo

Row 11 1 selv, p1, M1 p-st, p8, p2tog tbl, bind off 5 sts, p to last 2 sts, M1 p-st, p1, k1 tbl—36 sts.

Row 12 1 selv, k23 tbl, place rem 12 sts on holder (right front leg) and cont to work on right side and right hind leg.

Right hind leg

Row 13 (WS) Bind off 8 sts, work to end.

Row 14 1 selv, k1 tbl, M1, k tbl to end—17 sts.

Row 15 Bind off 7 sts, work to end—10 sts.

Row 16 1 selv, k1 tbl, M1, k6 tbl, k2tog, cast on 1 st—11 sts.

Row 17 1 selv, work to last 2 sts, M1 p-st, p1, 1 selv—12 sts.

Row 18 1 selv, k1 tbl, M1, k7 tbl, k2tog, 1 selv—12 sts.

Row 19 1 selv, work to last 3 sts, p2tog tbl, 1 selv—11 sts.

Row 20 1 selv, ssk, k5 tbl, k2tog, 1 selv—9 sts.

Rows 21 and 23 Rep row 19.

Row 22 1 selv, work to last 3 st, k2tog, 1 selv—6 sts

Row 24 1 selv, ssk, k2tog, 1 selv—4 sts.

Row 25 1 selv, p2tog tbl, 1 selv—3 sts.

Row 26 K3tog. Fasten off.

Right front leg

Transfer 12 sts from holder (right front leg) to needle to work next row from RS.

Row 12 (RS) Cast on 1 st, k10 tbl, M1, k1 tbl, 1 selv—14 sts.

Rows 13 Work to last 3 sts, p2tog tbl, 1 selv.

Row 14 Work to last 3 sts, k2tog, 1 selv—12 sts.

Row 15 1 selv, p2tog, p6, p2tog tbl, 1 selv—10 sts.

Rows 16 and 18 Rep row 14.

Row 17 Rep row 13.

Row 19 1 selv, [p1, bind off 1 st] 2 times, p2tog, 1 selv—4 sts.
Bind off rem sts in pat.

Turn work 180 degrees. With RS facing, pick up and k 41 sts along center edge. Turn.

LEFT SIDE

Rows 1 and 3 (WS) 1 selv, p2tog, work to end.

Row 2 (RS) 1 selv, ssk, work to end.

Row 4 Work even—38 sts.

Row 5 Work to last 2 sts, M1 p-st, p1, 1 selv.

Row 6 Work to last 3 sts, k2tog, 1 selv.

Rows 7 and 9 Rep row 5.

Rows 8 and 10 Work even.

Row 11 1 selv, p1, M1 p-st, p21, bind off 5 sts, p2tog, p to last 3 sts, M1 p-st, p1, 1 selv—36 sts.

Row 12 1 selv, k1 tbl, M1, k10 tbl, cast on 1 st—14 sts.

Place rem 24 sts on holder (left side and back leg) and cont on 14 sts for left front leg.

Left front leg

Row 13 1 selv, P2tog, work to end.

Rows 14, 16, and 18 1 selv, ssk, work to end.

Rows 15, 17, and 19 1 selv, p2tog, p to last 3 sts, p2tog tbl, 1 selv—10 sts.

Row 20 1 selv, k1 tbl, bind off 1 st, k1 tbl, k2tog, pass first knit st over k2tog. Fasten off rem 7 sts. Transfer 24 sts from holder (left side and back leg) to work next row from WS.

Left back leg

Row 12 (WS) Join yarn, 1 selv, p to end—24 sts.

Row 13 Bind off 8 sts, work to end—16 sts.

Row 14 1 selv, p1, M1 p-st, work to end.

Row 15 Bind off 7 sts, work to end.

Row 16 1 selv, p1, M1 p-st, p6, p2tog tbl, cast on 1 st—11 sts.

Row 17 Work to last 2 sts, M1, k1 tbl, 1 selv.

Row 18 1 selv, p1, M1 p-st, work to last 3 sts, p2tog tbl, 1 selv—12 sts.

Row 19 Work to last 3 sts, k2tog, 1 selv.

Row 20 1 selv, p2tog, work to last 3 sts, p2tog tbl, 1 selv—9 sts.

Rows 21 and 23 Rep row 19.

Rows 22 and 24 Rep row 20.

Row 25 1 selv, k1, 1 selv.

Row 26 P3tog. Fasten off.

Front of Face

Note Front face is worked from bottom of neck to top of head.

Cast on 3 sts. Work in twisted St st with 1 selv each side as foll:

Row 1 (RS) 1 selv, (K1, k1 tbl, K1) in next st, 1 selv—5 sts.

Row 2 1 selv, [p1, M1 p-st] twice, p1, 1 selv—7 sts.

Rows 3, 5, 7, 9, and 11 Work even.

Rows 4, 6, 8, and 10 1 selv, p1, M1 p-st, work to last 2 sts, M1 p-st, work to end—15 sts.

Rows 11 and 12 Work even.

Row 13 1 selv, k1 tbl, M1, work to last 2 sts, M1, work to end—17 sts.

Rows 14 and 15 Work even.

Row 16 Rep row 4—19 sts.

Rows 17–19 Work even.

Row 20 Rep row 4—21 sts.

Rows 21–40 Work even.

Row 41 1 selv, k2tog, work to last 3 sts, ssk, 1 selv—19 sts.

Rows 42–44 Work even.

Row 45–48 Rep rows 41–44—17 sts.

Row 49 Rep row 41—15 sts.

Rows 50–53 Work even.

Row 54 1 selv, p2tog tbl, p to last 3 sts, p2tog, 1 selv—13 sts.

Rows 55–70 Work even.

Row 71 Rep row 41—11 sts.

Rows 72 and 73 Work even.

Row 74 Rep row 54—9 sts.

Rows 75 and 76 Work even.

Row 77 and 79 Rep row 41—5 sts.

Rows 78 and 80 Work even.

Row 81 1 selv, S2KP, 1 selv.
Row 82 1 selv, p1, 1 selv.
Row 83 (RS) S2KP.
Fasten off last st.

Right Side of Body

Note Right side of body is worked from top of head/back to bottom of legs.

TOP OF HEAD

Cast on 5 sts. Work in twisted St st with 1 selv each side as foll:
Row 1 (WS) 1 selv, p1, M1 p-st, p to last 2 sts, M1 p-st, p1, 1 selv—7 sts.
Row 2 (RS) 1 selv, k1 tbl, M1, k4 tbl, 1 selv, cast on 2 sts—10 sts.
Rows 3 and 5 Rep row 1.
Row 4 1 selv, k1 tbl, M1, work to last st, M1, 1 selv. Place sts on st holder.

BACK

Cast on 8 sts. Work in twisted St st with 1 selv each side as foll:
Row 1 (RS) 1 selv, k1 tbl, M1, work to last 2 sts, M1, k1 tbl, 1 selv, cast on 4 sts—14 sts.
Row 2 1 selv, p1, M1 p-st, work to end, cast on 2 sts—17 sts.
Row 3 Rep row 1—23 sts.
Row 4 1 selv, p1, work to last 2 sts, M1 p-st, p1, 1 selv—24 sts.

JOIN TOP OF HEAD AND BACK

Row 5 (RS) 1 selv, work to end, cast on 3 sts, work 16 sts from st holder—43 sts.
Rows 6 and 8 Rep row 4.
Rows 7 and 9 Work to last 2 sts, M1, k1 tbl, 1 selv—47 sts.
Row 10 1 selv, p1, M1 p-st, work to end—49 sts.
Row 11 Work to end, cast on 2 sts—51 sts.
Rows 12 and 14 Rep row 10—52 sts.
Row 13 Rep row 11—54 sts.
Rows 15 and 17 Rep row 7.

Row 16 Rep row 10.
Row 18 Work even.
Row 19 Rep row 7.
Rows 20–23 Work even.
Row 24 Work to last 3 sts, p2tog, 1 selv—57 sts.
Rows 25–27 Work even.
Row 28 Rep row 24—56 sts.
Rows 29 and 30 Work even.
Row 31 Work to last 4 sts, ssk, k1 tbl, 1 selv—55 sts.
Row 32 Work even.
Row 33 1 selv, k1 tbl, M1, work to end—56 sts.
Row 34 1 selv, p2tog tbl, p15, p2tog, slide these first 18 sts to st holder for lower muzzle; bind off 1 st, work to end.

LOWER BODY

Cont on 37 sts, work as foll:
Row 35 (RS) 1 selv, k1 tbl, M1, work to end, cast on 1 st—39 sts.
Row 36 (WS) 1 selv, p1 tbl, M1 p-st, work to end.
Row 37 1 selv, k1 tbl, M1, work to end—41 sts.

Row 38 Work to last 2 sts, M1 p-st, p1tbl, 1 selv.
Row 39 1 selv, k1 tbl, M1, work to last 2 sts, M1, k1 tbl, 1 selv—44 sts.
Row 40 Rep row 38—45 sts.

LEGS

Row 41 (RS) 1 selv, k10 tbl, ssk (12 sts for hind leg), bind off 20 sts, work to end (12 sts for front leg).

FRONT LEG

Work only sts for front leg as foll:
Row 42 (WS) 1 selv, p1, M1 p-st, p8, p2tog, cast on 1 st—13 sts.
Row 43 Work even.
Row 44 Work to last 3 sts, p2tog, k1 tbl.
Row 45 Work to last 2 sts, M1, k1 tbl, 1 selv.
Row 46 Work even.
Row 47 1 selv, k2tog, work to last 3 sts, ssk, 1 selv.
Row 48 Bind off 3 sts, work to end—8 sts.
Row 49 P1 tbl, k2tog, work to end—7 sts.
Row 50 Bind off 4 sts work to end—3 sts.
Row 51 K3tog. Fasten off last st.

HIND LEG

Work sts for hind leg as foll:
Row 42 (WS) Cast on 1 st, work to last 3 sts, p2tog, 1 selv—12 sts.
Row 43 1 selv, k2tog, work to last 3 sts, ssk, 1 selv.
Row 44 1 selv, p2tog tbl, work to end.
Row 45 1 selv, k2tog, work to end—8 sts.
Rows 46 and 48 Rep row 44.
Row 47 Rep row 43—5 sts.
Row 49 1 selv, k3tog, 1 selv—3 sts.
Row 50 P3tog.
Fasten off last st.

LOWER MUZZLE

With RS facing, slide sts for lower muzzle to needle, cast on 1 st—19 sts.

Twist-Stitch Hippo

Row 35 (RS) 1 selv, ssk, work to end.
Row 36 1 selv, p2tog tbl, work to last 3 sts, p2tog, 1 selv.
Row 37 1 selv, [k2tog tbl] twice, work to end—14 sts.
Row 38 1 selv, p2tog tbl, p8, p2tog tbl, 1 selv.
Row 39 1 selv, k2tog, work to end.
Row 40 1 selv, p2tog tbl, p5, p2tog tbl, 1 selv—9 sts. Bind off in pat.

Left Side of Body
Note Side of body is worked from top of head/back to bottom of legs.

TOP OF HEAD
Cast on 5 sts. Work in twisted St st with 1 selv each side as foll:
Row 1 (WS) 1 selv, p1, M1 p-st, p1, M1 p-st, p1, 1 selv st, cast on 2 sts—9 sts.
Row 2 (RS) Work to last 2 sts, M1, k1 tbl, 1 selv—10 sts.
Rows 3 and 5 1 selv, p1, M1 p-st, p to last 2 sts, M1 p-st, p1, 1 selv.
Row 4 1 selv, k1 tbl, M1, work to last st, M1, 1 selv. Place sts on st holder.

BACK
Cast on 8 sts. Work in twisted St st with 1 selv each side as foll:
Row 1 (WS) 1 selv, p1, M1 p-st, p4, M1 p-st, p1, 1 selv, cast on 5 sts—15 sts.
Row 2 (RS) Work to end, cast on 2 sts—17 sts.
Row 3 1 selv, p1, M1 p-st, p14, 1 selv, cast on 5 sts—23 sts
Row 4 1 selv, work to last 2 sts, M1, work to end—24 sts.

JOIN TOP OF HEAD AND BACK
Row 5 (WS) 1 selv, p23, cast on 3 sts, work 16 sts from st holder—43 sts.

Rows 6 and 8 1 selv, k1 tbl, M1, work to last 2 sts, M1, k1 tbl, 1 selv.
Rows 7 and 9 1 selv, work to last 2 sts, M1 p-st, p1, 1 selv.
Row 10 1 selv, k1 tbl, M1, work to end—50 sts.
Row 11 Work to end, cast on 2 sts—52 sts.
Row 12 Rep row 10.
Row 13 Rep row 11—55 sts.
Rows 14 and 16 Rep row 10.
Rows 15 and 17 Rep row 7—59 sts.
Row 18 Work even.
Row 19 Rep row 7—60 sts.
Rows 20–23 Work even.
Row 24 1 selv, work to last 3 sts, k2tog, 1 selv—59 sts.
Rows 25–27 Work even.
Row 28 Rep row 24.
Rows 29 and 30 Work even.
Row 31 Work to last 3 sts, p2tog, 1 selv.
Row 32 Work even.
Row 33 1 selv, p1, M1 p-st work to end—58 sts.
Row 34 1 selv, k2tog, k15 tbl, ssk, slide these first 18 sts to st holder for lower muzzle; k2 tbl, bind off 1 st, work to end.

LOWER BODY
Cont on 37 sts, work as foll:
Row 35 (WS) 1 selv, p1 tbl, M1 p-st, p35, cast on 1 st for selv—39 sts.
Row 36 (RS) 1 selv, k1 tbl, M1, work to end—40 sts.
Row 37 1 selv, p1, M1 p-st, work to end.
Row 38 1 selv, work to last 2 sts, M1, k1 tbl, 1 selv.
Row 39 1 selv, p1, M1 p-st, work to last 2 sts, M1 p-st, p1, 1 selv—44 sts.
Row 40 Rep row 38—45 sts.
Row 41 1 selv, p10, p2tog (12 sts for hind leg), bind off 20 sts, work to end (12 sts for front leg).

FRONT LEG
Work only sts for front leg as foll:
Row 42 (RS) 1 selv, k1 tbl, M1, k8 tbl, ssk, cast on 1 st—13 sts.
Row 43 Work even.
Row 44 1 selv, work to last 2 sts, ssk, 1 selv.
Row 45 1 selv, work to last 2 sts, M1 p-st, p1, 1 selv.
Row 46 Work even.
Row 47 1 selv, p2tog tbl, p7, p2tog, 1 selv.
Row 48 Bind off 3 sts, work to end—8 sts
Row 49 1 selv, p2tog tbl, work to end.
Row 50 Bind off 4 sts, work to end.
Row 51 P3tog. Fasten off last st.

HIND LEG
Work sts for hind leg as foll:
Row 42 (RS) Cast on 1 st, work to last 3 sts, ssk, 1 selv—12 sts.
Row 43 1 selv, p2tog tbl, p to last 3 sts, p2tog, 1 selv.
Rows 44 and 46 1 selv, k2tog, work to end.
Row 45 1 selv, p2tog tbl, work to end.
Row 47 Rep row 43—5 sts.
Row 48 Rep row 44.
Row 49 1 selv, p2tog tbl, 1 selv.
Row 50 K3tog. Fasten off last st.

LOWER MUZZLE
With WS facing, slide sts for lower muzzle to needle, cast on 1 st—19 sts.
Row 35 (WS) 1 selv, p2tog tbl, work to end.
Row 36 1 selv, k2tog, work to last 2 sts, ssk, 1 selv—16 sts.
Row 37 1 selv, [k2tog tbl] twice, work to end—14 sts.
Rows 38 and 40 Rep row 36.
Row 39 Rep row 35. Bind off in pat.

Nostrils (Make 2)

Cast on 10 sts. Knit 1 row, purl 1 row. Cut yarn leaving a 12"/30.5cm tail. Thread tail through sts and draw sts together so strip forms curved circle with knit side inside the circle. Tie beg and tail ends together to fasten circle.

Finishing

Lightly block pieces along curled edges. Join underbelly with legs as foll: With WS tog, align right side of body with right half of underbelly, matching points B (under neck) and C (back rear) (see diagrams). Pin front and back hind legs in place. Using whipstitch, sew seams. Rep for left side of body and legs.

Join front of face with sides as foll: With WS tog, align and pin front of face edges beg at point B (top of neck), around muzzle, to point A (bottom of neck) (see diagram). Whipstitch in place.

At opening, fill with stuffing, beg with legs, then muzzle, then body.

For back closure, whip stitch all edges to sew back seam from point B (top of head) to point C (back rear).

Attach ears as foll: With knit side facing outwards, sew ears to each side near top of head in a diagonal (see diagram), or in desired position.

Attach nostrils as foll: Use tail ends to sew to front muzzle with circle edge angled toward center of face (see photo). With black yarn, embroider eye with French knot, wrapping 5 times, on left side. Weave end underneath 2 times to fasten, then weave in end into stuffing to conceal, coming out at other side for opposite eye. Make 2nd eye in same manner, pulling yarn slightly to create dimple in first eye.

TAIL

Cut 6 strands of yarn, each 13"/33cm long. Weave each strand evenly into same spot at seam (see diagram) with center of strand at seam creating two groups of yarn. Knot together strands from each section to create tail.

Cut a separate strand to tie tail ends together, then trim as desired. ∎

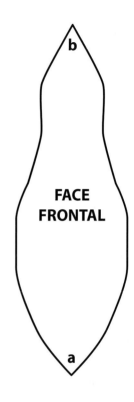

FACE
FRONTAL

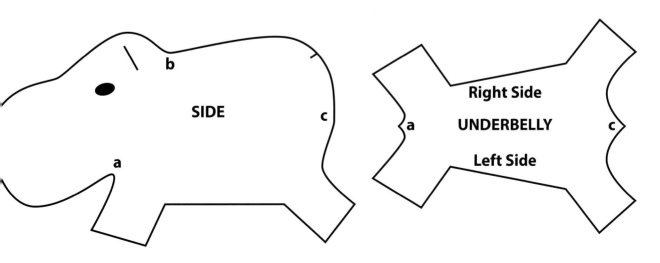

SIDE

Right Side

UNDERBELLY

Left Side

Dragon Puppet

With its bright colors and fanciful shapes,
this delightful dragon puppet adds drama to storytime.

DESIGNED BY PHYLLIS ROWLEY

Knitted Measurements
Approx 8½"/21.5cm long and 6"/15cm wide around hand, to fit a child's hand

Materials
▪ 1 3½oz/100g ball (each approx 220yd/200m) of Cascade Yarns *220 Superwash* (superwash wool) each in #208 Treetop (A), #887 Wasabi (B), #808 Sunset Orange (C), and #821 Daffodil (D) ⬤
▪ One set (4) size 5 (3.75mm) double-pointed needles (dpn), *or size to obtain gauge*
▪ Stitch markers
▪ Embroidery needle
▪ Small amount of black embroidery floss

Stitch Glossary
MB (make bobble) K into front, back, front, back and front of the same st (to make 5 sts from 1 st), turn, p5; turn, k5; turn, p2tog, p1, p2tog; turn, SK2P—1 st rem.

Note
Puppet is constructed beg at the tail by working back and forth in rows, then joined to work in rnds to end of head. A purl st is worked along the center of

back for placement of the scales and wings that are knit separately.

Body
TAIL
Beg at tail edge with A, cast on 5 sts.
Row 1 (RS) K1, p1, pm, k1 (center st), pm, p1, k1.
Row 2 P1, [k1, p1] twice.
Inc row 3 Work in rib to center marker, M1, sm, k1, sm, M1, work in rib to end.
Row 4 Work in rib to 1 st before center marker, p1, sm, p1, sm, p1, rib to end.
Row 5 Rep inc row 3.
Row 6 P1, *k1, p1; rep from * to end.
Rep rows 3–6 three times more —21 sts.

NECK
Next row (RS) Cast on 16 sts, then k these sts and k sts to center marker, sm, p1, re-move 2nd marker, k to end of row—37 sts. Join to work in rnds, divide sts over 3 dpn (12 sts, 12 sts, 13 sts), and pm for beg of rnd.
Next rnd K to center marker, sm, p1, k to end of rnd.
Cont to work in this way, rep the last rnd, until piece measures 5"/12.5cm from the 16-st cast-on. Cut A.

SHAPE BACK OF HEAD
Slide sts around on the dpn so that beg of next rnd is 9 sts to the right of the marker and rejoin A at this new beg point. Work back and forth in short rows as foll:
Row 1 (RS) Sl 1, k to marker, sm, p1, k9, turn.
Row 2 (WS) Sl 1, p to center st, k1, sm, p9, turn.
Rows 3–6 Rep rows 1 and 2 twice more.
Row 7 Sl 1, k to marker, sm, p1, k2, ssk, k1, turn.
Row 8 Sl 1, p to the st before marker, k1, sm, p2, p2tog, p1, turn.
Row 9 Sl 1, k to marker, sm, p1, k3, ssk, k1, turn.
Row 10 Sl 1, p4, k1, p3, p2tog, p1, turn.
Row 11 Sl 1, k to marker, sm, p1, k4, ssk, k1, turn.
Row 12 Sl 1, p5, k1, p4, p2tog, p1, turn.
Row 13 Sl 1, k to marker, sm, p1, k to end of row.
Cont around, pick up and k 6 sts along the side of the flap, k the body sts around, and pick up and k 6 sts along the other side of the flap — 43 sts.
Place marker and cont working in rnds.
Rnd 1 K1, MB, k3, sm, p1, k3, MB, k6, k2tog, k18, ssk, k to end of rnd.

Gauge
24 sts and 33 rows/rnds to 4"/10cm over St st using size 5 (3.75mm) needles.
Take time to check gauge

Dragon Puppet

Rnd 2 K5, sm, p1, k9, k2tog, k18, ssk, k4.
Rnd 3 K5, sm, p1, k8, k2tog, k18, ssk, k3—37 sts.
Rnd 4 Knit.
Next rnd K to 4 sts before the end of the rnd.
This is the beg of top of mouth opening.

TOP OF MOUTH
Row 1 (RS) K to marker, sm, p1, k9, turn—19 sts.
Work back and forth in rows as foll:
Row 2 P to center st, k1, p to end.
Row 3 K2, ssk, k to center st, p1, k to last 4 sts, k2tog, k2.
Rep the last 2 rows until 3 sts rem.
Rep row 2. Bind off. Cut yarn.

LOWER MOUTH
Rejoin A to the 18 sts left unworked and knit the next row on RS.
Next row Purl.
Next row K2, ssk, k to last 4 sts, k2tog, k2.
Rep the last 2 rows until 4 sts rem.
Purl 1 row. Bind off. Cut yarn.

Wings (Make 2)
With D, cast on 10 sts.
Row 1 (RS) Kfb, k to last 2 sts, k2tog.

Row 2 Knit.
Rep the last 2 rows for 10 rows more.
Next row (RS) K2tog, k to last st, kfb.
Next row Knit.
Rep last 2 rows for 10 rows more. Bind off.

Tongue
With C, cast on 6 sts.
Rows 1 and 3 Knit.
Row 2 Bind off 2 sts, k to end.
Row 4 Cast on 3 sts, k to end—7 sts.
Row 5 Knit. Bind off.

Mouth
With C, cast on 3 sts.
Row 1 (RS) Kfb, k to last st, kfb.
Row 2 Purl.
Rep last 2 rows 5 times more—15 sts.
Next row (RS) K2tog, k to last 2 sts, k2tog.
Next row Purl.
Rep the last 2 rows until 3 sts rem. Bind off.

Scales
With B, beg at the head edge, cast on 2 sts.
Knit 1 row.
Next row Kfb, k to end. Knit 1 row.
Rep the last 2 rows once more—4 sts.
Next row Bind off 2 sts, k to end—2 sts.
Knit 1 row.
Next row Kfb, k to end—3 sts. Knit 1 row.
Rep the last 2 rows 3 times more—6 sts.
Next row Bind off 4 sts, k to end—2 sts.
Knit 1 row.
*Next row Kfb, k to end—3 sts. Knit 1 row.
Rep the last 2 rows until there are 7 sts.
Next row Bind off 5 sts, k to end.
Knit 1 row*.
Rep between *'s until there are a total of 8 scales from beg. Bind off.

Finishing
Pin the scales in place along the center st of the body with the largest scale beg at the tail and the smallest scale at the top of the head above the eyes. Sew the scales in place. Sew wings on each side of scales, beg 3rd scale from the top (see photo). Sew tongue into center of mouth, then sew the mouth into the mouth opening. With embroidery floss, embroider the 2 bobble eye centers with straight sts. ■

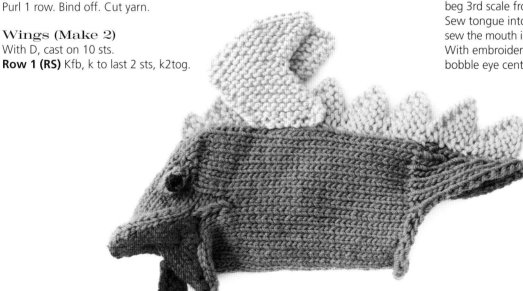

Lazy Llama

Fringed fur and a jaunty neckscarf
give this long-legged llama extra style.

DESIGNED BY AMY BAHRT

Knitted Measurements

Approx 10"/25.5 cm tall and 6"/15 cm long

Materials

- 1 3½oz/100g hank (each approx 50yd/138m) of Cascade Yarns *220 Superwash Aran Splatter* (superwash) in #3 Weathered (A) (4)
- 1 3½oz/100g hank (each approx 50yd/138m) of Cascade Yarns *220 Superwash Aran* (superwash merino wool) in #818 Mocha (B) (4)
- 1 3½oz/100g ball (each approx 220yd/200m) of Cascade Yarns *220 Superwash* (superwash wool) in #1997 Spring Bud (C) (3)
- One pair each sizes 6 and 7 (4 and 4.5mm) needles, *or size to obtain gauge*
- One size G/6 (4mm) crochet hook
- Embroidery needle
- Polyester stuffing
- 4 pipe cleaners (optional, for leg support)

Body

FIRST PIECE

With larger needles and A, cast on 22 sts.

Rows 1–14 Foll chart 1, work even in St st (k on WS, p on WS).

Row 15 (RS) K2tog, k to end.

Row 16 P10; join a separate length of A and bind off 11 sts, fasten off last st. Turn work.

Row 17 (RS) K2tog, k to end—9 sts.

Row 18 P to last 2 sts, p2tog—8 sts.

Row 19 Knit.

Row 20 P to last 2 sts, p2tog—7 sts.

Rows 21–28 Work even in St st.

Row 29 (RS) K to last st, kfb—8 sts.

Row 30 Cast on 2 sts, p to end—10 sts.

Row 31 K to last st, kfb.

Row 32 Pfb, p to end—12 sts.

Rows 33 and 34 Work even in St st.

Row 35 K to last 2 sts, k2tog.

Row 36 P2tog, p to end—10 sts.

Row 37 K to last 3 sts, SK2P—8 sts.

Row 38 Purl. Bind off.

SECOND PIECE

Note The second body piece is made foll chart as a mirror image of the first piece. With larger needles and A, cast on 22 sts.

Rows 1–14 Foll chart 1, work even in St st.

Row 15 (RS) K to last 2 sts, k2tog.

Row 16 Bind off 11 sts, p to end—10 sts.

Row 17 K to last 2 sts, k2tog.

Row 18 P2tog, p to end—8 sts.

Row 19 Knit.

Row 20 P2tog, p to end—7 sts.

Rows 21–28 Work even in St st.

Row 29 (RS) Kfb, k to end—8 sts.

Row 30 P to last 2 sts, [pfb] twice—10 sts.

Row 31 Kfb, k to end.

Row 32 P to last st, pfb—12 sts.

Rows 33 and 34 Work even in St st.

Row 35 K2tog, k to end—11 sts.

Row 36 P to last 2 sts, p2tog.

Row 37 Bind off 2 sts, k to end—8 sts.

Row 38 Purl. Bind off.

Gauge

18 sts and 24 rows to 4"/10 cm over St st using larger needles.
Take time to check gauge

Lazy Llama

Legs (Make 4)
With larger needles and B, cast on 8 sts.
Work in garter st (k every row) for 5 rows.
Change to A and cont in St st until piece
measures 3¾"/9.5cm from beg.
Bind off, leaving a long end for seaming later.

Tummy
With larger needles and A, cast on 18 sts.
Work, foll chart 2. Knit 1 row.
Row 2 (WS) Pfb, p to last st, pfb.
Row 3 Knit.
Row 4 Pfb, p to last st, pfb—22 sts.
Rows 5–7 Work even in St st.
Row 8 P2tog, p to last 2 sts, p2tog.
Row 9 Knit.
Row 10 P2tog, p to last 2 sts,
p2tog—18 sts. Bind off.

Ears (Make 2)
With larger needles and A, cast on 3 sts.
Knit 1 row, purl 1 row.
Next row (RS) Kfb, k1, kfb—5 sts.
Work 3 rows even in St st.
Next row K2tog, k1, k2tog—3 sts.
Purl 1 row. K3tog. Bind off.

Scarf
With smaller needles and C, cast on 4 sts.
Row 1 (RS) [K1, p1] twice.
Row 2 [P1, k1] twice.
Rep these 2 rows for seed st for 8"/20.5cm.
Bind off.

Finishing
With C, embroider eyes foll chart 1 for
placement on both sides of head.
Seam body pieces tog on WS, turn
inside out. Sew ears to head foll chart
for placement. Sew sides of each leg tog
(using pipe cleaner, bent at the foot, to
stabilize, if desired). Stuff each leg, then
pin to tummy foll chart 2 for placement.
Pin tummy to lower edge of body, then
seam, leaving an opening for stuffing.
Stuff body, close seam.
For body shag fur, cut approx two
hundred 5"/12.5cm lengths of B. With
crochet hook, fold each strand in half
and pull through st on body to make the
fringe. Beg along the top seam, knotting
in every other st and then alternating sts
every 2 rows until approx 1"/2.5cm from
the bottom of the body. Trim as desired.
Work opposite side of body in same way.
For top of head, cut twenty-four
2½"/6.5cm lengths of B. Tie these ends
tog tightly at the center to form a loose
"hair pompom" and sew in between the ears.
For tail, cut thirty-two 3"/7.5cm lengths of B.
Tie these ends tightly in center to form a
loose "tail pompom" and attach at the
back end.
Wrap scarf around neck, using a strand
of C to wrap tightly around center to
cinch scarf in place. ■

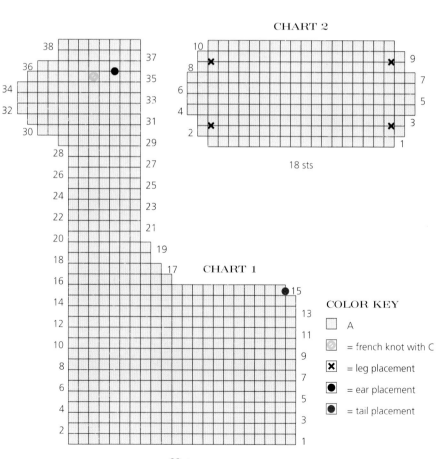

CHART 2

18 sts

CHART 1

22 sts

COLOR KEY

☐ A

= french knot with C

✖ = leg placement

● = ear placement

● = tail placement

Robot Pillow

Every future scientist needs a robot sidekick
—especially one that is plush, soft, and full of love.

DESIGNED BY MATTHEW SCHRANK

Knitted Measurements
Approx 11"/28cm wide x 18"/45.5cm high, from head to toe

Materials
1 3½oz/100g hank (each approx 150yd/138m) of Cascade Yarns *220 Superwash Aran* (superwash wool) each in #1946 Silver Grey (A) and #900 Charcoal (B) (4)

Small amounts in #240 Jasmine Green (C) and #242 Deep Sea Coral (D)

One pair size 8 (5mm) needles, *or size to obtain gauge*

One set (4) size 8 (5mm) dpn

Bobbins, stitch marker

Tapestry needle, polyester stuffing

Note
Use a separate bobbin of yarn for each block of color. When changing colors, twist yarns on WS to prevent holes in work.

Body
For front, with A, cast on 50 sts. Work in St st (k on RS, p on WS) for 10 rows.
Row 11 (RS) With A, k6; with B, k38; with A, k6.
Rows 12 & 13 Work even, matching colors.

Row 14 With A, p6; with B, p2; with A, p34; with B, p2; with A, p6. Cont in St st, matching colors, until piece measures 8½"/21.5cm from beg, end with a WS row.
Next 3 rows Rep rows 11–13. Cut B. With A only, cont in St st for 10 more rows. Bind off.
For back, with A, cast on 50 sts. Work in St st until same length as front. Bind off.

Head
For back, with A, cast on 25 sts.
Work in St st for 21 rows. Bind off.
For front, with A, cast on 25 sts.
Beg with a RS row, follow face chart in St st for 21 rows, end with a RS row. Bind off.

Arms and Legs (Make 4)
With A, cast on 16 sts and divide over 3 dpn. Join, taking care not to twist sts, and pm for beg of rnd. Work in St st (k every rnd), as foll: [2 rnds A, 1 rnd B] 5 times. Cut B, cont with A only as foll:
Dec rnd 1 [K2, k2tog] 4 times—12 sts.
Dec rnd 2 [K1, k2tog] 4 times—8 sts.
Dec rnd 3 [K2tog] 4 times—4 sts.
Cut yarn, draw through rem sts, and pull to secure. Stuff and seam cast-on sts to create flat seam.

Finishing
Note Seams are worked to show on RS. Sew front and back of body tog, leaving opening. Stuff body and sew rem seam. Sew arms and legs to body (see photo). Sew front and back of head tog, leaving opening. Stuff head, sew rem seam, and attach to body.
With C and tapestry needle, duplicate st 3 buttons foll chart. With 2 strands D held tog, embroider heart with straight sts. ■

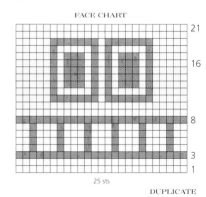

FACE CHART

21

16

8

3
1

25 sts

DUPLICATE STITCH

COLOR KEY
☐ A ■ B
▨ duplicate stitch in C

20

10

1

4 sts

Gauge
18 sts and 24 rows to 4"/10cm over St st using size 8 (5mm) needles.
Take time to check gauge

Zig Zag Toy

It wiggles and squiggles and wins giggles, and this stuffed toy
is just waiting for your child's imagination to concoct dozens of fun ways to play.

DESIGNED BY CLEO MALONE

Knitted Measurements
Circumference Approx 14"/35.5
Height Approx 20"/51cm high

Materials
- 2 3½oz/100g hanks (each approx 150yd/138m) of Cascade Yarns *220 Superwash Aran* (superwash wool) in #817 Aran (A) (4)
- 1 3½oz/100g hank (each approx 150yd/137.5m) of Cascade Yarns *220 Superwash Aran Splatter* (superwash merino wool) in #10 Primary (B) (4)
- Small amount of black yarn for eyes
- One set (5) size 7 (4.5mm) needles, *or size to obtain gauge*
- One size 7 (4.5mm) crochet hook
- Stitch markers
- Tapestry needle
- Scrap yarn
- Polyester stuffing

Note
When changing colors, twist yarns on WS to prevent holes in work.

Zig Zag Toy
With A, cast on 72 sts using provisional cast-on (see page 182) and knit 1 row. Divide sts evenly over 4 dpn. Join, taking care not to twist sts, and pm for beg of rnd.

BEGIN CHART
Note Each 4-st rep is always worked 6 times each.
*Work rnds 1–6 of chart 6 times, then work rnds 7–12 six times. Rep from * once more. With A, knit 3 rnds. Graft sts tog with Kitchener st (see page 182).

Finishing
Stuff toy. Remove provisional cast-on, dividing sts evenly over 2 dpn, and graft tog with Kitchener st.
With black yarn, embroider eyes over purl dots (see photo). ∎

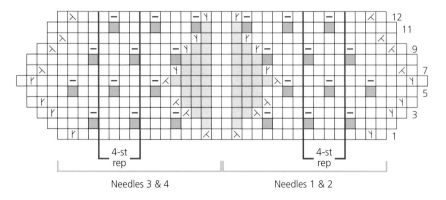

4-st rep   4-st rep

Needles 3 & 4   Needles 1 & 2

COLOR KEY
☐ A
▧ B

STITCH KEY
☐ knit
⊟ purl
M1L
M1L
k2tog
ssk
☐ no stitch

Gauge
22 sts and 29 rows to 4"/10cm over St st using size 7 (4.5mm) needles.
Take time to check gauge.

17

Argyle Bear

It's hard to decide which is cuter: this sweet-faced teddy
or his pint-sized argyle "sweater" that's knitted right on.

DESIGNED BY KARIN KING

Knitted Measurements
Approx 14"/35.5cm tall

Materials
◻ 2 1¾oz/50g hanks (each approx
137yd/125m) of Cascade Yarns *220
Superwash Sport* (superwash merino wool)
in #1946 Silver Grey (A) ⬛
◻ 1 hank each in #900 Charcoal (B),
#238 Angel Blue (C), and #897 Baby
Denim (D)
◻ One pair size 3 (3.25mm) needles,
or size to obtain gauge
◻ Bobbins
◻ Polyester stuffing

Notes
1) Argyle chart is worked in St st (k on
RS, p on WS). Use separate bobbins
of yarn for each block of color. When
changing colors, twist yarns on WS to
prevent holes in work.
2) Color B lines are worked in duplicate
st after pieces are finished.

Stitch Glossary
M1R (make 1 right) Insert LH needle
from back to front under the strand
between last st worked and next st on LH

needle. Knit into the front loop to twist
the st—1 st inc'd.
M1L (make 1 left) Insert LH needle from
front to back under the strand between last
st worked and next st on LH needle. Knit
into the back loop to twist the st—1 st inc'd.

Head
With A, cast on 7 sts using long-tail cast on.
Row 1 (RS) Holding both the tail and
working yarn together, k to last st, drop
tail and k last st with working yarn only.

Treat each loop on needle as separate
st—13 sts.
Row 2 and all WS rows except row 16
Purl.
Row 3 [K1, M1R] 6 times, [k1, M1L] 6
times, k1—25 sts.
Row 5 K1, M1R, k8, M1R, pm, k7, pm,
M1L, k8, M1L, k1—29 sts.
Rows 7, 9, 11, and 13 K1, M1R, k to
next marker, M1R, sm, k7, sm, M1L, k to
last st, M1L, k1—45 sts. Remove markers
Row 15 K17, M1R, k2, M1R, k7, M1L,
k2, M1L, k17—49 sts.
Row 16 P15, p2tog tbl, p15, p2tog,
p15—47 sts.
Row 17 K3, [k1, k2tog] 4 times, k3,
M1R, k2, M1R, k7, M1L, k2, M1L, k3,
[ssk, k1] 4 times, k3—43 sts.
Row 19 K15, M1R, k2, M1R, k9, M1L,
k2, M1L, k15.
Row 21 K17, M1R, k2, M1R, k9, M1L,
k2, M1L, k17—51 sts.
Row 23 K18, M1R, k2, M1R, k11, M1L,
k2, M1L, k18.
Row 25 K20, M1R, k2, M1R, k11, M1L,
k2, M1L, k20—59 sts.
Row 27 K6, [M1R, k1, M1R, k2] 5 times,
M1R, k17, M1L, [k2, M1L, k1, M1L] 5
times, k6—81 sts.

Gauge
24 sts and 32 rows to 4"/10cm over St st using size 3 (3.25mm) needles.
Take time to check gauge.

Argyle Bear

Rows 28–42 Work even in St st.

Row 43 K1, [k4, k2tog, k4] 4 times, [k4, ssk, k4] 4 times.

Row 45 K1, [k3 k2tog, k4] 4 times, [k3, ssk, k4] 4 times—65 sts.

Row 47 K1, [k3, k2tog, k3] 4 times, [k3, ssk, k3] 4 times.

Row 49 K1, [k2, k2tog, k3] 4 times, [k2, ssk, k3] 4 times—49 sts.

Row 51 K1, [k2, k2tog, k2] 4 times, [k2, ssk, k2] 4 times.

Row 53 K1, [k1, k2tog, k2] 4 times, [k1, ssk, k2] 4 times—33 sts.

Row 55 K1, [k1, k2tog, k1] 4 times, [k1, ssk, k1] 4 times—25 sts.

Row 57 K1, [k2tog, k1] 4 times, [ssk, k1] 4 times—17 sts.

Row 59 K1, [k2tog] 4 times, [ssk] 4 times—9 sts.

Cut yarn, leaving a 24"/61cm long tail. Thread tail through rem sts and pull tog tightly. Stuff firmly with small pieces of stuffing, shaping nose and face.

Sew seam, leaving a 2"/5cm opening at the base of the neck.

Ears (Make 2)

With A, cast on 8 sts.

Row 1 (RS) Kfb, k5, kfb, k1—10 sts.

Row 2 and all WS rows except rows 12 and 14 Purl.

Row 3 K1, M1R, k8, M1L, k1.

Row 5 K1, M1R, k10, M1L, k1.

Row 7 K1, M1R, k12, M1L, k1—16 sts.

Row 9 Knit.

Row 11 K2, k2tog, k8, ssk, k2.

Row 12 P2, p2tog tbl, p6, p2tog, p2—12 sts.

Row 13 Knit.

Row 14 (WS) Knit (for ridge at base).

Row 15 K1, M1R, k5, M1L, K5, M1L, k1

Row 17 K1, M1R, k13, M1L, k1—17 sts

Row 19 Knit.

Row 21 K1, k2tog, K11, ssk, k1—15 sts

Row 23 K1, k2tog, K9, ssk, k1.

Row 25 K1, k2tog, K7, ssk, k1—11 sts.

Row 27 k2tog, bind off to last 2 sts, ssk, bind off remaining st, leaving a long tail for sewing and attaching.

Fold ears in half and sew tog with knit side out. Sew ears to top of head, appro 3"/7.5cm apart, curving ears slightly inward as you sew.

Nose, Eyes, and Mouth

With B, cast on 7 sts.

Knit 1 row, purl 1 row.

Next row K1, ssk, k1, k2tog, k1.

Next row P2tog, p1, p2tog—3 sts.

Cut yarn and pull through rem sts.

Sew nose to middle of head.

With B, embroider satin stitch eyes approx 2"/5cm up from upper edge of nose. Embroider mouth with back stitch.

Body

With A, cast on 24 sts.

Row 1 K4, [kfb] 15 times, k5—39 sts.

Row 2 and all WS rows unless otherwise instructed Purl.

Row 3 [K2, M1R, k2] 4 times, k2, M1R,

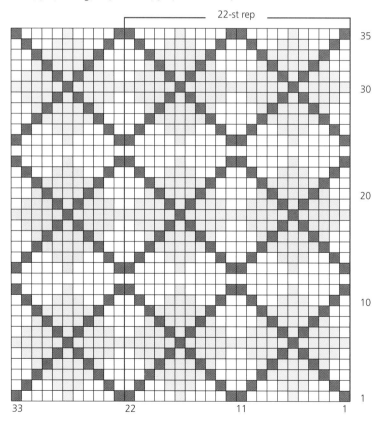

22-st rep

35

30

20

10

1

33   22   11   1

COLOR KEY

☐ A ■ B ☐ C ☐ D

3, M1L, k2, [k2, M1L, k2] 4 times.

ows 4–12 Work even in St st.
ow 13 K11, [M1R, k1] 4 times, k19, ‹1, M1L] 4 times, k11—57 sts.
ow 14 Purl.

EGIN CHART
ow 15 (RS) K1 (selvage st), work 22-st ≥p twice, then work last 11 sts of chart, 1 (selvage st).
ont in chart pat as established through row ‹5. Cut all colors but A. Purl 1 row on WS.
Next row K15, [ssk] twice, k19, [k2tog] vice, k15—53 sts.

EGIN SHORT ROWS
ext row (WS) P15, turn, k to end.
ext row (WS) P14, p2tog, p to end.
ext row (RS) K15, turn, p to end.
ext row (RS) K14, k2tog, k to end.
ext row (WS) P15, turn, k to end.
ext row (WS) P14, [p2tog] twice, p to end.
ext row (RS) K15, turn, p to end—49 sts.
ext row (RS) K6, ssk, k6, ssk, k2tog, 7, k2tog, k14, k2tog, k6—44 sts.
ext row (WS) Purl.
ext row (RS) [Ssk] 11 times, [k2tog] 11 times.
ext row (WS) Purl.
ext row (RS) [Ssk] 5 times, [k2tog] 6 mes—11 sts.
ut yarn and draw through rem sts.
≥w back seam of bear using mattress titch, stuffing firmly as you go, making ure not to stuff so firmly that argyle sts ecome distorted. Leave cast-on edge pen. Sew head to body, adding more tuffing to body and head as needed to nake join sturdy.

Right Arm
Vith A, cast on 8 sts.
ow 1 Knit.
ow 2 and all WS rows except rows

10 and 12 Purl.
Row 3 K1, M1R, k2, M1R, k2, M1L, k2, M1L, k1—12 sts.
Row 5 K1, M1R, k to last st, M1L, k1.
Rows 7, 9, and 11 Rep row 5—20 sts.
Rows 10 and 12 P1, M1L, p to last st, M1R, p1—24 sts.

BEGIN CHART
Row 1 (RS) K1 (selvage st), work 22-st rep twice, k1 (selvage st).
Cont in chart pat as established through row 35. Cut all colors but A. Purl 1 row, knit 1 row, then purl 1 row.
Next row (RS) [K1, ssk] 4 times, [k1, k2tog] 4 times—16 sts.
Next row (WS) Purl.
Next row (RS) [Ssk] 4 times, [k2tog] 4 times—8 sts.
Cut yarn and draw through rem sts. Sew sleeve seam using mattress st, stuffing as you go. Attach to body at neck.

Left Arm
Work as for right arm, reversing colors in argyle chart.

Right Leg
With A, cast on 13 sts.
Row 1 Knit.
Row 2 and all WS rows Purl.
Row 3 K1, [M1L, k1] 11 times, k1—24 sts.
Row 5 [K1, M1L, k1] 12 times—36 sts.
Row 7 [K1, M1L, k2] 12 times—48 sts.
Row 9 *K1, p1; rep from * to end.
Rows 10–18 Work even in St st.
Row 19 K6, [ssk] 10 times, k9, [k2tog] 4 times, k5.
Row 21 K8, [ssk] 4 times, k18—30 sts.
Next row (WS) Purl.

BEGIN CHART
Row 1 (RS) With A, k4; work first 11 sts

of chart; with A, k to end.
Cont in chart pat as established through row 23. Cut all colors but A. Purl 1 row on WS.
Bind off 2 sts at beg of next 2 rows. Dec 1 st each side of every RS row 4 times, then each side of every row 3 times—12 sts.
K2tog across last RS row. Bind off, leaving long tail to attach leg to body.

Left Leg
Work as for right leg through row 18.
Row 19 K5, [ssk] 4 times, k9, [k2tog] 10 times, k6.
Row 21 K18, [k2tog] 4 times, k8—30 sts.
Next row (WS) Purl.

BEGIN CHART
Row 1 (RS) With A, k14; work first 11 sts of chart; with A, k to end.
Cont in chart pat as established through row 23. Cut all colors but A. Complete as for right leg.
Sew leg seams with mattress st, stuffing as you go. Join legs to lower part of body, facing forward, allowing bear to sit. ∎

Penguin Bowling

Tuxedo-clad penguins form the well-dressed pins
in this hip version of bowling—fun for adults and kids alike!

DESIGNED BY PAT OLSKI

Knitted Measurements
Approx 13"/33cm high

Materials
2 3½oz/100g hanks (each approx
150yd/138m) of Cascade Yarns *220
Superwash Aran* (superwash merino wool)
in #871 White (MC) (4)
1 hank each #815 Black (A) and #822
Pumpkin (B)
Small amount of gray yarn for
snowflake embroidery
One set (5) size 7 (4.5mm)
double-pointed needles (dpn),
or size to obtain gauge
One pair size 7 (4.5mm) needles
for wing piece
Stitch markers
Stitch holders
Polyester stuffing
Piece of cardboard or plastic for base
cut into a circle 3"/8cm diameter
Tapestry needle

Notes
1) Insert a cardboard or plastic circle
into the base of each penguin for extra
stability.
2) Stuff ball and each penguin as you work.

Penguins (Make 3)
BOTTOM CIRCLE
With dpn and B, cast on 8 sts. Divide sts
evenly over 4 needles. Join, being careful
not to twist sts, and pm for beg of rnd.
Rnd 1 Knit.
Rnd 2 Kfb in each st around—16 sts.
Rnds 3–5 Knit.
Rnd 6 Kfb in each st around—32 sts.

Rnds 7–10 Knit.
Rnd 11 [K3, kfb] 8 times—40 sts.
Rnd 12 Knit.
Turning rnd 13 Purl.
Knit 7 rnds. Cut B. Join A and knit 7 rnds.
Cut A. Join MC and knit 25 rnds.

SHAPE BODY
Rnd 1 [K3, k2tog] 8 times—32 sts.
Rnds 2–4 Knit.
Rnd 5 [K2, k2tog] 8 times—24 sts.
Rnds 6–8 Knit.
Rnd 9 [K4, k2tog] 4 times—20 sts.
Rnds 10–12 Knit.
Cut MC. Join A and knit 1 rnd.
Work in k1, p1 rib for 5 rnds. Knit 1 rnd.

HEAD
Cut A, and join MC.
Rnd 1 Knit.
Rnd 2 [K4, kfb] 4 times—24 sts.
Rnd 3 Knit.
Rnd 4 [K2, kfb] 8 times—32 sts.
Rnd 5 Knit.
Rnd 6 [K7, kfb] 4 times—36 sts.
Rnds 7–9 Knit.
Dec rnd 10 [K7, k2tog] 4 times—32 sts.
Rnd 11 Knit.
Cut MC, and join A.

Gauge
18 sts and 24 rows/rnds to 4"/10cm over St st using size 7 (4.5mm) needles.
Take time to check gauge.

Penguin Bowling

Rnd 12 Knit.
Dec rnd 13 [K2, k2tog] 8 times—24 sts.
Rnd 14 Knit.
Rnd 15 [K4, k2tog] 4 times—20 sts.
Rnds 16–17 Knit.
Rnd 18 [K2, k2tog] 5 times—15 sts.
Rnd 19 [K1, k2tog] 5 times—10 sts.
Stuff head.
Cut yarn, leaving an 8"/20cm tail.
Thread tail twice through rem 10 sts, cinch closed, and secure end.

WINGS
With straight needles and A, cast on 22 sts.
Row 1 (RS) K to last st, sl 1 wyif.
Row 2 and all WS rows P to last st, sl 1 wyif.
Inc row 3 (RS) K2, M1, k to last 2 sts, M1, k1, sl 1 wyif—2 sts inc'd.
Rows 5, 7, 9, 11, and 13 Rep inc row 3—34 sts at end of row 13.
Rows 15, 17, and 19 (RS) Rep row 1.
Dec row 21 K1, [k3, k2tog] 6 times, k2, sl 1 wyif—28 sts.
Row 23 K to last st, sl 1 wyif.
Row 25 K1, [k2, k2tog] 6 times, k2, sl 1 wyif—22 sts.
Row 27 K to last st, sl 1 wyif.
Row 29 K2, [k2, k2tog] 4 times, k3, sl 1 wyif—18 sts.
Row 31 K to last st, sl 1 wyif.
Row 32 P to last st, sl 1 wyif.
Bind off, leaving long tail for sewing onto penguin.

Finishing
Sew top of wing pieces around neck with opening at center front (see photo).
With A, make a single duplicate st at center top of face and 2 French knot eyes.
With B, make nose by embroidering a duplicate st with one straight st in the center.

TUFT
Wrap color A yarn around 2 fingers 4 or 5 times. Take a piece of color A yarn and tie wrapped yarn into a bundle. Cut ends of bundle open and secure to top of head. Trim to desired size and tease yarn to separate plies.

Snowball
With dpn and MC, cast on 6 sts. Divide sts evenly over 4 needles. Join, being careful not to twist sts, and pm for beg of rnd.
Rnd 1 Knit.
Rnd 2 Kfb in each st around—12 sts.
Rnds 3, 5, 7, 9, 11, 13, 15, and 17 Knit
Rnd 4 [K1, kfb] 6 times—18 sts.
Rnd 6 [K2, kfb] 6 times—24 sts.
Rnd 8 [K3, kfb] 6 times—30 sts.
Rnd 10 [K4, kfb] 6 times—36 sts.
Rnd 12 [K5, kfb] 6 times—42 sts.
Rnd 14 [K6, kfb] 6 times—48 sts.
Rnd 16 [K7, kfb] 6 times—54 sts.
Rnd 18 [K8, kfb] 6 times—60 sts.
Rnds 19–22 Knit.
Rnd 23 [K8, k2tog] 6 times—54 sts.
Rnd 25 [K7, k2tog] 6 times—48 sts.
Rnd 27 [K6, k2tog] 6 times—42 sts.
Rnd 29 [K5, k2tog] 6 times—36 sts.
Rnd 31 [K4, k2tog] 6 times—30 sts.
Rnd 33 [K3, k2tog] 6 times—24 sts.
Rnd 35 [K2, k2tog] 6 times—18 sts.
Rnd 37 [K1, k2tog] 6 times—12 sts.
Rnd 39 [K2tog] 6 times—6 sts.
Stuff ball. Cut yarn, leaving a long tail. Using tapestry needle, thread tail through rem 6 sts, cinch closed, and secure.

Finishing
Using grey yarn and photo as guide, embroider snowflake as foll:
Work stem st lines along each of the 6 inc segments, then add straight st.
Fasten off and weave in ends. ∎

49

Cuddly Owl

Tiny tots will hoot and holler
when they see this huggable, snuggleable owl toy.

DESIGNED BY AUDREY DRYSDALE

Knitted Measurements
Approx 10"/25.5cm high

Materials
- 1 3½oz/100g ball (each approx 220yd/200m) of Cascade Yarns *220 Superwash* (superwash wool) each in #816 Gray (A), #892 Space Needle (B), and #871 White (C) (3)
- Small amount of #1952 Blaze (D)
- One set (5) size 6 (4mm) double-pointed needles (dpn), *or size to obtain gauge*
- One pair size 6 (4mm) needles
- Two 1"/2.5cm black buttons

Note As buttons are a choking hazard, embroider eyes if making for a child.
- Stitch markers
- Polyester stuffing

Body
With A and dpn, cast on 4 sts.
Set-up row 1 Kfb in each st—8 sts.
Divide sts evenly over 4 dpn. Join to work in rnds, being careful to not twist sts, and pm for beg of rnd.
Rnd 1 Kfb in each st—16 sts.
Rnd 2 and every other rnd Knit.
Rnd 3 *K2, M1; rep from * around—24 sts.

Rnd 5 *K3, M1; rep from * around—32 sts.
Rnd 7 *K4, M1; rep from * around—40 sts.
Cont in this way to inc 8 sts evenly every other rnd until there are 88 sts.
Work even in St st (k every rnd) until piece measures 4¾"/12 cm from beg.

SHAPE NECK
Rnd 1 *K9, k2tog; rep from * around—80 sts.
Rnd 2 and every other rnd Knit.
Rnd 3 *K8, k2tog; rep from * around—72 sts.
Rnd 5 *K7, k2tog; rep from * around—64 sts.
Rnd 7 *K8, M1; rep from * around—72 sts.
Rnd 9 *K9, M1; rep from * around—80 sts.
Rnd 11 *K10, M1; rep from * around—88 sts.
Work even in St st until piece measures 9"/23 cm from beg.

Head
EAR TUFT
**Row 1 (RS) K16, turn.
Work back and forth in St st (k on RS, p on WS) over these 16 sts as foll:
Row 2 (WS) P1, p2tog tbl, p to last 3 sts, p2tog, p1.
Row 3 K1, k2tog, k to last 3 sts, ssk, k1.
Rep rows 2 and 3 once more—8 sts.
Next row P1, p2tog tbl, p2, p2tog, p1—6 sts.
Next row K1, k2tog, ssk, k1—4 sts.
Next row P2tog tbl, p2tog—2 sts.
Next row K2tog. Fasten off.******

Gauge
22 sts and 30 rnds and 4"/10cm over St st using size 6 (4mm) needles.
Take time to check gauge.

145

Cuddly Owl

TOP OF HEAD
***Rejoin A to rem sts.
Row 1 (RS) K28. Turn.
Work back and forth in St st over these 28 sts as foll:
Row 2 (WS) Bind off 4 sts, p to end.
Row 3 Bind off 4 sts, k to end.
Rep rows 2 and 3 twice more. Bind off rem 4 sts.***
Rejoin A to rem sts. Rep from ** to ** for 2nd ear tuft. Rep from *** to *** for 2nd half of top of head. Sew top of head seam, leaving opening to insert stuffing. Stuff head and body.
Sew opening closed.

Chest
With B and straight needles, cast on 2 sts.
Row 1 (RS) Kfb, k1—3 sts.
Rows 2 and 4 Knit.
Row 3 [Kfb] twice, k1—5 sts.
Row 5 Kfb, k to last 2 sts, kfb, k1.
Row 6 Knit.
Rep last 2 rows 12 times more—31 sts.
Work even in garter st (k every row) for 8 rows.
Next row (RS) K1, k2tog, k to last 3 sts, k2tog, k1.
Next 5 rows Knit.
Rep last 6 rows 3 times more—23 sts.
Work even in garter st until piece measures 6"/15cm from lower point.
Bind off. Sew to body as shown in photo.

Eyes (Make 2)
With C and straight needles, cast on 3 sts.
Row 1 (WS) Kfb in each st—6 sts.
Row 2 and all RS rows Knit.
Row 3 [K1, M1] 5 times, k1—11 sts.
Row 5 [K2, M1] 5 times, k1—16 sts.
Row 7 [K3, M1] 5 times, k1—21 sts.
Cont in this way to inc 5 sts evenly every other row until there are 41 sts.
Next row Knit.

Bind off knitwise on WS. Sew bound-off edge to cast-on edge. Sew to head as shown in photo. Embroider eyes or sew buttons in position.

Beak
With D, cast on 9 sts.
Row 1 (WS) Knit.
Row 2 K1, k2tog, k to last 3 sts, k2tog, k1
Row 3 Knit.
Rows 4 and 5 Rep rows 2 and 3—5 sts.
Row 6 K1, k3tog, k1—3 sts.
Row 7 Knit.
Row 8 K3tog.
Fasten off. Sew to head as shown in photo.

Wings (Make 4)
Note WS/RS is not important.
With A and straight needles, cast on 2 sts.
Row 1 Kfb, k1—3 sts.
Row 2 Knit.
Row 3 Kfb, k to end—4 sts.
Rows 4–23 Rep last 2 rows 10 times—14 sts.
Rows 24, 26, and 28 Knit.
Row 25 Bind off 7 sts, k to end—7 sts.
Row 27 Cast on 5 sts, k to end—12 sts
Row 29 K1, k2tog, k to end—11 sts.
Rows 30–47 Rep last 2 rows 9 times—2 sts
Row 48 K2tog. Fasten off.
Matching shapes, sew two wings pieces tog to create one wing. Sew straight edge to side of body (see photo). ■

50

The Curious Caterpillar

This cleverly-constructed caterpillar is cuddly and curious
—and just the right size to wiggle alongside your little cutie-pie.

DESIGNED BY CHRISTINE MARIE CHEN

Knitted Measurements
Approx 14"/35.5cm long

Materials
- 1 3½oz/100g hank (each approx 150yd/138m) of Cascade Yarns *220 Superwash Aran* (superwash merino wool) each in #802 Green Apple (A) and #820 Lemon (B) **④**
- One set (4) size 7 (4.5mm) double-pointed needles (dpn), *or size to obtain gauge*
- One size H/8 (5mm) crochet hook
- Stitch marker
- Polyester stuffing
- Small amount of black felt
- Five ⅝" Velcro® disks
- Fabric glue or sewing needle and thread

Note
Caterpillar is made up of 6 segments of 2 medallions each, which are worked in the round from the outer edge and sewn together.

Medallion 1 (Make 2)
With A, cast on 70 sts and divide over 3 dpn. Join, being careful not to twist sts, and pm for beg of rnd.
Rnd 1 Knit.
Rnd 2 [K12, k2tog] 5 times—65 sts.
Rnd 3 Knit.
Rnd 4 [K11, k2tog] 5 times—60 sts.
Rnd 5 Knit.
Rnd 6 [K10, k2tog] 5 times— 55 sts.
Rnd 7 [K9, k2tog] 5 times—50 sts.
Rnd 8 [K8, k2tog] 5 times—45 sts.
Rnd 9 [K7, k2tog] 5 times—40 sts.
Rnd 10 [K6, k2tog] 5 times—35 sts.
Rnd 11 [K5, k2tog] 5 times—30 sts.
Rnd 12 [K4, k2tog] 5 times—25 sts.
Rnd 13 [K3, k2tog] 5 times—20 sts.
Rnd 14 [K2, k2tog] 5 times—15 sts.
Rnd 15 [K1, k2tog] 5 times—10 sts.
Rnd 16 [K2tog] 5 times—5 sts.
Cut yarn, leaving a long tail. Thread tail through rem sts to close.
With RS held together, sew the 2 medallions together, leaving a small opening.
Turn inside out, stuff, and sew closed.

Medallion 2 (Make 2)
With A, cast on 60 sts and divide over 3 dpn. Join, being careful not to twist sts, and pm for beg of rnd.
Knit 1 rnd. Beg with rnd 6, complete as for Medallion 1.

Medallion 3 (Make 2)
With A, cast on 50 sts and divide over 3 dpn. Join, being careful not to twist sts, and pm for beg of rnd.
Knit 1 rnd. Beg with rnd 8, complete as for Medallion 1.

Medallion 4 (Make 2)
With A, cast on 40 sts and divide over 3 dpn. Join, being careful not to twist sts, and pm for beg of rnd.
Knit 1 rnd. Beg with rnd 10, complete as for Medallion 1.

Medallion 5 (Make 2)
With A, cast on 30 sts. Join, being careful not to twist sts, and pm for beg of rnd.
Knit 1 rnd. Beg with rnd 12, complete as for Medallion 1.

Gauge
20 sts and 24 rnds to 4"/10cm over St st using size 7 (4.5mm) needles.
Take time to check gauge.

The Curious Caterpillar

Medallion 6 (Make 2)

With A, cast on 20 sts and divide over 3 dpn. Join, being careful not to twist sts, and pm for beg of rnd. Knit 1 rnd. Beg with rnd 14, complete as for Medallion 1.

Eyes (Make 2)

With B, cast on 30 sts. Complete as for Medallion 5, but do *not* sew pieces tog.

Antennae (Make 2)

With 2 dpn and B, cast on 3 sts. *Knit one row. Without turning work, slide the sts back to the opposite end of needle to work next row from RS.
Pull yarn tightly from the end of the row. Rep from * until I-cord measures 13"/33cm. Cut yarn, leaving a tail.
Thread tail through open sts to close.

Finishing

Sew eyes, mouth, and antenna to medallion 1 for head. With B and crochet hook, ch 13 on medallion 1 for mouth (see photo).
Cut small circles of black felt and glue or sew to center of eyes.
Sew or glue Velcro® disks to the centers of the Medallions so they can be stuck together to form caterpillar. ■

51

Life-Size Lucy

Clad in a pint-sized sweater vest, this cutie-pie is all set to be your child's best friend.

DESIGNED BY LORI STEINBERG

Knitted Measurements
Height Approx 38"/96.5cm

Materials
- 2 3½oz/100g hanks (each approx 50yd/138m) of Cascade Yarns *220 Superwash Aran* (superwash merino wool) each in #845 Denim (A), #809 Really Red (B), and #817 Aran (D) (4)
- One hank each in #201 Sesame (C) and #815 Black (E)
- One size 9 (5.5mm) circular needle, 24"/40cm long, *or size to obtain gauge*
- One set (4) size 9 (5.5mm) double-pointed needles (dpn)
- One size I/9 (5.5mm) crochet hook
- Cable needle (cn)
- Stitch markers
- Scrap yarn
- Polyester stuffing

Stitch Glossary
6-st LC Place 3 sts on cn and hold to front, k3, k3 from cn.

Stripe Pattern
2 rnds B, 1 rnd A, 2 rnds B, 1 rnd A. Rep these 8 rnds for stripe pat.

Cable Pattern
(over 10 sts)
Row 1 (RS) P2, k6, p2
Row 2 and all WS rows K2, p6, k2.
Row 3 P2, 6-st LC, p2.
Row 5 Rep row 1.
Row 6 Rep row 2.
Rep rows 1–6 for cable pat.

DOLL
LEGS (Make 2)
With A, cast on 32 sts and divide over 3 dpn as foll: 16 sts on Dpn #1 and 8 sts each on Dpn #2 and #3. Join, being careful not to twist sts, and pm for beg of rnd. Work in St st (k every rnd) until piece measures 13"/33cm from beg.
Cut A, join B. Cont in St st for 3½"/9cm.
Shape Toe
Dec rnd *Dpn #1*: K1, SKP, k to last 3 sts, k2tog, k1; *Dpn #2*: k1, SKP, k to end; *Dpn #3*: k to last 3 sts, k2tog, k1—4 sts dec'd.
Rep dec rnd every *other* rnd 3 times more, then *every* rnd once—12 sts.
Place sts on dpn #2 and #3 onto one needle and join to the 6 sts on dpn #1 using 3-needle bind-off (see page 182).
Stuff lightly and set aside.

ARMS (Make 2)
With B, cast on 28 sts divided as foll: 14 sts on Dpn #1 and 7 sts each on Dpn #2 and #3. Join, being careful not to twist sts, and pm for beg of rnd.
Work in St st and stripe pat until piece measures 10"/25.5cm from beg, end with 1 row B. Cut A and B, and join C. Work 12 rnds in C.

Gauge
16 sts and 24 rnds to 4"/10cm over St st using size 9 (5.5mm) needle.
Take time to check gauge.

Shape Hand

Dec rnd *Dpn #1*: K1, SKP, k to last 3 sts, k2tog, k1; *Dpn #2*: k1, SKP, k to end; *Dpn #3*: k to last 3 sts, k2tog, k1 — 4 sts dec'd. Rep dec rnd every *other* rnd once more, then *every* rnd twice — 12 sts.

Place sts on Dpn #2 and #3 onto one needle and join to the 6 sts on Dpn #1 using 3-needle bind-off (see page 182). Stuff lightly and set aside.

BODY

With circular needle and A, cast on 84 sts. Join, being careful not to twist sts, and pm for beg of rnd. Work in St st until body measures 6½"/16.5cm. Join B. Beg with 2 rnds B, work in stripe pat for 6"/15cm.

Divide to Shape Shoulders

Next row (RS) Bind off 6 sts, k36. Turn. Work back and forth on one side only as foll:

Next row Bind off 6 sts, p to end. Cont in stripe pat, bind off 5 sts at beg of next 2 rows. Place rem 20 sts on scrap yarn to hold for neck. Rep for other side. Sew shoulder seams. Stuff body lightly. Sew legs and arms to body, using photo as a guide.

HEAD

With C, cast on 40 sts and divide over 3 dpn. Join, being careful not to twist sts, and pm for beg of rnd.

Work in St st, inc 4 sts evenly around every 4th rnd 4 times — 72 sts.

Work even until piece measures 5"/12.5cm from beg. Cut C. Join E. Work 6 rows even.

Shape Head

Next rnd *K2, k2tog; rep from * around — 54 sts.

Knit 1 rnd.

Next rnd *K1, k2tog; rep from * around — 36 sts.

Knit 1 rnd.

Next rnd *K2, k2tog; rep from * around — 27 sts.

Next rnd *K1, k2tog; rep from * around — 18 sts.

Next rnd [K2tog] 9 times around — 9 sts. Cut yarn, leaving a long tail. Thread tail through open sts and pull tight to close top.

Finishing

Divide 40 sts on scrap yarn for neck over 4 dpn. Join A and pm for beg of rnd. Work 6 rnds in St st. Bind off.

Stuff head. Check body stuffing and adjust if necessary. Sew head to body with beg of head rnd at center back.

HAIR

With E, cut approx 60 strands 36"/91.5cm long. Attach hair along back of neck, creating hair line around face, by attaching strands as foll: fold strand in half over crochet hook, draw loop through stitch along back of neck, draw ends of strand through loop and pull to tighten. When all strands have been attached, gather hair into a high side ponytail. Wrap strands of A tightly around ponytail for holder. Cut more strands of E and attach to fill in bare spaces, threading through ponytail holder. Trim ponytail. Using photo as guide, embroider face.

SWEATER VEST

BACK

With D, cast on 44 sts.

Next row (RS) *K1, p1; rep from * to end. Rep last row 5 times more for k1, p1 rib. Cont in St st (k on RS, p on WS) until piece measures 17"/43cm from beg. Bind off.

FRONT

Cast on and work rib as for back. Cont in St st, working cable pat over center 10 sts, until piece measures 11"/28cm from beg, end with a WS row.

Divide for neck

Work in pat over next 20 sts, k2tog, join 2nd ball of D, SKP, k to end.

Next row (WS) Work both sides at once with separate balls of yarn, purl.

Dec row With first ball, k to last 2 sts, k2tog; with 2nd ball of yarn, SKP, k to end. Cont in St st, rep dec row every other row until 11 sts rem for each shoulder. Work even until piece measures same as back. Bind off.

Finishing

Sew shoulder seams and lay piece flat. Place a marker 6"/15cm either side of left shoulder seam.

With circular needle and RS facing, pick up and k 36 sts between markers for sleeve trim. Work 3 rows in k1, p1 rib. Bind off. Rep for right side side.

NECK TRIM

With circular needle and RS facing, beg at right back shoulder, pick up and k 22 sts along back neck, pick up and k 19 sts along left front neck, pick up and k 1 st at center of v-neck and mark this st, pick up and k 19 sts along right front neck — 61 sts.

Next row (WS) *P1, k1; rep from * to marked st; p marked st; **p1, k1; rep from ** to end

Next row K the knit sts and p the purl sts (for K1, P1 rib) to 1 st before the marked st; SK2P; rib to end. Rib 1 row more. Bind off. Sew side seams, including sleeve trim. Sew neck trim seam.

Put sweater vest on doll. ∎

Funny Bunny

A plush and cushiony bunny doubles as a portable neck pillow perfect for every member of the family.

DESIGNED BY JACQUELINE VAN DILLEN

■■□□

Knitted Measurements
Height Approx 16"/40.5cm
Circumference Approx 16"/40.5cm

Materials
- 1 3½oz/100g hank (each approx 220yd/200m) of Cascade Yarns *220 Superwash Effects* (superwash wool) in #4 Teals, #6 Stormy Sea, or #14 Forest (4)
- Small amount of red yarn for mouth embroidery
- One pair size 6 (4mm) needles, *or size to obtain gauge*
- Two ⅝"/15mm buttons

Note As small buttons are a choking hazard, embroider eyes if making for a child.
- Contrast color thread
- Polyester stuffing
- Tapestry needle
- Plastic baggie, partially filled with rice (for weighing the base)

Rabbit
Beg at base with chosen yarn color, cast on 4 sts.
Row 1 (RS) Kfb in each st—8 sts.
Row 2 and all even-numbered rows through row 12 Purl.
Row 3 Kfb in each st—16 sts.
Row 5 [K1, kfb] 8 times—24 sts.
Row 7 [K1, kfb] 12 times—36 sts.
Row 9 [K2, kfb] 12 times—48 sts.
Row 11 [K2, kfb] 16 times—64 sts.
Row 13 [K4, kfb, k1] 10 times, k4—74 sts.
Row 14 Pfb, p to last 2 sts, pfb, p1—76 sts.
Work even until piece measures 12½"/32cm from beg.

SEPARATE FOR EARS
Next row (RS) Bind off 2 sts, k until there are 34 sts on needle, bind off 4 sts, k to end.
Next row Bind off 2 sts, p until there are 34 sts on needle, turn, leaving rem sts on hold. Work even on these 34 sts for one ear until it measures 4"/10cm from beg of the ear.

Shape top of ears
Dec row (RS) [K2, SKP, k9, k2tog, k2] twice—30 sts.
Next row and all WS rows Purl.

Dec row (RS) [K2, SKP, k7, k2tog, k2] twice—26 sts.
Dec row (RS) [K2, SKP, k5, k2tog, k2] twice—22 sts.
Dec row (RS) [K2, SKP, k3, k2tog, k2] twice—18 sts.
Dec row (RS) [K2, SKP, k1, k2tog, k2] twice—14 sts.
Dec row (RS) [K2, SK2P, k2] twice—10 st
Last dec row (RS) [K1, SK2P, k1] twice—6 sts.
Cut yarn, leaving a long end, draw throug sts twice and pull up tightly to finish.
Rejoin yarn to work 2nd ear in same way.

Finishing
Sew both ear seams. Embroider or sew button approx 2½"/6.5cm down from center of base of each ear. With tapestry needle and doubled strand of red yarn, make a cross hatch mouth (see photo). Starting from the bottom, seam approx 4"/10cm of back from bottom. Insert baggi with rice into base, then partially stuff the rabbit.
Seam rest of back, leaving a small opening Stuff remainder of body and ears, seam rest of back. ■

Gauge
22 sts and 32 rows to 4"/10cm over St st using size 6 (4mm) needles.
Take time to check gauge.

53

Swirly Eyes

Knit mainly in the round, kids will love
this whimsical creature with googly, giggly eyes.

DESIGNED BY CHARLES GANDY

Knitted Measurements
Length Approx 16"/40.5cm
Circumference 10"/25.5cm

Materials
▪ 1 1¾oz/50g hank (each approx 137yd/125m) of Cascade Yarns *220 Superwash Sport* (superwash merino wool) each in #882 Plum Crazy (A), #871 White (B), and #807 Raspberry (C)
▪ 1 set (5) size 5 (3.75mm) double-pointed needles (dpn), *or size to obtain gauge*
▪ Stitch marker
▪ Polyester stuffing
▪ 1"/2.5cm pompom maker

Note
Slip the first st in the 2nd rnd of each color stripe for a "jogless join."

Body
With A, cast on 48 sts, dividing evenly over 4 dpn. Join, being careful not to twist sts, and pm for beg of rnd.
Knit 6 rnds A. Knit 6 rnds B. Rep these 12 rnds twice more.
Join C and knit 6 rnds. Cut C.
[Knit 6 rnds B, knit 6 rnds A] 7 times. Cut B.
Divide sts evenly over 2 dpn. Turn tube inside out and use 3 needle bind-off (see page 182) to join halves.
Turn piece RS out.

Eyes (Make 2)
Count 5 stripes down from bound-off edge and 4 sts in from RH edge. Place the RH leg of the next 6 sts of the top rnd of the stripe on 1 dpn; place the corresponding 6 sts of the bottom rnd of the stripe on a 2nd dpn; with 3rd and 4th dpn, pick up the center of the sts in 3 rnds between the top and bottom dpn—18 sts in rnd.
Place marker for beg of rnd.
With A, beg with bottom dpn and [knit 6 rnds A, knit 6 rnds B] 5 times.
Join C and knit 6 rnds. Cut C.
Knit 6 rnds B, knit 6 rnds A. Cut yarn, leaving a long tail of A. Thread tail through open stitches. Do *not* cinch closed.
Work 2nd eye in same way at 4 sts from LH side.

Finishing
With C, make two 1"/2.5cm pompoms.
Stuff body and sew cast-on edge closed.
Stuff each eye lightly and cinch tops closed. Twist eye into a knot and pull tight to keep in place (see photo).
Twist 2nd eye into a knot in the opposite direction and pull tight to keep in place.
Sew pompoms firmly to ends of eyes. ▪

Gauge
24 sts and 32 rnds to 4"/10cm over St st using size 5 (3.75mm) needles.
Take time to check gauge.

Bobcat Family

One pattern knit up in three yarns and using three different needle sizes creates this fetching family of felines.

DESIGNED BY WEI WILKINS

■■■□

Knitted Measurements
Height Approx 7 (8,10)"/18 (20.5, 25)cm
Circumference Approx 7½ (9, 10½)"/19 (23, 26.5)cm

Materials
▪ 1 1¾oz/50g hank (each approx 137yd/125m) of Cascade Yarns *220 Superwash Sport* (superwash merino wool) each in #873 Extra Creme Cafe (A), #818 Mocha (B) and #817 Aran (C) (**3**)
▪ 1 3½oz/100g ball (each approx 220yd/200m) of Cascade Yarns *220 Superwash* (superwash wool) each in #873 Extra Creme Cafe (A), #818 Mocha (B) and #817 Aran (C) (**3**)
▪ 1 3½oz/100g hank (each approx 150yd/138m) of Cascade Yarns *220 Superwash Aran* (superwash merino wool) each in #873 Extra Creme Cafe (A), #818 Mocha (B) and #817 Aran (C) (**4**)
▪ Small amount of matching yarn weights in black
▪ One pair each sizes 4, 5, and 7 (3.5, 3.75, and 4.5mm) needles, *or size to obtain gauges*
▪ One set (4) of sizes 4, 5, and 7 (3.5, 3.75, and 4.5mm) double-pointed needles (dpn)
▪ Six .47"/12mm animal eyes
Note As animal eyes are a choking hazard, embroider eyes if making for a child.
▪ Stitch markers
▪ Tapestry needle
▪ Polyester stuffing
▪ Extra-hold hair gel

Notes
1) Each bobcat is worked from the same instructions but with a different yarn weight and needle size to create the three different finished sizes.
2) All parts are worked in St st in rows.

Legs (Make 2)
SOLID SEGMENT
Beg at top edge with A, cast on 11 sts.
Work in St st (k on RS, p on WS) for 4 rows.
Dec row (RS) K1, k2tog, k to end—10 sts.
Work 3 rows even.
Dec row (RS) K to last 3 sts, ssk, k1—9 sts.
Work 3 rows even.
Dec row (RS) K1, k2tog, k to end—8 sts.
Work 7 rows even.

Inc row (RS) K2, [M1, k2] 3 times—11 sts.
Work 3 rows even.
Dec row (RS) K2, S2KP, k1, S2KP, k2—7 sts.
Purl 1 row. Bind off rem sts knitwise.

STRIPED SEGMENT
Beg at top edge with C, cast on 9 sts, and work 2 rows in St st. Work 2 rows with B.
Dec row (RS) With C, k2tog, k to end—8 sts.
Work 3 rows with C.
Dec row (RS) With B, k to last 2 sts, ssk—7 sts.
Work 1 row with B. Work 2 rows with C.
Dec row (RS) With C, k2tog, k3, ssk—5 sts.
Work 1 row with C, 2 rows with B, then 4 rows with C.
Inc row (RS) With B, k2, [M1, k1] 3 times—8 sts.
Work 3 rows with B.
Dec row (RS) K1, S2KP, k1, ssk, k1—5 sts.
Bind off rem sts purlwise.

Arms (Make 2)
SOLID SEGMENT
Beg at top edge with A, cast on 5 sts.

Gauges
24 sts and 28 rows to 4"/10 cm over St st using size 4 (3.5 mm) needles and *220 Superwash Sport*.
20 sts and 26 rows to 4"/10 cm over St st using size 5 (3.75 mm) needles and *220 Superwash*.
18 sts and 22 rows to 4"/10 cm over St st using size 7 (4.5 mm) needles and *220 Superwash Aran*.
Take time to check gauges.

Work in St st for 2 rows.
Inc row (RS) K1, M1, k3, M1, k1—7 sts.
Inc row (WS) P1, M1, p5, M1, p1—9 sts.
Work 6 rows even.
Dec row (RS) K1, k2tog, k3, ssk, k1—7 sts.
Work 9 rows even.
Inc row (RS) K1, M1, k5, M1, k1—9 sts.
Work 3 rows even.
Dec row (RS) K1, S2KP, k1, S2KP, k1—5 sts.
Work 1 row. Bind off rem sts knitwise.

STRIPED SEGMENT
Beg at top edge with C, cast on 4 sts.
Work in St st for 2 rows.
Inc row (RS) With B, k1, M1, k2, M1, k1—6 sts.
Inc row (WS) P1, M1, p4, M1, p1—8 sts.
Work 4 rows with C, 2 rows with B, 2 rows with C.
Dec row (RS) With C, k2tog, k4, ssk—6 sts.
Work 1 row with C, 2 rows with B, then 4 rows with C.
Inc row (RS) With B, M1, k6, M1—8 sts.
Work 3 rows with B.
Dec row (RS) With B, k1, S2KP, k1, ssk, k1—5 sts.
Work 1 row even. Bind off rem sts knitwise.

Back
Beg at top (neck) edge with A, cast on 8 sts. Work in St st for 2 rows.
Inc row (RS) K1, [M1, k2] 3 times, M1, k1—12 sts.
Work 3 rows even.
Inc row (RS) K2, [M1, k2] 5 times—17 sts.
Work 3 rows even.
Inc row (RS) K2, [M1, k3] 5 times—22 sts.
Work 3 rows even.
Inc row (RS) K3, [M1, k5] 3 times, M1, k4—26 sts.
Work 25 rows even.

Dec row (RS) K1, k2tog, k to last 3 sts, ssk, k1—24 sts.
Work 3 rows even.
Dec row (RS) K1, k2tog, k to last 3 sts, ssk, k1—22 sts.
Work 3 rows even.
Dec row (RS) K1, k2tog, k to last 3 sts, ssk, k1.
Purl 1 row.
Rep last 2 rows twice more—16 sts.
Knit 1 row. Bind off sts purlwise.

Front
Beg at lower edge with C, cast on 10 sts.
Work in St st for 2 rows.
Inc row (RS) K to last st, M1, k1.
Purl 1 row.
Inc row (RS) K1, M1, k to end.
Purl 1 row.
Rep the last 4 rows once more—14 sts.
Inc row (RS) K to last st, M1, k1.
Work 3 rows even.
Inc row (RS) K1, M1, k to end—16 sts.
Work 7 rows even.
Dec row (RS) K to last 2 sts, ssk.
Purl 1 row.
Dec row (RS) K2tog, k to end—14 sts.
Purl 1 row.
Rep the last 4 rows 4 times more—6 sts.
Bind off sts knitwise.

Head
Note Head is made in one piece with seam running up center back.
Beg at lower (neck) edge with A, cast on 23 sts. Work in St st for 2 rows.
Inc row (RS) K3, [M1, k2] 10 times—33 sts.
Purl 1 row.
Inc row (RS) K3, [M1, k3] 10 times—43 sts.
Purl 1 row.

BEGIN CHART
Row 1 (RS) K10, pm, work row 1 of chart over 23 sts, pm, k10.
Rows 2–14 Cont to work chart over center 23 sts with rem sts in A on each side.
Row 15 (RS) K9, remove marker and S2KP, cont across foll chart to 2 sts before next marker, S2KP removing marker, k9—39 sts.
Cont with A only over all sts as foll:
Purl 1 row.
Dec row (RS) K8, S2KP, k17, S2KP, k8—35 sts.
Purl 1 row.
Dec row (RS) K7, S2KP, k15, S2KP, k7—31 sts.
Purl 1 row.
Divide sts over 2 dpn, 15 sts for front of head and 16 sts for back of head. Set aside

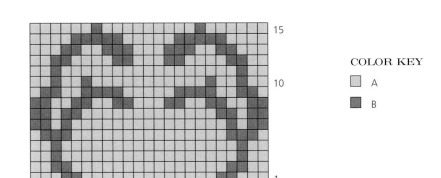

23 sts

COLOR KEY
■ A
■ B

MUZZLE

With C, cast on 9 sts. Work in St st for 2 rows.
Inc row (RS) K1, M1, k to last st, M1, k1—11 sts.
Purl 1 row.
Rep the last 2 rows once more—13 sts.
Work 2 rows even.
Dec row (RS) K5, S2KP, k5—11 sts.
Purl 1 row. Bind off 4 sts, S2KP, bind off all sts.

NOSE

With black yarn, cast on 5 sts. Work 2 rows in St st.
Dec row (RS) K1, S2KP, k1—3 sts.
S2KP and fasten off last st, leaving long end.

EARS (Make 2)

Striped back of ear
Beg at attaching edge with B, cast on 13 sts.
Work 2 rows in St st.
Dec row 3 (RS) K1, k2tog, k to last 3 sts, ssk, k1—11 sts.
Row 4 (WS) Purl.
With C, rep rows 3 and 4 once—9 sts.
With B, rep rows 3 and 4 twice—5 sts.
Next row (RS) With B, k1, S2KP, k1—3 sts.
Purl 1 row. S2KP and fasten off rem st, leaving long tail.

Solid front of ear
Beg at attaching edge with C, cast on 11 sts. Work 2 rows in St st.
Dec row (RS) K2tog, k to last 2 sts, ssk—9 sts.
Purl 1 row.
Rep last 2 rows once more—7 sts.
Dec row (RS) K2tog, k to end.
Purl 1 row.
Dec row (RS) K to last 2 sts, ssk—5 sts.
Purl 1 row.

Next row (RS) K1, S2KP, k1—3 sts.
S2KP and draw yarn through rem st.

Tail

Beg at attaching edge with A, cast on 10 sts. Work 2 rows with A, 2 rows with B, 4 rows with A, and 2 rows with B.
Dec row (RS) With A, k1, k2tog, k to end—9 sts.
With A, work 3 rows in St st. Cut A.
Dec row (RS) With B, k6, ssk, k1—8 sts.
With B, work 3 rows in St st. Cut B.
Change to black and work 2 rows in St st.
Cut yarn leaving a long end, draw through sts twice, and pull tightly to finish.

Finishing

Sew back of body to front of body, leaving neck edge open. Stuff body.
Seam tog fronts and backs of legs, stuff, and join to body as in photo. Seam fronts and backs of arms tog, stuff, and join to body as in photo. Using Kitchener st (see page 182), join top of head sts tog. Sew muzzle and nose to face. Sew on or embroider eyes. With black yarn, embroider mouth using stem sts as in photo.
Sew back of head seam, stuff, and sew to top of body at neck opening.
Sew tail seam, stuff and sew to body at back as in photo. Sew tog fronts and backs of ears, stuff, and sew to head. With black yarn, braid and attach 3 strands of yarn at ear tips. Apply hair gel to tips and trim as desired. ■

55

Fair Isle Doll

Enjoy a Fair Isle frenzy of colorful patterning on this whimsical doll,
then add fun finishing touches like purple loopy hair and a stitched-on smile.

DESIGNED BY MARI TOBITA

Knitted Measurements
Approx 14"/35.5cm high

Materials
▪ 1 3½oz/100g balls (each approx
220yd/200m) of Cascade Yarns *220
Superwash* (superwash wool) each in
#807 Raspberry (A), #835 Pink Rose (B),
#902 Soft Pink (C), #805 Violet (D),
and #1986 Purple Hyacinth (E) (3)
▪ One set (5) size 6 (4mm) double-pointed
needles (dpn), *or size to obtain gauges*
▪ Small amounts of black and red yarn
for embroidery
▪ Stitch markers
▪ Stitch holders
▪ Polyester stuffing

Notes
1) Doll body is knit in the round from top
down beginning with the neck. The head is
then picked up and worked from the neck.
2) When changing colors, twist yarns on
WS to prevent holes in work. Carry color
not in use loosely across back.

Stitch Glossary
LS (loop stitch) K1 but do not drop
st from LH needle, [bring yarn to front
between needles and wrap clockwise
around the left thumb making a 2"/5cm
loop, then bring yarn to back and k into
same st on LH needle tbl] twice, sl st off
LH needle —3 sts made in 1 st.

Doll
Beg at the neck with A, cast on 28 sts
and divide evenly over 4 dpn. Join, taking
care not to twist sts, and pm for beg of
rnd. Knit 2 rnds.
Next rnd Join B and work as foll: k10 (body),
pm, k4 (arm), pm, k10 (body), pm, k4 (arm)

BEGIN BODY AND ARM CHARTS
Working body chart (for body sts) and
arm chart (for arm sts), work rnds 1 and
2. Cont working charts and AT THE SAME
TIME work shoulder shaping as foll:
Inc rnd 3 [Sm, k1, M1, k to 1 st before
marker, M1, k1] 4 times—36 sts.
Cont working charts in this way through
rnd 13—92 sts.
Work rnd 14, removing all markers
except beg of rnd marker.

BODY
Cont to work row 15 of Body Chart as
foll: *K26, slip next 20 sts to st holder
for arm, cast on 4 sts; rep from * once
more—60 sts.

Gauges
22 sts and 30 rows/rnds to 4"/10cm over St st using size 6 (4mm) needles.
24 sts and 27 rows/rnds to 4"/10cm over St st and Fair Isle chart using size 6 (4mm) needles.
Take time to check gauges.

Fair Isle Doll

Work row 16 of Body Chart to 2 sts before marker, place new beg of rnd marker. Remove old marker. Cont in chart A for 22 rnds. Remove marker. Cut yarn.

Legs
BEGIN LEG CHART
Slip 15 sts to RH needle, then place next 30 sts on st holder. Attach E yarn at end of slipped sts, cast on 3 sts to join rem sts, and work next rnd as foll: K35, pm for new beg of rnd—33 sts.
Cont leg chart to end—28 sts.

SHAPE END OF LEG
Rearrange sts over 3 dpn (10 sts, 9 sts, 9 sts). With D, work 4 rnds even.
Next rnd Work k2tog over the last 2 sts of each needle until 3 sts rem on each needle.

Cut yarn, draw through rem sts, and pull tightly to secure end.
Work 2nd leg as first, reversing all shaping.

Arms
Cont working arm chart as foll:
Slip 20 sts from holder onto 2 needles, join yarn at center of body underarm, pick up and k 2 sts. Work arm chart, then pick up and k 2 sts from body under-arm—24 sts. Divide sts evenly over 3 dpn and pm for new beg of rnd.
Cont arm chart to end—20 sts.

HAND
With color C, knit 4 rnds. Rearrange sts over 3 dpn (7 sts, 7 sts, 6 sts).
Dec rnd K to last 2 sts of each needle, k2tog—3 sts dec'd.

Rep dec rnd 3 times more.
Cut yarn, draw through rem sts, and pull tightly to secure end.

Work 2nd arm as first. Stuff body.

Head
With RS facing and B, pick up and k 28 sts around inside neck edge below first 2 A rows (these 2 rows will roll to outside t form collar), and divide evenly over 4 dpn. Join and pm for beg of rnd.
Join C and knit 16 rnds.

HAIR
Join E and cont back and forth in rows ir loop st as foll:
Row 1 (WS) K1, pm, p8, pm, p2tog, p7 pm, p2tog, p7, pm, k1—26 sts.
Row 2 (RS) K1, [sm, work LS in each st to 2 sts before marker, k2tog using this dec'd st to make next LS] 3 times, sm, k1—3 sts dec'd.
Row 3 K1, [sm, p3tog to marker] 3 times, sm, k1.
Rep last 2 rows 3 times more—14 sts.
Next row (RS) *K2tog; rep from * to end—7 sts.
Cut yarn, draw tail rem sts, and pull tight to secure end.
Stuff head and sew seam.

Finishing
Embroider eyes with black yarn and mouth with red yarn (see photo). ■

LEG CHART

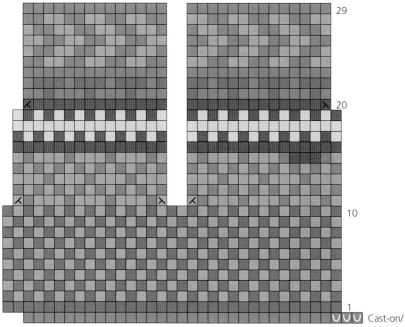

29

20

10

1

⌄⌄⌄ Cast-on/ pick up row

BODY CHART

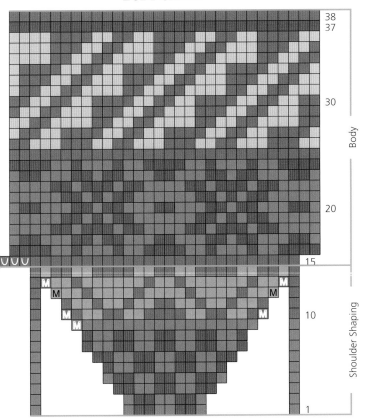

ARM CHART

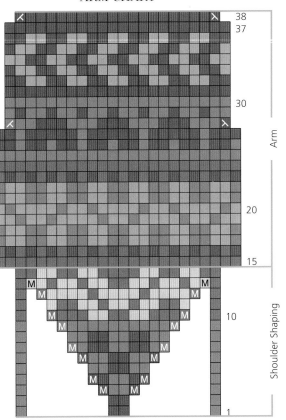

KEY

■	A
■	B
□	C
■	D
■	E
M	M1
⊼	k2tog
⊻	ssk
∪	loop cast-on 1 st

56

Nesting Dolls

These supersweet toys inspired by the charming folk dolls of eastern Europe will make a colorful addition to the nursery.

DESIGNED BY PAT OLSKI

Knitted Measurements

Approx 12 (14)"/30.5 (35.5)cm tall

Materials

▓ 1 3½oz/100g ball (each approx 220yd/200m) of Cascade Yarns *220 Superwash* (superwash wool) in #809 Really Red (A), #834 Strawberry Pink (B), #886 Citron (C), #844 Periwinkle (D), #910A Winter White (E), and #1920 Pumpkin Spice (F) **(3)**
▓ Small amount of black yarn for eyes
▓ One set (5) size 5 (3.75mm) double-pointed needles (dpn), *or size to obtain gauge*
▓ One pair size 5 (3.75mm) needles
▓ One size F/5 (3.75mm) crochet hook
▓ Polyester stuffing
▓ Cardboard or plastic circle 3 (4)"/7.5 (10)cm diameter
▓ Stitch marker

Small Doll

BASE
With A, cast on 8 sts and divide evenly over 4 dpn. Join, taking care not to twist sts, and pm for beg of rnd.
Rnd 1 Knit.
Rnd 2 Kfb in every st—16 sts.

Rnds 3–5 Knit.
Rnd 6 Kfb in every st—32 sts.
Rnds 7–10 Knit.
Rnd 11 [K3, kfb] 8 times—40 sts.
Rnd 12 Knit.
Turning rnd 13 Purl.

BODY
Knit 7 rnds A, 1 rnd B.

Inc rnd With B, knit, inc 4 sts evenly around—44 sts.
Knit 3 rnds B, 3 rnds C, 1 rnd D.
Inc rnd With D, knit, inc 4 sts evenly around—48 sts.
Knit 1 rnd D.
Fair Isle rnd 1 K1 D, [k1 A, k3 D] 11 times, k1 A, k2 D.
Fair Isle rnd 2 [K3 A, k1 D] 12 times.
Next rnd Rep Fair Isle rnd 1.
Knit 3 rnds D, 1 rnd A, 3 rnds B.
Next 2 rnds [K1 C, k3 B] 12 times.
Next 2 rnds K3 B, [k3 C, k5 B] 5 times, k3 C, k2 B.
Next 2 rnds K2 B, [k5 C, k3 B] 5 times, k5 C, k1 B.
Next 2 rnds K2 B, [k2 C, k1 B, k2 C, k3 B] 5 times, k2 C, k1 B, k2 C, k1 B.
Next 2 rnds K2 B, [k1 C, k3 B, k1 C, k3 B] 5 times, k1 C, k3 B, k1 C, k1 B.
Knit 2 rnds B, 1 rnd A, 3 rnds D, 2 rnds C
Place cardboard or plastic in base of doll
Stuff doll to needles.
Dec rnd With C, knit, dec 4 sts evenly around.
Rep dec rnd once more—40 sts.
Knit 1 rnd C, 1 rnd A.
Next 3 rnds With A, *K1, p1; rep from * around.

Gauge

22 sts and 28 rnds to 4"/10cm over St st using size 5 (3.75mm) needles.
Take time to check gauge.

56 Nesting Dolls

HEAD

Knit 2 rnds E.

Inc rnd With E, knit, inc 4 sts evenly around—44 sts.

Knit 9 rnds E, 2 rnds F.

Dec rnd With F, [k9, k2tog] 4 times around—40 sts.

Knit 1 rnd F.

Stuffing as you go, cont to shape head as fo▮

Dec rnd With F, [k3, k2tog] 8 times—32 st▮

Knit 1 rnd F.

Dec rnd With F, [k2, k2tog] 8 times—24 st▮

Dec rnd With F, [k2, k2tog] 6 times—18 st▮

Knit 1 rnd F.

Dec rnd With F, [k1, k2tog] 6 times—12 st▮

Knit 1 rnd F. Cut yarn, leaving a long tail▮ Finish stuffing. Thread tail through rem sts and pull tight to close.

HEADSCARF

With straight needles and A, cast on 46 sts. Knit 5 rows.

Next row (WS) K3, p to last 3 sts k2, sl 1 wyif.

Next row (RS) K to last st, sl 1 wyif.

Rep last 2 rows for St st with garter st borders for 5 rows more.

Dec row (RS) K5, [k2tog, k7] 4 times, k to last st, sl 1 wyif—42 sts.

Work 1 row even in pat.

Dec row K5, [k2tog, k4] 6 times, sl 1 wyif—36 sts.

Rib row (WS) *K1, p1; rep from * to en▮

Next 5 rows K the knit sts and p the purl sts.

Next row (WS) K3, p to last 3 sts, k1, sl1 wy▮

Inc row (RS) K3, k to last 3 sts, inc 5 sts▮ evenly across, k2, sl 1 wyif—41 sts.

Work even for 15 rows in St st with 3-st▮ garter st borders as established.

Shape Top

Row 1 (RS) K8, [k2tog, k4] 5 times, k2, sl 1 wyif—36 sts.

ow 2 and all WS rows Work even in pat.

ow 3 K3, [k2tog, k3] 6 times, k2, sl 1
yif—30 sts.

ows 4–6 Work in pat.

ow 7 K4, [k2tog, k3] 4 times, k2tog,
3, sl 1 wyif—25 sts.

ow 9 K3, [k2tog] 9 times, k3, sl 1
yif—16 sts.

ow 11 K3, [k2tog, k1] 3 times, k to last
, sl 1 wyif—13 sts. Bind off.

inishing

old headscarf and sew top seam. Place
arf on doll and sew edges at ribbed
ction of neck. With crochet hook, make
12"/30.5cm chain and sew to seam of
bed section. Tie in a bow.

sing photo as guide, embroider the foll:
ench knots with black for eyes; French
ots with E and D for flowers at centers
hearts and over the dots between the
arts; lazy daisy stitches with D for leaves
 each side of every flower; lazy daisy
tches with C for leaves at bottom of first
ir Isle pat; and mouth and cheeks with B.

arge Doll

ASE

ork as for small doll base through rnd
0—32 sts.

nd 11 [K1, kfb] 16 times around—48 sts.
it 2 rnds. Purl 1 rnd for turning.

ODY

it 7 rnds A, 2 rnds B.

ext rnd With B, knit, inc 8 sts evenly
ound—56 sts.

it 3 rnds B, 3 rnds C, 5 rnds D.

ir Isle rnd 1 K1 D, [k1 A, k3 D] 13
nes, k1 A, k2 D.

ir Isle rnd 2 *K1 A, k1 D; rep from *
ound.

ep Fair Isle rnd 1.

it 1 rnd D.

Next rnd With D, knit, inc 4 sts evenly
around—60 sts.
Knit 3 rnds D, 1 rnd A, 4 rnds B.
Next 2 rnds [K1 C, k4 B] 12 times.
Next rnd [K1 C, k3 B, k3 C, k3 B] 6 times.
Next 2 rnds K3 B, [k5 C, k5 B] 5 times,
k5 C, k2 B.
Next 2 rnds K2 B, [k7 C, k3 B] 5 times,
k7 C, k1 B.
Next rnd K2 B, [k3 C, k1 B, k3 C, k3 B]
5 times, k3 C, k1 B, k3 C, k1 B.
Next rnd K3 B, [k2 C, k1 B, k2 C, k5 B]
5 times, k2 C, k1 B, k2 C, k2 B.
Knit 3 rnds B, 1 rnd A, 1 rnd D.
Dec rnd With D, knit, dec 6 sts evenly
around—54 sts.
Knit 1 rnd D, 2 rnds C.
Place cardboard or plastic circle in bottom
of doll. Stuff doll to needles.
Dec rnd With C, knit, dec 6 sts evenly
around—48 sts.
Knit 2 rnds C.
Dec rnd With C, knit, dec 6 sts evenly
around—42 sts.
Knit 2 rnds C, 1 rnd A.
Next 5 rnds With A, *k1, p1; rep from
* around.

HEAD

Inc rnd With E, knit, inc 6 sts evenly
around—48 sts.
Knit 1 rnd E.
Inc rnd With E, knit, inc 8 sts evenly
around—56 sts.
Knit 17 rnds E, 5 rnds F.
Stuffing as you go, cont to shape head
as foll:
Dec rnd [K5, k2tog] 8 times—48 sts.
Knit 3 rnds F.
Dec rnd [K4, k2tog] 8 times—40 sts.
Dec rnd [K2, k2tog] 10 times—30 sts.
Dec rnd [K1, k2tog] 10 times—20 sts.
Dec rnd [K2tog] 10 times—10 sts.
Cut yarn, leaving long tail. Finish stuffing.

Thread tail through rem sts and pull tight
to close.

HEADSCARF

With straight needles and A, cast on 60
sts. Knit 5 rows.
Next row (WS) K3, p to last 3 sts k2, sl
1 wyif.
Next row K to last st, sl 1 wyif.
Rep last 2 rows for St st with 3-st garter
st borders, for 3 rows more.
Dec row K5, [k2tog, k6] 6 times, k2tog,
k4, sl 1 wyif—53 sts.
Work 3 rows in pat.
Dec row K5, [k2tog, k5] 6 times, k2tog,
k3 sl 1 wyif—46 sts.
Work 3 rows in pat.
Dec row K5, [k2tog, k8] 4 times, sl 1
wyif—42 sts.
Rib row (WS) *K1, p1; rep from * to end.
Next 5 rows K the knit sts and p the purl sts.
Inc row (RS) K5, k and inc 6 sts evenly
across to last 5 sts, k4, sl 1 wyif—48 sts.
Work 1 row in pat.
Inc row K5, k and inc 6 sts evenly across
to last 5 sts, k4, sl 1 wyif—54 sts.
Work 18 rows in pat.

SHAPE TOP

Row 1 K5, [k2tog, k4] 8 times, sl 1
wyif—46 sts.
Row 2 and all WS rows K3, p to last 3
sts k2, sl 1 wyif.
Row 3 K5, [k2tog, k4] 6 times, k4, sl 1
wyif sts—40 sts.
Row 5 K5, [k2tog, k3] 6 times, k4, sl 1
wyif sts—34 sts.
Row 7 K5, [k2tog, k2] 6 times, k4, sl 1
wyif sts—28 sts.
Row 9 K3, [k2tog] 12 times, sl 1 wyif—
16 sts. Bind off.

Finishing

Work same as for small doll. ■

Cloud Pillow

Sweet dreams are guaranteed when cuddled up with this adorable cloud-shaped pillow. Its smiling face is sure to put your tot on cloud nine!

DESIGNED BY MATTHEW SCHRANK

Knitted Measurements
Width Approx 16"/40.5cm
Height Approx 7"/18cm

Materials
▥ 1 3½oz/100g hank (each approx 150yd/138m) of Cascade Yarns *220 Superwash Aran* (superwash wool) in #875 Feather Grey (A) (4)
▥ Small amount in black for embroidery
▥ One pair size 8 (5mm) needles, *or size to obtain gauge*
▥ Tapestry needle
▥ Polyester stuffing

Front
Cast on 72 sts. Work in St st (k on RS, p on WS) for 22 rows.

FIRST BUMP
Row 23 (RS) K18 sts, turn, leave rem sts on hold. Cont on these 18 sts only as foll:
Rows 24, 26, and 28 Purl.
Row 25 K1, k2tog, k12, ssk, k1.
Row 27 K1, k2tog, k10, ssk, k1.

Row 29 K1, k2tog, k8, ssk, k1.
Row 30 P1, p2tog, p6, p2tog tbl, p1.
Row 31 k1, k2tog, k4, ssk, k1.
Row 32 P1, p2tog, p2, p2tog tbl, p1.
Row 33 K1, k2tog, ssk, k1.
Row 34 Bind off rem 4 sts purlwise.
Cut yarn. Reattach yarn to sts on hold to work next row from RS as foll:
Work in St st over rem 54 sts for 11 rows, end on a RS row.

LAST BUMP
Beg with a WS row, work first 18 sts only same as for rows 24–34 of first bump.

LEFT INSIDE BUMP
Reattach yarn to work next row from WS as foll:
Next row (WS) P18, turn, leave rem sts on hold.
Work same as for rows 24–34 of first bump.

RIGHT INSIDE BUMP
Reattach yarn to work next row from WS as foll:

Work in St st for 5 rows, then same as for rows 25–34 of first bump.

Back
Work as for front, reversing positions of inside bumps.

Center Strip
Cast on 16 sts and work in St st for 40"/101.5cm. Place sts on hold.

Finishing
Block pieces. With black yarn, embroider eyes and mouth with chain st to front (see photo).
Pin one long side of center stripe along lower edge of back, around side, top and other side of back piece so that the 16 st on hold meet up with the cast-on edge. Adjust length of strip if necessary, then bind off rem sts.
Sew bound-off and cast-on sts of strip tog
Sew strip in place on back and front piece leaving an opening for stuffing.
Stuff then sew closed. ∎

Gauge
18 sts and 24 rows to 4"/10cm over St st using size 8 (5mm) needles.
Take time to check gauge.

Dino Hatchling

This delightful toy asks the age-old question:
which came first, the dinosaur or the egg?

DESIGNED BY MEGAN KREINER

Knitted Measurements

Dinosaur Approx 8"/20.5cm long and
5½"/14cm tall
Egg Approx 6"/15cm tall and
4½"/11.5cm wide

Materials

- 1 3½oz/100g hank (each approx
150yd/138m) of Cascade Yarns *220
Superwash Aran* (superwash merino
wool) in #1998 Aqua (A) (4)
- 1 3½oz/100g ball (each approx 220yd/
200m) of Cascade Yarns *220 Superwash*
(superwash wool) in #887 Wasabi (B) (3)
- Small amount each in #871 White (C),
#815 Black (D), and #864 Christmas
Green (E)
- One set (5) size 4 (3.5mm) double-point-
ed needles (dpn), *or size to obtain gauge*
- One pair size 4 (3.5mm) needles
- Stitch markers
- Tapestry needle
- Polyester stuffing
- Scrap yarn

Dinosaur

BODY

With dpn and A, cast on 6 sts. Divide sts
evenly over 3 dpn. Join, taking care not
to twist sts, and pm for beg of rnd.
Rnd 1 [Kfb] 6 times—12 sts.
Rnd 2 Knit.
Rnd 3 [Kfb] 12 times—24 sts.
Rnd 4 Knit.
Rnd 5 [K1, M1, k1] 12 times—36 sts.

Cut four 6"/15cm lengths of contrast
scrap yarn. Use a different strand for
placement of each leg opening on the
next rnd.
Rnd 6 *With A, k3; with scrap yarn, k5,
then sl these sts back to LH needle; with
A, k7; with scrap yarn, k5, then sl these
sts back to LH needle; with A, k8; rep
from * once more.
Rnd 7 Knit.
Rnd 8 [K2, M1, k1] 12 times—48 sts.
Rnd 9 Knit.
Rnd 10 [K3, M1, k1] 12 times—60 sts.
Cut an 8"/20.5cm length of contrast
scrap yarn for placement of the tail on
the next rnd.
Rnd 11 With A, k25; with waste yarn,
k10, then sl these sts back to LH needle;
with A, k35.
Rnds 12, 14, 16, and 18 Knit.
Rnd 13 [K8, k2tog] 6 times—54 sts.
Rnd 15 [K7, k2tog] 6 times—48 sts.
Rnd 17 [K6, k2tog] 6 times—42 sts.
Rnd 19 [K5, k2tog] 6 times—36 sts.
Cut an 8"/20.5cm length of contrast scra[p]
yarn for placement of neck on next rnd.
Rnd 20 With A, k31; with scrap yarn, k5[,]
then sl these sts back to LH needle; with[]
A, k5.

Gauge

24 sts and 34 rnds to 4"/10cm over St st worked in rnds using size 4 (3.5 mm) needles and *220 Superwash*.
Take time to check gauge.

Dino Hatchling

Rnd 21 Cont with scrap yarn from previous rnd, k5, then sl these sts back to LH needle; with A, k36.
Rnd 22 [K4, k2tog] 6 times—30 sts.
Rnd 23 Knit.
Rnd 24 [K3, k2tog] 6 times—24 sts.
Rnd 25 Knit.
Rnd 26 [K2, k2tog] 6 times—18 sts.
Rnd 27 [K1, k2tog] 6 times—12 sts.
Stuff the body, then cut A, draw through rem 12 sts on needles twice, and pull up tightly to close.

LEGS (Make 4)
With a dpn, carefully remove scrap yarn for one leg and sl the 5 sts from the lower 5 loops and top 5 loops to separate dpn—10 sts.
Rnd 1 [With A, pick up and k1 st between dpn, k5 from dpn] twice—12 sts.
Divide sts evenly over 3 dpn.
Rnd 2 Knit.
Rnd 3 [K1, M1, k1] 6 times—18 sts.
Rnds 4–7 Knit.
Rnd 8 Purl.
Rnd 9 [K1, k2tog tbl] 6 times—12 sts.
Rnd 10 Knit.
Stuff the leg.
Rnd 11 (K2tog) 6 times—6 sts.
Cut yarn, draw through rem sts twice and pull up tightly to close.

NECK AND HEAD
With a dpn, carefully remove scrap yarn for neck and sl the 10 sts from the lower 10 loops and top 10 loops to separate dpn—20 sts.
Rnd 1 [With A, pick up and k 2 sts between dpn, k10 from dpn] twice—24 sts.
Divide sts evenly over 3 dpn.
Rnds 2–5 Knit.
Rnd 6 [K4, k2tog] 4 times—20 sts.
Rnds 7–16 Knit.

Rnd 17 [K1, M1, k1] 10 times—30 sts.
Rnd 18 Knit.
Rnd 19 [K2, M1, k1] 10 times—40 sts.
Rnds 20–24 Knit.
Rnd 25 [K2, k2tog] 10 times—30 sts.
Rnds 26–32 Knit.
Rnd 33 [K1, k2tog] 10 times—20 sts.
Rnd 34 Knit.
Rnd 35 [K2tog] 10 times—10 sts.
Stuff the neck and head. Cut yarn, draw through rem sts twice, and pull up tightly to close.

TAIL
With a dpn, carefully remove scrap yarn for tail and sl the 10 sts from the lower 10 loops and top 10 loops to separate dpn—20 sts.
Rnd 1 [With A, pick up and k 2 sts between dpn, k10] twice—24 sts.
Divide sts evenly over 3 dpn.
Rnds 2–4 Knit.
Rnd 5 [K4, k2tog] 4 times—20 sts.
Rnd 6 Knit.
Rnd 7 [K3, k2tog] 4 times—16 sts.
Rnds 8 and 9 Knit.
Rnd 10 [K2, k2tog] 4 times—12 sts.
Rnds 11 and 12 Knit.
Rnd 13 [K1, k2tog] 4 times—8 sts.
Rnds 14–16 Knit.
Stuff the tail. Cut yarn, pull through the rem sts twice, and pull up tightly to close.

Finishing

Bend the head down towards the front neck and sew the back of the chin to create the head shape as in photo.
Using tapestry needle and D, and foll photo, embroider the mouth with a long stitch (tacked at both corners), the 2 eyes (both sides) with satin st, the 2 eyebrows with a short stitch tacked at center and the 2 nostrils with a lazy daisy loop for

each one. For the spots that are shown in the photo along the back and tail, using tapestry needle and C, embroider 11 spots (4 small, 4 medium and 3 large scattered along the back and tail with a long st worked in a circle then filled in with satin at the centers.

Egg

EGG BOTTOM
With B, cast on 6 sts and divide evenly over 3 dpn. Join, taking care not to twist sts, and pm for beg of rnd.
Rnd 1 [Kfb] 6 times—12 sts.
Rnd 2 and all even rnds to 18 Knit.
Rnd 3 [Kfb] 12 times—24 sts.
Rnd 5 [K3, M1, k1] 6 times—30 sts.
Rnd 7 [K4, M1, k1] 6 times—36 sts.
Rnd 9 [K5, M1, k1] 6 times—42 sts.
Rnd 11 [K6, M1, k1] 6 times—48 sts.
Rnd 13 [K7, M1, k1] 6 times—54 sts.
Rnd 15 [K8, M1, k1] 6 times—60 sts.
Rnd 17 [K9, M1, k1] 6 times—66 sts.
Rnd 19 [K10, M1, k1] 6 times—72 sts.
Rnds 20–30 Knit.
Rnd 31 [K10, k2tog] 6 times—66 sts.
Rnds 32–34 Knit.
Rnd 35 [K9, k2tog] 6 times—60 sts.
Rnds 36–38 Knit.
Rnd 39 [K8, k2tog] 6 times—54 sts.
Rnds 40–42 Knit.
Rnd 43 [K7, k2tog] 6 times—48 sts.
Rnd 44 Knit.
Bind off sts to complete egg bottom.
Cut a 14"/36cm length of scrap yarn.

EGG BOTTOM LINER
Work as for egg bottom.

EGG TOP
With straight needles and B, cast on 48 sts.
Row 1 (RS) With B, K4; with scrap yarn, k40, sl these sts back to LH needle; with B, k44.

Divide sts evenly over 4 dpn. Join, taking care not to twist sts, and pm for beg of rnd.

Rnd 2 Knit.

Rnd 3 [K6, k2tog] 6 times—42 sts.

Rnds 4–6 Knit.

Rnd 7 [K5, k2tog] 6 times—36 sts.

Rnds 8–10 Knit.

Rnd 11 [K4, k2tog] 6 times—30 sts.

Rnds 12 and 13 Knit.

Rnd 14 [K3, k2tog] 6 times—24 sts.

Rnd 15 Knit.

Rnd 16 [K2tog, k2tog] 6 times—18 sts.

Rnd 17 Knit.

Rnd 18 [K1, k2tog] 6 times—12 sts.

Cut yarn. Pull end through rem sts twice, and pull up tightly to close.

Work egg opening as foll:
With dpn, carefully remove the scrap yarn and sl the 40 sts from lower loops and 40 sts from top loops to separate dpn—80 sts.

Rnd 1 [With B, pick up and k 2 sts between dpn, bind off those 2 sts; bind off 40 sts] twice.

EGG TOP LINER
With dpn, cast on 48 sts and divide evenly over 4 dpn. Join, taking care to not twist sts, and pm for beg of rnd.
Work as for egg top, beg with rnd 2.

Finishing
With WS held tog, sew liners into egg bottom and egg top. At egg opening on top egg, sew to bottom egg.
Foll the photo, using tapestry needle and B, embroider 5 spots (1 large, 2 medium, 2 small) on the egg and 2 spots (1 large, 1 small) on the egg top.
Use a long st worked in a circle then filled in with satin sts at the centers. ■

175

Cat with Sweater

Even a furry kitty cat can get chilly,
so be sure to knit up a cozy sweater for your feline pal.

DESIGNED BY AUDREY DRYSDALE

Knitted Measurements
Approx 13½"/34.5cm high

Materials
▓ 1 1¾oz/50g hank (each approx 137yd/125m) of Cascade Yarns *220 Superwash Sport* (superwash merino wool) each in #875 Feather Gray (A), #219 Moon Rock (B), #817 Aran (C), and #1941 Salmon (D) ❸
▓ One pair size 5 (3.75mm) needles, *or size to obtain gauge*
▓ One set (5) size 5 (3.75mm) double-pointed needles (dpn)
▓ Pink, black, and green embroidery floss
▓ Stitch markers
▓ Stitch holders
▓ Tapestry needle
▓ A small amount of contrasting scrap yarn
▓ Polyester stuffing

Notes
1) Wind small balls of yarn for each block of color.
2) When changing colors, twist yarns on WS to prevent holes in work.

Legs (Make 2)
With B and 2 dpn, cast on 4 sts.
Row 1 (RS) Kfb into each st—8 sts.
Divide sts over 3 dpn (2 sts, 3 sts, 3 sts). Join, taking care not to twist sts, and pm for beg of rnd.
Rnd 1 Kfb into each st—16 sts.
Rnds 2 and 4 Knit.
Rnd 3 [K2, M1] 8 times—24 sts.
Rnd 5 [K3, M1] 8 times—32 sts.
Knit 8 rnds. Cut B. With A, work even in St st (k every rnd) until leg measures 5"/12.5cm.
Next rnd Bind off 3 sts, k to end of rnd. Leave rem 29 sts on holder. Stuff leg.

Body
Join legs as foll:
Next rnd With A, k29 of first leg, then k29 of 2nd leg. Place marker to mark join (center back)—58 sts.
Work even in St st until body measures 2¾"/7cm from joining.
Dec rnd 1 *K12, k2tog, k13, k2tog; rep from * once more—54 sts. Knit 2 rnds.
Dec rnd 2 *K7, k2tog; rep from * around—48 sts. Knit 5 rnds.
Dec rnd 3 *K6, k2tog; rep from * around—42 sts. Knit 5 rnds.

Dec rnd 4 *K5, k2tog; rep from * around—36 sts.
Knit 7 rnds. Stuff body.

Neck and Head
Next rnd *K2tog; rep from * around—18 sts. Knit 1 rnd.
Next rnd *Kfb into each st—36 sts. Knit 1 rnd.
Cont to work in rows as foll:
Row 1 (RS) *K6, M1; rep from * to end—42 sts. Turn.
Row 2 (WS) Purl.
Row 3 With A, k2, [M1, k5] twice; with C, [k6, M1] twice, k6; with A, [k5, M1] twice, k2—48 sts.
Row 4 With A, p14; with C, p20; with A, p14.
Row 5 With A, k14; with C, k20; with A, k14.
Rep last 2 rows 7 times more.

SHAPE TOP OF HEAD
Row 1 (RS) With A, [k3, k2tog] twice, k4; with C, [k2, k2tog, k3, k2tog] twice, k2; with A, k4, [k2tog, k3] twice—40 sts.
Row 2 Purl, matching colors.
Row 3 With A, [k2, k2tog] twice, k4; with C, [k1, k2tog. k2, k2tog] twice, k2; with A, k4, [k2tog, k2] twice—32 sts.
Cut C.

Gauge
24 sts and 32 rows/rnds to 4"/10cm over St st using size 5 (3.75mm) needles.
Take time to check gauge.

Row 4 With A, purl.

Row 5 [K1, k2tog] twice, k4, [k2tog, k1, k2tog] twice, k6, [k2tog, k1] twice—24 sts.

Row 6 Purl.

Row 7 *K2tog, k1; rep from * to end—18 sts.

Row 8 Purl.

Row 9 *K2tog; rep from * to end—9 sts. Cut A and draw tightly through rem 9 sts. Sew center back seam of head leaving opening for stuffing. Stuff head. Sew opening closed. Embroider face with embroidery floss (see photo). Embroider whiskers with B.

Arms (Make 2)

With B and 2 dpn, cast on 4 sts.

Set-up row (RS) Kfb into each st—8 sts. Divide sts over 3 dpn (2 sts, 3 sts, 3 sts). Join, taking care not to twist sts, and pm for beg of rnd.

Rnd 1 *Kfb into each st—16 sts.

Rnds 2 and 4 Knit

Rnd 3 *K4, M1; rep from * around—20 sts. Cut B. With A, cont in St st until arm measures 4½"/11 cm. Stuff arm.

Next rnd *K3, k2tog; rep from * around—16 sts. Bind off. Sew arms to sides of body approx ¾"/2cm below neck.

Tail

With B and 2 dpn, cast on 4 sts.

Set-Up Row (RS) Kfb into each st—8 sts. Divide sts on 3 dpn (2 sts, 3 sts, 3 sts). Join to work in the rnd, taking care not to twist sts, and pm for beg of rnd.

Rnd 1 Kfb into each st—16 sts.

Rnds 2–4 Knit. Cut B. With A, cont in St st until tail measures 6½"/16.5 cm. Stuff tail.

Next rnd *K2, k2tog; rep from * around—12 sts. Bind off. Sew tail to back of body approx 1½"/4 cm above lower leg join.

Ears (Make 2)

LARGER PIECES (Make 2)

With B, cast on 9 sts. Knit 4 rows.

Next row K1, k2tog, k to last 3 sts, ssk, k1.

Next row Knit.

Rep last 2 rows once more—5 sts.

Next row Knit.

Next row K1, k3tog, k1—3 sts.

Next row Knit.

Next row K3tog. Fasten off.

SMALLER PIECES (Make 2)

With C, cast on 5 sts. Knit 2 rows.

Next row K1, k3tog, k1—3 sts.

Next row Knit.

Next row K3tog.

Fasten off. Sew smaller ear to larger ear. Sew ears in position to head.

Sweater

BACK

**With D and straight needles, cast on 32 sts. Work in St st (k on RS, p on WS) for 4"/10cm, end with a WS row.

Shape armholes

Bind off 4 sts at beg of next 2 rows—24 sts.** Work even until armholes measure 1¾"/4.5cm, end with a WS row.

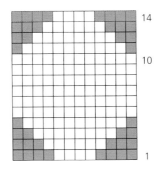

Shape shoulders

Bind off 2 sts, k20, bind off rem 2 sts. Slip 20 rem sts to holder.

FRONT

Work from ** to ** as for back. Work even until armholes measure 6 rows less than armholes on back, end with a WS row.

Shape neck

Next row (RS) K4, k2tog (neck edge), turn. Leave rem sts on holder.

Dec 1 st at neck edge on next 3 rows—2 sts. Work 2 rows even. Bind off.

With RS facing, leave center 12 sts on holder, join yarn to rem sts, ssk, k to end.

Dec 1 st at neck edge on next 3 rows—2 sts. Work 2 rows even. Bind off.

Embroidery

With C, work duplicate st slightly off center on front. Then, work ball of yarn over duplicate st section, using satin stitch for wraps and chain stitch for strand of loose yarn (see photo).

SLEEVES (Make 2)

With D and straight needles, cast on 21 sts. Work in St st for 3½"/9cm. Bind off.

Finishing

Sew right shoulder seam.

ROLLED NECK

With RS facing, D, and pair of needles, pick up and k 44 sts evenly around neck edge (including sts on holders). Beg on a purl row, work 7 rows in St st. Bind off. Sew left shoulder and neck seam.

Sew in sleeves. Sew side and sleeve seams, allowing lower edges to curl. ■

60

Turtle Trio

A sweet trio of turtles double as rattles simply by adding a toy rattle insert.
They're so huggable, they function just as well as stuffed lovies.

DESIGNED BY JESIE OSTERMILLER

Knitted Measurements

Length Approx 6"/15cm, including head
Circumference Approx 10½"/26.5cm, at highest point, stuffed.

Materials

- 1 3½oz/100g hank (each approx 220yd/200m) of Cascade Yarns *220 Superwash Effects* (superwash merino wool) each in #14 Forest (A), #04 Teals (B), and #02 Graphite (C) (4)
- One set (5) size 6 (4mm) double-pointed needles (dpn), *or size to obtain gauge*
- Six ¼"/6mm black buttons
Note As buttons are a choking hazard, embroider eyes if making for a child.
- Polyester stuffing
- 3 toy rattle inserts (if desired)
- Stitch marker

Shell

With C, cast on 6 sts and divide evenly over 3 dpn. Join, being careful not to twist sts, and pm for beg of rnd.
Inc rnd 1 [Kfb] 6 times—12 sts.
Rnd 2 Knit.
Inc rnd 3 [Kfb] 12 times—24 sts.
Rnd 4 Knit.

Rnd 5 With B, knit.
Inc rnd 6 [Kfb, k2] 8 times—32 sts.
Rnd 7 Knit.
Rnd 8 With C, knit.
Inc rnd 9 [Kfb, k3] 8 times—40 sts.
Rnd 10 Knit.
Rnds 11 and 12 With B, knit.
Inc rnd 13 [Kfb, k7] 5 times—45 sts.
Cont in St st as foll: 3 rnds C, 3 rnds B, 1 rnd A.

Inc rnd 21 [Kfb, k1] 22 times, k1—67 sts.
Knit 2 rnds. Bind off.

UNDERSIDE OF SHELL
With WS facing, edge of shell towards you, and A, pick up and k 63 sts along inc rnd 21 of shell. Divide sts over 4 dpn and pm for beg of rnd.
Rnd 1 Knit.
Rnd 2 [K2tog, k1] 21 times around—42 sts.
Rnd 3 K4, k2tog, k9, ssk, k8, k2tog, k9, ssk, k4—38 sts.
Rnd 4 Knit.
Rnd 5 K3, k2tog, k9, ssk, k6, k2tog, k9, ssk, k3—34 sts.
Rnd 6 Knit.
Rnd 7 K2, k2tog, k9, ssk, k4, k2tog, k9, ssk, k2—30 sts.
Rnd 8 Knit.
Rnd 9 K1, k2tog, k9, ssk, k2, k2tog, k9, ssk, k1—26 sts.
Rnd 10 K2tog, k9, ssk, k2tog, k9, ssk—22 sts.
Lightly stuff, including toy rattle if desired. Divide rem sts evenly over 2 dpn. Cut yarn, leaving a 20"/51cm tail for grafting. Graft sts tog using Kitchener stitch (see page 182).

Gauge

20 sts and 28 rnds to 4"/10cm over St st using size 6 (4mm) needles.
Take time to check gauge.

Turtle Trio

Legs (Make 4)

With A, cast on 10 sts. Divide sts over 3 dpn. Join, being careful not to twist sts, and pm for beg of rnd. Knit 2 rnds.

Inc rnd K5, [kfb] 5 times—15 sts.
Knit 4 rnds.

Dec rnd K5, [k2tog] 5 times—10 sts.

Dec rnd [K2tog] 5 times—5 sts.
Cut yarn, leaving a long tail. Thread tail through rem sts to close. Stuff lightly. Sew cast-on edge closed.

Head

With A, cast on 18 sts. Divide sts over 3 dpn as foll: 9 sts on Dpn #1, 4 sts on Dpn #2, 5 sts on Dpn #3.
Join, being careful not to twist sts, and pm for beg of rnd. Knit 5 rnds.
Work short rows (see page 183 for instructions on w&t) on Dpn #1 as foll:

Row 1 (RS) K8, w&t.
Row 2 (WS) P7, w&t.
Row 3 K6, w&t.
Row 4 P5, w&t.
Row 5 (RS) Knit to end of rnd, picking up all wraps.
Knit 4 rnds over all sts.

Dec rnd [K2tog] 9 times—9 sts.
Knit 1 rnd.

Dec rnd [K2tog] 4 times, k1—5 sts.
Cut yarn, leaving a long tail. Thread tail through rem sts to close. Stuff lightly.

Tail

With top of shell facing up and A, pick up and k 5 sts directly under curved edge of turtle shell. Work I-cord tail as foll:
*Knit one row. Without turning work, slide the sts back to the opposite end of needle to work next row from RS. Pull yarn tightly from end of row. Rep from * twice.

Next row Cont as for I-cord, k2tog, k1, ssk—3 sts.

Next row K3tog—1 st.
Fasten off.

Finishing

Sew cast-on edges of legs to underside of shell, using photo as a guide.
Sew head to body with short row shaping on bottom, then sew on legs.
Embroider or sew on buttons for eyes. ∎

Techniques

Kitchener Stitch

Cut a tail at least 4 times the length of the edge that will be grafted together and thread through a tapestry needle. Hold needles together with right sides showing, making sure each has the same number of live stitches, and work as follows:

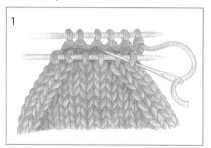

1) Insert tapestry needle purlwise through first stitch on front needle. Pull yarn through, leaving stitch on needle.

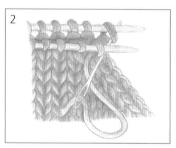

2) Insert tapestry needle knitwise through first stitch on back needle. Pull yarn through, leaving stitch on needle.

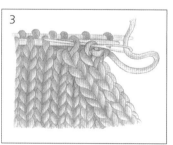

3) Insert tapestry needle knitwise through first stitch on front needle, pull yarn through, and slip stitch off needle. Then, insert tapestry needle purlwise through next stitch on front needle and pull yarn through, leaving this stitch on needle.

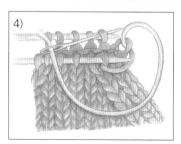

4) Insert tapestry needle purlwise through first stich on back needle, pull yarn through, and slip stitch off needle. Then, insert tapestry needle knitwise through next stitch on back needle and pull yarn through, leaving this stitch on needle.

Repeat steps 3 and 4 until all stitches on both front and back needles have been grafted. Fasten off and weave in end.

Three-Needle Bind-Off

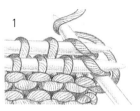

1) Hold pieces together on two needles. Insert third needle knitwise into the first stitch of each needle and wrap yarn knitwise.

2) Knit these two stitches together and slip them off the needles. *Knit the next two stitches together in the same manner.

3) Slip the first stitch on third needle over the second stitch and off needle. Rep from * in step 2 as many times as necessary to bind off required number of stitches.

Provisional Cast-On

With scrap yarn and crochet hook, chain the number of stitches to cast on, plus a few extra. Cut a tail and pull the tail through the last chain stitch. With knitting needle and yarn, pick up and knit the stated number of stitches through the "purl bumps" on the back of the chain. To remove scrap chain, when instructed, pull out the tail from the last crochet stitch. Gently and slowly pull on the tail to unravel the crochet stitches, carefully placing each released knit stitch on a needle.

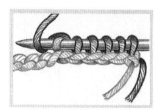

Techniques

Embroidery Stitches

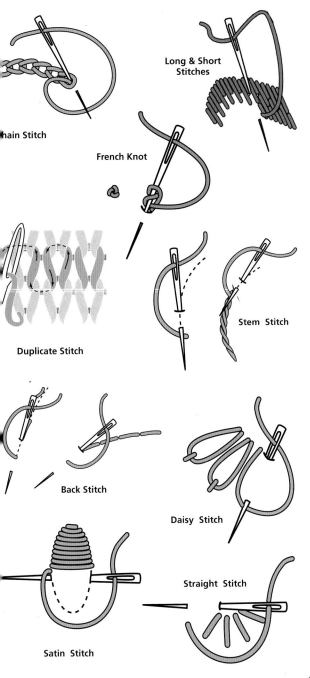

Chain Stitch

Long & Short Stitches

French Knot

Duplicate Stitch

Stem Stitch

Back Stitch

Daisy Stitch

Satin Stitch

Straight Stitch

Short Row Wrapping (wrap and turn—w & t)
Knit (Purl) side

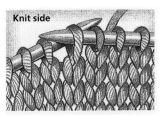
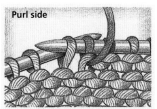

1) With yarn in back, slip next st purlwise.

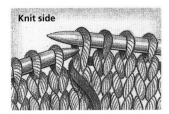
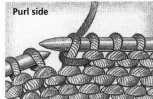

2) Move yarn between the needles to the front (back).

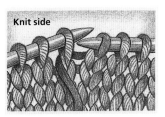
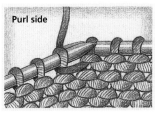

3) Slip the same st back to the left-hand needle. Turn work, bring yarn to the purl (knit) side between needles. One st is wrapped

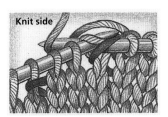
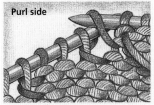

4) When short rows are completed, hide all wraps as follows: work to just before wrapped stitch, *For knit side*: Insert right-hand needle under the wrap and knitwise into the wrapped stitch, knit them together. *For purl side*: Insert right-hand needle from behind into the back loop of the wrap and place it on the left-hand needle; purl wrap together with stitch on needle.

index

33

72

98

134